The Abuse of Power

Law in Society Series
EDITED BY C. M. CAMPBELL AND PAUL WILES

Negotiated Justice
J. BALDWIN AND M. McCONVILLE

The Social Control of Drugs
PHILIP BEAN

Decisions in the Penal Process
A. KEITH BOTTOMLEY

Law and State
KEVIN BOYLE, TOM HADDEN, PADDY HILLYARD

Law and Society: Readings in the Sociology of Law
Edited by COLIN CAMPBELL and PAUL WILES

Magistrates' Justice
PAT CARLEN

Censorship and Obscenity
J. C. H. DAVIES AND R. DHAVAN

Deviant Interpretations: Problems in Criminological Theory
Edited by DAVID DOWNES and PAUL ROCK

Female Sexuality and the Law
SUSAN S. M. EDWARDS

Pollution, Social Interest and the Law
NEIL GUNNINGHAM

The Politics of Abolition
THOMAS MATHIESEN

Social Needs and Legal Action
PAULINE MORRIS, RICHARD WHITE, PHILIP LEWIS

Crime and Conflict
HAROLD E. PEPINSKY

Marx and Engels on Law and Laws
PAUL PHILLIPS

Sexism and the Law
ALBIE SACHS AND JOAN HOFF WILSON

Law in the Balance: Legal Services in the Eighties
Edited by PHILIP A. THOMAS

Order and Dispute: An Introduction to Legal Anthropology
SIMON ROBERTS

The Abuse of Power

Civil Liberties in the United Kingdom

PATRICIA HEWITT

MARTIN ROBERTSON · OXFORD

© Patricia Hewitt, 1982

First published in 1982 by
Martin Robertson & Company Ltd.,
108 Cowley Road, Oxford OX4 1JF.

British Library Cataloguing in Publication Data

Hewitt, Patricia
The abuse of power.
1. Civil Rights—Great Britain
I. Title
323.4'0941   JN906

ISBN 0-85520-379-X
ISBN 0-85520-380-3 Pbk

Photoset in 11/12pt Palatino by Enset Limited, Midsomer Norton
Printed and bound in Great Britain by The Pitman Press, Bath

For my mother, Hope Hewitt

Contents

Acknowledgments

In a book covering a wide variety of issues I have, inevitably, drawn extensively on the works of other writers. My debt to them is acknowledged throughout. I am extremely grateful to the editors of this series, Colin Campbell and Paul Wiles, and to Michael Hay at Martin Robertson for their involvement in the planning of this book and their very constructive comments on earlier drafts. I want also to thank all my colleagues on the staff and Executive Committee of NCCL and, in particular, Harriet Harman for her assistance with chapter 5 and for allowing me to disturb her files, which provided much of the material for that and other chapters; Sarah Spencer, whose own research on police accountability has been invaluable; Catherine Scorer for her comments on chapter 7; Anne Dunn, for her tireless help with checking references; and Anna Coote for her encouragement. Most of all, I want to thank Bill Birtles for his criticisms and his support and for the use of his extensive library.

Foreword

This book is about the struggle to protect and preserve civil liberties in Britain. The author has almost unrivalled authority to write about the threats to existing rights and freedom. She has a unique insight into the debates and developments, progress and failures of recent years; this is combined with practical experience in resisting these threats and constructing adequate and workable solutions to newly pressing problems.

It is interesting how struggles about the defence of liberties and rights for people have so often, in the past, reflected lessons first learnt elsewhere. In the 1960s the fight by black people in the United States of America for civil rights became a touchstone for similar struggles in other countries, and ultimately in the arena of international politics. The tactics and ideals of that movement were studied and transplanted into different contexts and used to tackle different issues. Nowadays it is sometimes difficult to remember the origins of the civil rights movement in Northern Ireland, and the reactionary response to the claims then made; they are worth recalling all the same, since they were the opening scene for the tragic saga of horror and violence which continues even now.

It is sad to have to admit that the contemporary period in Britain may prove to be a similar focus for civil rights struggles elsewhere. If ideas and tactics are, in important ways, forged in struggle and during conflict, then Britain today has many of the necessary ingredients to influence the opposing responses to turmoil elsewhere. No Western state has so much experience of urban terrorism nor has any developed to such a degree the technology of counter-force and control. Few European countries have the same explosive mixture of indigenous black citizens facing ingrained racial prejudice and structural discrimination. No other advanced industrial society has suffered the same wild gyrations in its

political economy as a result of trying to redevelop a rapidly declining industrial base while stubbornly clinging to dreams of former
power and glory. The instability of high inflation and then of mass
unemployment has strained the social order in alarming ways. The
danger is that the threats to the political order produced by these
stresses will not, or not always, be met in a liberal way. A state
under threat is not the best guardian of civil liberties. There is a
constant temptation to try to decipher and adopt the easy or quick
or expedient solution. The negotiation and resolution of conflict
through political processes could come to be replaced by control
based upon suppression. The borderline is narrow, difficult to
perceive and subtle; severe oppression can spring from folly and
misjudgement just as readily as from wickedness and hatred.

The challenges now presented to the enjoyment of civil liberties
in Britain represent a formidable list. The judgements called for,
and the decisions made, will be of great significance. Patricia
Hewitt is General Secretary of the National Council for Civil
Liberties. She has had to steer and mobilize its activities during this
very testing period. Her knowledge and insight are based on
practical experience. How civil rights campaigners act and what
success they achieve will be important to all living in Britain. Their
actions could also provide a model for others in the future. Let us
hope it is a good model.

Colin Campbell
Paul Wiles
1981

Introduction

It is still widely believed that Britain leads the world in civil liberties. 'It's a free country,' people say, sceptical about evidence to the contrary. This book explores the gulf between this myth – the myth that this is a tolerant country, respectful of the rights of minorities, watchful of the principles of justice, ever-ready to challenge and restrict the growth of state power – and the reality.

Three examples illustrate the point. *Habeas corpus* is the most famous symbol of British liberty. But it has failed to protect black migrants settled in this country from arbitrary power. Under Labour and Conservative Governments alike, the Home Office has asserted – and the courts have upheld – a power to arrest without warrant an immigrant settled in this country; the power to imprison him on suspicion of being an illegal entrant; the power to deny him bail, to detain him for an indefinite period and to deport him without ever having laid charges against him or brought him before a court. In 1980 alone, over a thousand people were the victims of this abuse of power.

A similar excess of executive power, sanctioned this time by Parliament itself, is to be found in the system of exclusion orders created by the 1976 Prevention of Terrorism Act, under which a citizen of the United Kingdom born in Northern Ireland may be arrested, detained, deported to Belfast and banned from ever re-entering Great Britain – all without any criminal charge being made against him and with no right to a court hearing. Over two hundred people have already been exiled through the use of a power which resembles closely the system of internment without trial that defaced the administration of law in Northern Ireland between 1971 and 1975.

The rule of law, whose principles are supposedly central to this country's unwritten constitution, demands that power should be accountable. In the case of exclusion orders, Parliament – which should itself be holding government to account – has instead placed government above the law. In the case of the removal of suspected illegal immigrants, the courts have refused to enforce the law against the government. My third example is the impotence of elected representatives and the courts to ensure that the police are answerable to the law that they are meant to enforce. It is not yet true that a police officer who has broken the law always escapes with impunity. But it has happened so often, and in such serious cases, that we are now witnessing a general breakdown of the system of accountability and not the occasional failure. The police officer who killed a New Zealand teacher, Blair Peach, at a demonstration in Southall in 1979 has never been prosecuted or disciplined. Other officers responsible for serious assaults on members of the public on the same day have not been prosecuted or disciplined. The senior police officers in charge on that day have not been called to account publicly for the breakdown of police behaviour. When an investigation was ordered into the use by the Merseyside police of CS gas canisters designed to punch through barricades against a crowd of rioters in July 1981, the investigation was headed by Merseyside's own Chief Constable, Ken Oxford. The massive development of the police surveillance capability over the last decade has taken place with no legal restraint, no public supervision whatsoever, and the police have denied to the public the information about their activities which could make such supervision effective.

Of course, it is true that this is not the Argentine, where thousands of the regime's opponents have disappeared, or the Soviet Union, where dissidents have been confined to psychiatric hospitals, or South Africa, with its system or white supremacy. But that is hardly a proud boast. The claim of the British establishment – a claim generally believed to be true – is not that this country is better than the worst excesses of repressive government, but that we set the standards of freedom by which we judge others.

It is not to be expected that abuses of power will never occur. The issue is whether those abuses are sanctioned or whether they are stopped. Detention without trial, internal exile, forcible expulsions and a police force which can break the law with impunity – all of which exist in the United Kingdom today – are the characteristics of a police state. And although civil and political rights have not been extinguished, although Britain is not a police state, neither Parliament, nor the courts, nor governments supposedly dedicated to strengthening human rights have shown themselves capable in the last decade of recognizing, let alone checking, the abuse of power. There have been honourable exceptions, of course: MPs, for instance, who have fought to bring Ministers under their control; local councillors who have tried to assert their authority over the police; journalists who have stood out against threat of imprisonment. Some battles have been won, but the real struggle against the extension of state power has barely been engaged.

There is in this country no Bill of Rights which sets a limit to the powers of government, Parliament and the courts. Nor (as I argue in chapter 10) would proposals recently made for a new Bill of Rights necessarily improve matters. There is thus no limit to what new incursions may be sanctioned by a majority in Parliament or in a court. Our freedoms exist in the gap between prohibitions – and the prohibitions are rapidly closing the gap. In chapters 4 and 5 I examine the growing restrictions on freedom of expression and peaceful protest, and in chapter 6 the system of emergency powers which has spread from Northern Ireland to the rest of the country. But our freedoms are not defined only by the absence of restrictions on what the citizen may lawfully do: even more important, they are defined by restrictions on the power of the authorities. And when it comes to the police (whose position is examined in chapters 1, 2 and 3) and the treatment of black minorities (the subject of chapter 8) we find that the absence of effective restrictions on those in power is an even more serious threat than the restrictions directly imposed on our own freedom of action. Finally, as I argue in chapters 7 and 9, this country has failed to develop anything resembling an adequate system of protection for women and for minorities who suffer from discrimination.

This book deals with civil and political rights and not with the economic and social rights which are also an integral part of any full conception of 'human rights'. I have not tried to write a history of how civil and political rights have been fought for in this country: but I have written always in the knowledge that civil liberties are fought for, not given. It is fashionable among some sections of the left to dismiss civil liberties as bourgeois, liberal ideals – a notion which seriously misunderstands the struggles of the working class for political power and for curbs on the power of government. The right to *habeas corpus,* the right to jury trial, freedom of the press from the more overt forms of censorship and real advances in the rights of women have been carved out through centuries of political struggle – and it would be folly to pretend that the struggle was over.

I have written *The Abuse of Power* during a period of concerted attacks on our freedoms: when Government intransigence threatens to drive Northern Ireland into even more violent sectarian conflict; when protest marches are being banned with frightening regularity, and new criminal restrictions on demonstrations and pickets are threatened; when a Royal Commission has proposed to extend the powers of the police and to reduce already inadequate safeguards for the suspect; when new Immigration Rules have further undermined the right to family life of black citizens, and a new Nationality Act has further entrenched the racial discrimination of previous immigration laws; when many of the rights won by women are being dismantled; when the surveillance of those who criticize is being stepped up; and when the rioting in the cities during the summer of 1981 – the predicted response to bad policing, growing unemployment and often appalling living conditions – has led to the authorization of CS gas and water cannon, the threat of a new Riot Act and the operation of 'special courts' with scant regard for the defendants' rights to bail and legal representation.

This book has grown out of the years I have spent with the National Council for Civil Liberties (NCCL) in day-to-day defence of people's rights and freedoms. It therefore reflects the priorities and preoccupations of NCCL over the last decade, although it does not necessarily reflect NCCL policy. There are, of course, omissions, and I particularly regret that I have not been able to include a discussion of the rights of patients in mental hospitals. Nor have I tried to provide a theoretical account of civil liberties principles or to write an academic textbook. Instead I have set out to provide a map to the state of civil liberties in the United Kingdom today, a map which, I hope, will be used by those who wish to explore the erosion of our freedoms and to join the struggle in their defence.

I

The Police and Civil Liberties

1

Justice and the Criminal Law

The central aim of a criminal justice system should be the impartial enforcement of just laws. The process of law enforcement raises directly the issue of the relationship between the individual and the coercive powers of the state. The measures taken to reduce crime and to convict the guilty must not be allowed to destroy the limits placed on the state's right to interfere with the citizen's liberty; nor must the aim of detecting and convicting the guilty be pursued at the cost of the conviction or imprisonment of the innocent. A perfectly efficient system, one that always detects and punishes the guilty but never infringes the rights of the innocent, is impossible to achieve. Inefficiency that involves the conviction and punishment of the innocent destroys the integrity of the system: some tolerance of inefficiency in respect of those who are probably guilty is essential for the protection of all.

Unfortunately, the Royal Commission on Criminal Procedure – whose report,[1] published in January 1981, will form the basis of debate in this area for the next decade or more – was directed by its terms of reference towards a fallacious view of the 'balance' which must be struck by the criminal justice system. Asked to consider 'the interests of the community in bringing offenders to justice' on the one hand and 'the rights and liberties of persons suspected or accused of crime' on the other, the Commission failed to spell out the interests of the *community* in ensuring justice to the individual. The community as a whole has an even greater interest in avoiding the wrongful conviction of an innocent person that in securing the conviction of the guilty. The wrongful conviction of the innocent is a double danger to the community, not only because all risk suffering the same injustice but also because the conviction of an innocent suspect inevitably leaves the true culprit free. It is easy to make proposals which would increase the rate of convictions, but

3

the price of such proposals – generally made without regard to the quality of the convictions secured – would be an intolerable increase in the risk of punishing innocent people.

Discussion about the administration of justice is usually concerned with the methods of enforcing laws rather than with the content of those laws. But an unjust law cannot be improved by fair methods of enforcement. Indeed, it is an additional argument against laws that are unjust because of their vagueness or the scope they offer for capriciousness that they can never be fairly enforced. Before turning to the question of enforcement, therefore, I shall consider briefly what standards we should expect of the criminal law itself.

It is easy to understand why laws should be clear in their meaning and certain in their scope. Vague, open-ended laws, which make it impossible for the ordinary individual to know whether what he wants to do is criminal or not and which allow the authorities arbitrarily to select those whom they wish to accuse, are the stuff of which tyranny is made. Dicey argued[2] that the chief requirement of the rule of law is certainty: no one should be punished unless he has infringed a specific rule established before the offence was committed. Since the legitimacy of the law depends on its origins as well as on its substance, a further requirement should be added: that the law be made by those elected to make it and not by those appointed to enforce it. And yet the English law of conspiracy – established, reinterpreted and often dramatically extended by the judges – continues to offend on both counts.

Conspiracy charges starred in all of the major prosecutions against those whose politics or lifestyle offended conventional wisdom during the 1960s and early 1970s. Conspiracy to commit a criminal offence offered a convenient method of side-stepping maximum sentences laid down by Parliament; as a common law offence, conspiracy carried no maximum sentence, with the absurd result that a higher sentence could be imposed for agreeing to do something than for actually carrying out the plan. The conviction of Dennis Warren and Eric Tomlinson in 1974, who received sentences of three years' and two years' imprisonment respectively for conspiracy to intimidate (even though intimidation itself carried a maximum of three months' imprisonment under the 1875 Conspiracy and Protection of Property Act), eventually persuaded the Labour Government in 1977 to pass the Criminal Law Act, which restricted the maximum sentence on a conspiracy charge to the maximum that could be imposed for the substantive offence itself. But other evils of criminal conspiracy charges were left untouched, in particular the peculiar rules of evidence, which permit hearsay and details of the defendant's lifestyle and associates to be used by the prosecution.

In 1972 the Court of Appeal, in an extraordinary display of judicial creativity, decided that conspiracy to commit an unlawful act extended beyond criminal offences to all *civil* wrongs, including trespass. Its reason for rushing in where Parliament had never thought to tread was a sit-in by a number of students from Sierra Leone at their High Commission in London, protesting against their Government's policies. For nine months, until the House of Lords reversed the conviction, it was a criminal offence for two people taking a walk in the country to agree to take a short cut across a field![3] But the House of Lords decision still allowed charges for conspiracy to trespass or to commit any other tort if, in Lord Hailsham's words, the object of the agreement was 'the invasion of the public domain', or if the defendants intended to inflict on the property owner 'something more than purely nominal damage'. The 1977 Act finally killed off conspiracy to trespass, but only by replacing it with a number of more specific offences directed against student sit-ins, worker occupations of a factory, squatters and so on. In fact, civil procedures for eviction in such cases had already been dramatically extended (so that, for instance, the occupiers no longer need be named on the court summons), and it is not surprising that little use seems to have been made of the criminal offences created in 1977.

But the conspiracy laws are not confined to conspiracies to break the criminal law or to commit a civil wrong. Early in 1974 it was possible for a leading writer to comment: 'It is now beyond all doubt that the offences of conspiracy to effect a public mischief, conspiracy to corrupt public morals and conspiracy to outrage public decency are all crimes recognized by English law.'[4] By November the same year the Law Lords had changed the law again and held that conspiracy to effect a public mischief was no longer a crime known to the law. Their decision, although welcome for pruning the blossoming law of conspiracy, left a gap in the legal protection of privacy that has still not been filled. The case concerned two private detectives who placed a bugging device in a hotel bedroom. Although similar behaviour had been successfully charged as conspiracy to effect a public mischief in earlier cases, and despite the fact that in 1970 the House of Lords itself had referred to 'the established categories of public mischief',[5] the same court this time took the view that the offence was dangerously and unjustifiably broad.

Conspiracy to corrupt public morals or to outrage public decency, although previously regarded as a subdivision of conspiracy to effect a public mischief, continue to thrive. The Labour Government refused to add its abolition to other reforms of conspiracy law, and the recommendation by the Williams Committee on Obscenity for its abolition[6] is unlikely to be implemented. Prosecutions may still, therefore, be brought against the publisher or author of advertisements for homosexual friendships or for prostitution (whether homosexual or heterosexual) even though neither prostitution nor private homosexual activity between two adults is a criminal offence. In 1981 Tom O'Carroll was convicted and sentenced to two years' imprisonment for conspiracy to corrupt public morals, although his co-conspirators had been acquitted in a previous trial, at which the jury had also failed to agree on the charge against O'Carroll. The considerable controversy aroused by the case – O'Carroll was the secretary of the Paedophile Information Exchange (PIE) and had assisted in the publication of contact advertisements between adults who shared a sexual interest in children – overshadowed the deplorable nature of the conspiracy charge used by the prosecution. Conspiring to corrupt public morals is an offence incapable of definition or precise proof. Assisting adults to meet each other is not a crime, even if the purpose of the meeting is to exchange pornographic material. (Although the exchange of obscene material through the post is itself a criminal offence, it is the policy of the Director of Public Prosecutions – as revealed in this trial – not necessarily to prosecute in such cases when the material is solicited and no financial gain is involved.) If the purpose of the contact advertisements was, in fact, to facilitate sexual encounters between adults and those under age, then the adults involved could have been charged with specific offences and those who assisted them with inciting, or aiding and abetting, such offences. But a specific criminal charge would have required specific proof and would not have allowed the prosecution to rely on the general offensiveness of the material whose exchange apparently resulted from the PIE advertisements.

The particular targets of the conspiracy laws are political and sexual dissidents. The 'sus' law, although introduced for use against vagrants, was until recently used to a large extent against the young members of black communities of London and some other large cities. Like conspiracy, the offence of being a suspected person loitering with intent to commit an arrestable offence enabled the police to criminalize conduct which fell far short of any actual criminal offence. 'Proof' of the offence depended, in the vast majority of cases, on the evidence of police officers alone, without even the safeguard of jury trial. The law's vagueness and its arbitrary and capricious use led the Home Affairs Select Committee in 1980[7] unanimously to recommend its repeal. But the Government's Criminal Attempts Act 1981, although repealing the 'sus' offence, amended the law of attempt to provide, for instance, that attempted theft may be charged even where the 'completed' offence (such as theft from an empty pocket) is impossible to commit. As originally drafted, the Bill would also have made it an offence to 'interfere' with a parked car; the Act now limits the offence to cases in which there is an intention to steal from a car, to steal the car itself or to take and drive away the vehicle. Since both attempt and the new offence of interference carry with them the right to jury trial, it seems unlikely that they will be as uncertain or as unjust in practice as the old 'sus' law.

Elsewhere I deal with other unjust laws – for instance, the laws against obscenity (page 95) and against homosexuality (page 220). But this brief outline of some of the issues involved in substantive law reform may serve to remind us that thoroughgoing change in the operations of the police must include changes in the laws they enforce, as well as in the method of their enforcement.

The attack on the criminal justice system

Criticism of Britain's criminal justice system normally starts from the assumption that the system is tilted in favour of the criminal. In 1973 the then Metropolitan Police Commissioner, Sir Robert Mark, in his notorious Dimbleby Lecture,[8] criticized the pre-trial and trial process for what he described as its 50 per cent failure rate. The notion that all those charged with criminal offence are guilty and that the purpose of the trial is to confirm the police officer's decision continues to dominate much discussion in police circles and much of the evidence given by police bodies to the Royal Commission. But Sir Robert's figures produced an entirely distorted picture of the trial process, since he concentrated on the very small minority of cases which are dealt with by juries at the Crown Court and in which the defendant pleads guilty, and he ignored the majority of guilty pleas tried summarily by magistrates. In 1978, for instance, 57 per cent of all Crown Court cases involved a plea of guilty. Of the remainder (21,876 charges which were contested by the defendants), 47 per cent were acquitted (Sir Robert Mark's 'one in two'). But over 40 per cent of those acquittals were directed by the judge, on the grounds that there was inadequate evidence on which to base a prosecution, the remainder being acquittals by the jury. But these Crown Court cases were only a tiny proportion of criminal offences tried that year. Of 1.9 million cases dealt with by the magistrates' courts, nearly 95 per cent resulted in conviction.[9]

Central to Sir Robert Mark's proposals for reducing the 'failure rate' was the abolition of the suspect's right to remain silent under police questioning by providing that silence could be used as evidence of guilt at a subsequent trial. The proposal had been adopted in 1972 by the Criminal Law Revision Committee (CLRC), but the outcry, particularly from practising lawyers, ensured that the CLRC's report was never implemented. Abolition of the right to silence was firmly rejected by the Royal Commission some nine years later.

Before I turn to a detailed examination of police powers – and, particularly, the powers of arrest, detention and interrogation – it is worth recalling the case which led to the establishment of the Royal Commission. Far from suggesting that the rules under which the police operate were tilted in favour of the guilty, the case illustrated vividly how innocent people may come to be imprisoned and how inadequately existing procedures protect them.

Early in the morning of 22 April 1972 the fire brigade was called to a house in Catford, in south London. When the fire had been put out, the brigade found the body of a man, later identified as Maxwell Confait, who had been murdered. Two days later the police arrested and interviewed three young men: Colin Lattimore, who, although aged 18, was severely mentally subnormal; Ronald Leighton, aged 15; and Ahmet Salih, aged 14. On the basis of confession statements made in the absence of parents or solicitors and later repeated when their parents arrived at the police station, the three boys were charged with arson, and Lattimore and Leighton with the murder of Maxwell Confait. At the trial in November, at which the three pleaded not guilty, Lattimore was convicted of manslaughter on the grounds of diminished responsibility, Leighton of murder and all three of arson. Salih was ordered to be detained for four years, Leighton to be detained during Her

Majesty's Pleasure and Lattimore to be detained at Rampton Hospital for an indefinite period. Their applications for leave to appeal were refused. But subsequent examination of the evidence by a leading forensic pathologist, who was brought into the case by the National Council for Civil Liberties (NCCL) at the request of Lattimore's parents, revealed that the Home Office pathologist, whose evidence had been accepted by the trial court, had misjudged the effect of the fire upon the cooling of the dead man's body, thus misleading the court about the likely time of the murder – which must, in fact, have taken place much earlier in the evening, at a time for which Lattimore had a firm alibi. It was not until October 1975, however, and only after a sustained campaign led by the boys' MP, Christopher Price, that the Home Office referred the case back to the Court of Appeal, which quashed all the convictions. And it was not until 1981 that the boys were offered by the Home Office compensation of £65,000 between them for the three years that they had wrongly spent in detention.

Sir Henry Fisher, formerly a judge of the High Court, was appointed to investigate the circumstances leading to the trial. His report[10] revealed that Lattimore had been interrogated in breach of the Judges' Rules and Administrative Directions; that in the Metropolitan Public District, Direction 7 (that a suspect should be allowed to telephone a friend or solicitor and should be informed of his right to do so) was not observed – furthermore, that the very existence of Direction 7 was *unknown* to the senior police officers and lawyers appearing before his inquiry; that the Home Office pathologist had failed adequately to examine the crucial evidence concerning time of death; and that the Director of Public Prosecutions's department and counsel advising it should never have allowed the case to go to trial. By referring the issues raised in Sir Henry's report to a Royal Commission, the Home Secretary succeeded in avoiding any commitment to implementing his recommendations. Nor was any explanation ever forthcoming of how the Metropolitan Police had succeeded not only in breaking the Judges' Rules in one case – which might be understandable – but in ignoring completely the suspect's right to contact a solicitor.

Police powers of arrest

The criminal law itself must be clear and certain in order to avoid the injustices of arbitrary and retrospective use. Similarly, the powers of the police must be clear and certain in order to reduce the risk that they will be abused to punish someone who has not been convicted or to convict someone who is innocent.

Arrest and detention is itself a punishment. It is a punishment imposed on someone who may have committed no offence at all, who has been neither charged nor convicted of an offence, and who, even if charged and convicted, may not be sentenced to imprisonment. Some loss of liberty for some suspects before charge or trial is inevitable. But because detention involves the loss of one of the most basic of human rights, the right to liberty, its incidence should be kept to the minimum.

The present powers of the police to arrest without a warrant are extremely confused. A simple principle – that the police may arrest without a warrant someone reasonably suspected of committing an arrestable offence (i.e., one carrying a maximum of five years' or more imprisonment) – has been destroyed by the addition of over a hundred lesser offences. Some police forces are considerably more willing to use the power of summons, rather than that of arrest, in order to bring a suspect before the court. In 1978, for instance, 76 per cent of those charged with an indictable offence and 45 per cent of those charged with a summary offence had been arrested before being charged, although the vast majority had been released on bail to appear at court. The remainder of those charged – that is, 24 per cent of those charged with indictable offences and 55 per cent of those charged with summary offences – were brought to court by means of a summons. But in the Metropolitan Police district and in Greater Manchester fewer than 1 per cent of those charged with an indictable offence were brought to court by way of a summons. Yet in Thames Valley, West Yorkshire and a number of other police areas 40 per cent or more of those charged with an indictable offence were summonsed rather than arrested.[11] Although in a large urban area a higher proportion of suspects may be of no fixed abode or may be thought by the police to be likely to abscond before trial, the discrepancies beween different areas suggest that there is considerable room for reducing the number of arrests and for making greater use of the summons procedure.

The evidence to the Royal Commission of Sir David McNee, Metropolitan Police Commissioner, does indeed suggest that a greater use of the arrest power is a matter of police *policy* rather than external factors. Sir David argued that, except in minor traffic offences, the arrest and detention of the suspect made it easier for the police to investigate the offence.[12] But arresting, rather than summonsing, a suspect is not simply a matter to be decided according to the convenience of the police or – a different criterion – the interests of the community in seeing offenders brought to justice. Even a fairly brief period of arrest may have serious consequences for the suspect's family or for the suspect's own standing with an employer or within the community. The suspect who is arrested and detained is more likely to be refused bail than is a person summonsed for the same offence[13] – and thus more likely to suffer the extremely prejudicial effects of being held in custody before trial.

A crucial question for the Royal Commission, therefore, was whether or not the power of arrest should be used more or less frequently. On the one hand, Sir David McNee proposed a power of arrest for *all* imprisonable offences. On the other hand, NCCL argued for a return to the basic principle of a power of arrest only for offences carrying a maximum of at least five years' imprisonment, together with the common law power of arrest where a breach of the peace was reasonably anticipated. Following instead the proposal made by Professor Michael Zander that the police should be given a broader power of arrest, but urged to weigh up the question of whether or not the power was really needed in particular cases, the Royal Commission proposed to extend the power of arrest not only to all imprisonable offences but also to cases in which the offence cannot be punished by imprisonment but the offender refuses to identify himself. The Commission also believed, however, that the power of arrest should be used *less* frequently and therefore proposed that the newly extended powers of arrest should be coupled with a 'necessity principle' governing their use. Although the initial arrest would not be restrained, detention at a police station would be lawful only if it was necessary in order to identify the suspect so that a summons could be served on him; to prevent the continuation or repetition of the offence; to protect the suspect, or other people, or property; to secure or preserve evidence of the offence, or to obtain such evidence from the suspect by questioning him; or to prevent the person from absconding. (The Commission also suggested that the need to obtain identification would be the *only* grounds for the arrest and continued detention of someone seen committing an offence which is not punishable by imprisonment; it remains to be seen whether this restriction is carried through into legislation or practice.) To expect these criteria to *reduce* the number of arrests, when the power of arrest is itself being significantly extended, is indeed extraordinary. No doubt, some police forces will conscientiously scrutinize each case, having regard, as the Commission proposed, 'to the nature and seriousness of the offence, the nature, age and circumstances of the suspect, and the nature of the investigation that is required'. But it is inconceivable that the Metropolitan Police, with a stated policy of preferring arrest and detention to the use of the summons, would not find a way of bringing almost every case within the scope of inevitably broad criteria. Particularly disturbing is the proposal that the need to question the suspect, in order to obtain evidence, should itself be grounds for continued detention. As McConville and Baldwin, two of the academics involved in background research for the Commission, have commented: 'Unnoticed and under the guise of a *limiting* principle, the Royal Commission has thus proposed a new power to detain for questioning.'[14]

The British section of the International Commission of Jurists, Justice, has estimated[15] that by 1975 there were already over 7000 separate criminal offences in English law. Under the Commission's proposals, all will carry the power of arrest. Since it would be impossible for the police to arrest everyone suspected of committing any offence or even for them to attempt to establish the identity of anyone seen committing an offence that does not carry a sentence of imprisonment, the result will inevitably be that the power to arrest for a minor offence will be used arbitrarily. Young people, and particularly young black people, those of unconventional appearance or whose views are known to be unpopular, will be the especial victims of such arbitrary discretion. The only effective means of ensuring that the power of arrest is used less and not more often – an end which the Royal Commission itself endorsed – is to restrict the power of arrest to those more serious cases in which the loss of liberty is justified. The alternatives are to leave untouched the present confused collection of arrest powers or to find a new and simpler rule. The simplest alternative, which would leave the police with powers of arrest in all cases of any seriousness while requiring them to make more use of the summonsing procedure in other cases, is to restore the common law division between offences that justify arrest and those that do not by providing that any offence punishable with at least five years' imprisonment should carry a power of arrest. The statutory exceptions should be abolished, although the common law power of arrest for breach of the peace (restricted, as I propose on page 150, to situations where there is a 'clear and present danger' of a breach of the peace) should be codified and retained.

The detention of suspects

English law has virtually nothing to say about the detention of suspects by the police. Under the 1952 Magistrates' Courts Act, the police are required either to bail someone charged with an offence that is not serious or to bring him to court within twenty-four hours. Someone kept in custody after being charged with a serious offence must likewise be brought before a court 'as soon as practicable'. The Metropolitan Police Commissioner has asserted[16] that 'as soon as practicable' refers to the inquiries undertaken by the police *after* charge and not simply to the availability of the next court hearing – an interpretation which nullifies an already vague provision. In any case, the Act does not deal with the period *between* arrest and charge.

The police have not taken the inadequacies of the law as a licence to detain suspects for weeks at the police station. Most people who are arrested are released without charge (between 10 per cent and 20 per cent of those arrested, according to the Royal Commission)[17] or are charged and released on bail within a fairly brief period. But a three-month study within the Metropolitan Police District revealed that 212 people had been detained for over seventy-two hours,[18] while the Prevention of Terrorism Act 1976 authorizes detention without charge for up to seven days.[19]

In his evidence to the Royal Commission Sir David McNee proposed that the police should be permitted to detain an arrested person for up to seventy-two hours' questioning, with, presumably, a further twenty-four hours or longer elapsing between charge and appearance at court. Sir David envisaged that the police would be able to apply to a magistrate for an indefinite number of renewals of the seventy-two hour period of detention without the suspect having any right to be represented at the hearing or even to be informed of it. The Royal Commission, rightly, rejected Sir David's extraordinary proposals. Instead the Commission proposed that a senior police officer should review the case of an arrested person after six hours' detention in order to establish whether or not grounds for continued detention still existed (i.e., the 'necessity principle'), and that after twenty-four hours the suspect should be released or charged and either released on bail or brought before the next available court.

The Royal Commission was right in establishing a fixed time limit for the detention of suspects. But its proposal has two flaws. The first is that the time limit proposed would have no effect at all on the

experience of most people at present. As the Commission itself
points out, about three-quarters of those detained are dealt with
within six hours and 95 per cent within twenty-four hours.[20] By
contrast, the Thomson Committee, which reported in 1975 on
Scottish procedure, recommended a fixed period of six hours'
detention between arrest and charge or release, with no power for
the police to apply for an extension.[21] The Australian Law Reform
Commission[22] proposed a four-hour period, with a power to apply
to the magistrate for an extension of up to eight hours or, in
exceptional cases, a further extension on the authority of a
Supreme Court judge. The Australian Commission also proposed
that a suspect who had been charged should either be bailed or
brought before a magistrate within four hours; that he should have
a right to appeal against refusal of bail, if necessary by telephone to
a magistrate; and that if the appeal failed, he should be brought to
the first sitting of the nearest court. The American Law Institute's
Model Code of Pre-Arraignment Procedure in 1973[23] proposed a
limit of five hours' detention in the police station, with only two
hours for minor offences.

Even more serious, the Royal Commission's time limit of twenty-
four hours would not apply in the case of 'grave' offences. The
distinction between grave and other offences is central to the Royal
Commission's scheme. Those suspected of a grave offence, if not
charged after twenty-four hours, would have to be brought before
a magistrates' court, which could authorize a further twenty-four
hours' period of detention. The suspect would be legally represented, although the hearing itself would be in private. If a court
was unable to sit at the end of the twenty-four-hour period (for
instance, on a Sunday), an independent 'visitor' would see the
prisoner. At the end of the second period of detention the suspect
could be brought before the court again, which could again
authorize a further day's detention. This time the suspect would
have a right of appeal – although the Commission did not specify
who would hear the appeal – but if no appeal were made or if it
were unsuccessful, the magistrates' court could continue to
authorize an unlimited number of 24-hour detentions.

Although the Commission proposed fewer safeguards for those
suspected of grave offences, it is in these cases that the most
rigorous safeguards are needed, precisely because the consequences of a wrongful conviction are most severe. The Commission did not explore in any detail the circumstances that might
warrant continued detention. On the one hand, the desire of the

police to obtain a confession statement is *not* an acceptable reason for extended detention, particularly in view of the effect of detention on the validity of any confession obtained (see below, page 17). On the other hand, an extremely complex case, involving a large number of suspects all of whom had to be questioned, might require a period longer than twenty-four hours, even though the offences involved did not qualify as grave.

It was to counter the risk of indefinite detention that the writ of *habeas corpus* was enshrined in the 1679 Habeas Corpus Act. But *habeas corpus* no longer represents an adequate check on the abuse of power. Those most in need of its protection are least able to initiate proceedings. A suspect held incommunicado in a police station cannot instruct a lawyer to act on his behalf or even inform his family of his whereabouts. The family may not know how to find a solicitor to act for it or be able to afford legal fees for an application to the Divisional Court. According to Tom Sergeant, secretary of Justice,[24] some solicitors are reluctant to issue a writ in case the police charge their clients unjustifiably instead of releasing them a few days or hours later. Most seriously, the courts have fallen into the habit of adjourning *habeas corpus* applications – thus giving the police an additional day or more in which to detain the suspect and ensuring that the suspect is either charged or released by the time the adjourned application is heard. For instance, in 1975 an application made on behalf of Ronald Milhench, who had been held by the police for over forty-eight hours, was adjourned from Saturday morning until Monday morning – thus ensuring a further forty-eight hours' detention for the suspect! In 1979 of twenty-five applications, only nine were heard and only one granted.[25]

In one case in 1980, however, the court granted a writ of *habeas corpus* to a suspect who had been detained at Kentish Town police station for questioning even after being charged with a different offence. Despite the absence of a statutory time limit between arrest and charge, the court suggested that forty-eight hours would be the maximum it would tolerate.[26]

This more robust approach needs swift Parliamentary backing, which recognizes that urgency is of the essence of an application for *habeas corpus*. The jurisdiction of circuit judges should be extended to such applications, thus removing the difficulties of finding a High Court judge at short notice, and the court should have no power to adjourn an application except with the applicant's consent. At the most, if the court decides to grant the application, it should have the power to suspend operation of the writ for a few hours in order to allow the respondent time to appeal. Most important, in view of the recent decision of the House of Lords in a case affecting someone detained by the Home Office on suspicion of being an illegal entrant (see page 198), Parliament should restore to the detainor the burden of proof in a *habeas corpus* case. It should no longer be up to the suspect in a police station or the settled immigrant suspected of some years-old irregularity to prove his innocence.

Under the Commission's scheme, an application for *habeas corpus* could lie only where someone not suspected of a grave offence had been held without charge beyond twenty-four hours, or where someone suspected of a grave offence had either been held beyond the period authorized by the magistrates' court or not been brought before the magistrates at all. In view of the regrettable willingness of some magistrates to sanction almost any police application at all, the Royal Commission would have done better to direct itself, first, to a proper consideration of the circumstances which could justify extended detention and, second, to a reform of the *habeas corpus* procedure, instead of allowing magistrates to sanction continued detention and thus to nullify the protection of a *habeas corpus* writ.

The questioning of suspects

Detention in a police station is, of itself, a punishment. But the use of detention powers, the length of detention and the use of inter-rogation during detention are also of concern because of their effect on the integrity of the trial that may follow. Most people detained at a police station are disoriented and frightened. They often have no idea of how long they will be kept there; they may be worried about children and other members of the family; they may, rightly or wrongly, fear violence; they may be told that if they co-operate, they will get bail, and if they don't, they will be kept in custody even longer. Background research carried out for the Royal Commission revealed that very few detainees remain completely silent, and that six out of ten of those questioned make some confession or admission.[27] The Commission itself recognized the 'psychological pressures that custody in the police station generates' (para. 4.46) and rightly argued, in support of retaining the present rule on the right to silence:

It is not only that those extreme means of attempting to extort confessions, for example the rack and thumbscrew, which have sometimes disfigured the system of criminal justice in this country, are abhorrent to any civilized society, but that they and other less awful, though not necessarily less potent, means of applying pressure to an accused person to speak *do not necessarily produce speech or the truth*. (My emphasis.)[28]

The Confait case described above is a telling example of the risk that a 'confession' may not be the truth. Such a confession may be produced even in the face of compelling evidence to the contrary. For instance, in 1981 the *Guardian* published details of the case of Erroll Madden, a black youth arrested by the police late one night as he returned home from the cinema. After some hours' questioning, Madden signed a confession statement admitting the theft of two model cars that he had bought a few days previously – despite the fact that in his bag was the receipt for one of the models![29]

The Judges' Rules and Administrative Directions are concerned with the problem of ensuring that statements made under interrogation are voluntary – that is, not obtained by ill-treatment, threats or bribes. Their provisions are inadequate and, as Sir Henry Fisher found, often ignored. But the problem is not simply one of enforcing proper standards for the treatment and interrogation of suspects. The fundamental problem with the Judges' Rules is the assumption that statements made under police questioning can be truly voluntary.

The Tavistock Institute's research for the Royal Commission[30] strongly suggests that the notion of a 'voluntary' statement is meaningless. Even in the absence of physical force or overt threats or bribes, the combination of isolation, fear and simple techniques for questioning lead most suspects to talk. The researchers concluded that it is impossible to predict the degree of isolation or fear which will destroy the resistance of a particular suspect. We are, therefore, faced with a crucial choice about the nature of our criminal justice system. Are we satisfied with a system in which the majority of convictions depend on self-incriminating statements obtained from suspects in a state of acute psychological disadvantage, or do we wish to make sense of our existing notions of 'voluntary' statements and the safeguards which the Judges' Rules attempt to provide? The police would generally argue that in the absence of violence or explicit threats or inducements, any suspect's statement should be admissible as evidence, and that further restrictions or even the enforcement of existing safeguards would weaken the fight against crime. On the other hand, there must be serious doubts about the quality of convictions produced by the existing system; a real risk that, unknown to the public, a significant minority of people are wrongfully convicted on the basis of their own statements; and a further risk that the police will come to rely more and more on arrests and subsequent interrogation rather than on independent, corroborated evidence.

Since arrest and interrogation form an inescapable part of the process of enforcing the criminal law, the need is to provide and enforce adequate safeguards designed to maximize the reliability of evidence obtained through questioning and, therefore, to reduce the risk of wrongful pleas of guilty or wrongful convictions. The Royal Commission proposed the introduction of a Code of Practice to replace the present Rules and Directions – a Code specifically 'aimed at producing conditions of interview that minimize the risk of unreliable statements'. The intention is welcome. But the proposal fails on three grounds. First, the Code would be drafted by the Home Office and introduced by the Home Secretary through a statutory instrument incapable of amendment by Parliament. Since the Royal Commission generally failed to spell out its proposals in any detail, it would hardly be surprising if the new Code closely resembled the old Rules. Second, the Commission's proposals, even when made in detail, are often defective. The Commission, for instance, wished to strengthen the right of a suspect to see a solicitor. A duty solicitor scheme would be created under the legal aid system, and in most cases the present right of the police to deny access to a solicitor would be abolished. But the Commission then undermined its own arguments in favour of unrestricted right of access by reinstating the discretion of the police to refuse access in cases where the person is suspected of a 'grave' offence – the very cases for which access to a solicitor is most imperative. On tape recording the Commission is even weaker. Recognizing the delays and costs incurred by arguments about the police version of an interview, the Commission concluded that tape recording could produce more accurate records of interviews – but proposed that the only part of an interview to be recorded should be a 'summary' dictated by the interviewing officer, together with any comments added by the suspect!

But the Commission's proposals are weakest when it comes to the *enforcement* of the projected Code of Practice. There are, broadly, three ways of enforcing the standards laid down for the detention and interrogation of suspects. First, administrative means can be provided to investigate complaints by suspects and to observe and supervise police officers' conduct. Such means may be internal to the police – as is the present machinery for the investigation of complaints – or external, in the form, for instance, of a Police Ombudsman. Second, an aggrieved suspect may be able to sue a police officer for damages if, for instance, he has been assaulted or unlawfully detained. And, third, the rules of evidence may make inadmissible in any subsequent trial evidence obtained from the suspect in breach of the Code of Practice.

The Commission itself recognized the serious defects in the present police complaints machinery (described on page 70). It might also have acknowledged that although the Judges' Rules are already part of the Standing Orders of the Metropolitan Police, the disciplinary sanction did nothing to prevent the situation identified by Sir Henry Fisher in the Confait inquiry. The Commission also accepted that a civil action is likely to be expensive and difficult, particularly when the plaintiff has already been convicted of a criminal offence. Nonetheless, the Commission proposed to rely almost entirely on these two methods for the enforcement of its new rules on interrogation and detention.

But the method most likely to be effective in securing obedience to the rules is one that ensures that any breach of those rules has a direct effect on the trial of the suspect. As Mr Justice MacKenna said in 1976:

> if the police are allowed to use in court evidence which they have obtained from suspects to whom they have wrongly denied the right of legal advice, they will be encouraged to continue this illegal practice. If the police know that the answers to their questions will not be admitted if they have refused, without good reason, to allow their prisoner to see his solicitor, and that it is not a good reason that they hope that, unadvised, he will incriminate himself, there will, I think, be fewer complaints of the denial of this right.[31]

But this sanction – excluding evidence improperly obtained – is so inconsistently and uncertainly applied that it is hardly surprising if it does not loom large in the mind of the investigating officer. In the Confait case described earlier none of the boys' confession statements was excluded; indeed, defence counsel did not even attempt to have two of the statements ruled inadmissible. Confession statements obtained in breach of the Rules are so commonly accepted in evidence that the police and many journalists were shocked when the case against the suspected murderer of Michelle Booth in 1978 was abandoned after the judge excluded the suspect's confession as having been improperly obtained. (It appeared that the suspect, like Colin Lattimore in the Confait case, was mentally subnormal and that the confession had been obtained in the absence of a solicitor or any other independent adult.) What is urgently needed is a rule on the admissibility or exclusion of evidence that is clear, certain and regularly applied.

All that the Commission proposed was that evidence should be excluded only if it had been obtained by the use of violence, threats of violence, torture or inhuman or degrading treatment. All other evidence would be admissible, and the judge's present discretion to exclude 'involuntary' statements or evidence obtained in breach of the Rules would be abolished.

In support of this proposal the Commission argued, first, that an exclusionary rule can assist only in the small minority of cases in which a suspect contests the charge against him. But this is to misunderstand the fact that at the time of the interrogation itself a police officer is concerned primarily with obtaining evidence; he cannot know whether or not the suspect will plead guilty to any charge that may be laid. An officer who knows with utter certainty that any statement he obtains from the suspect will be useless as evidence unless he sticks to the rules is more likely to comply than one who believes, with good reason, that he can get away with ignoring them.

Second, the Commission looked to the experience of the exclusionary rule in the United States of America to argue that it results in the acquittal of the 'patently guilty' on technicalities and is, in any case, ineffective in preventing police misbehaviour. At least one Commissioner argued that an exclusionary rule can protect only the guilty and is of no help to the innocent.[32] The intellectual dishonesty in the Commission's argument is breathtaking. The American research from which it quotes[33] is concerned with the exclusionary rule as it relates to illegal *searches* and not with the exclusion of improperly obtained statements. Now, it is perfectly true that the legality or illegality of a search does not affect the nature of what is found. A knife is still a knife; a smoking gun remains a smoking gun, even if the police have broken down the door in order to find it. In relation to the product of illegal searches, it is true to say that a strict exclusionary rule will deny to the courts evidence of guilt. There are, nonetheless, strong arguments for excluding the fruit of illegal searches: the community should not benefit from police wrongdoing by obtaining a conviction on the basis of illegally obtained evidence, and the courts should discourage, as far as possible, police violation of the law. Oddly enough, the Commission itself accepted these arguments when it proposed the exclusion of evidence obtained in breach of the rules on search warrants: 'the right of members of the public to be free from general searches must be respected.'[34]

Unlike the product of illegal searches, however, the product of illegal questioning – a statement or confession made by the suspect – is directly affected by the means used to obtain it. The *reliability* of a 'confession' obtained from a suspect who has been denied access to a lawyer, or the right to contact his family, or adequate sleep or refreshments, must be open to extremely serious question. Far from an exclusionary rule's protecting only the guilty, as the Commission argued, the exclusion of a statement unfairly or improperly obtained is directly concerned with preventing the wrongful conviction of the innocent.

Sir Henry Fisher, in his report on the Confait case, did not go so far as to prescribe the automatic exclusion of any statement obtained in breach of the Judges' Rules. His recommendations, nonetheless, represent a minimum level of acceptable reform: no person should be convicted on the basis of any statement or confession obtained in breach of the Rules unless there is corroborative evidence *not* obtained in those circumstances; no child, young person or mentally handicapped person should be convicted on the basis of a confession or statement obtained in the absence of an independent adult unless there is properly obtained corroboration; and the trial judge be given discretion to exclude any statement obtained in breach of the Rules, regardless of whether or not the statement was 'voluntary' or whether or not there is other supporting evidence.[35] Instead of proposing at least the firm corroboration rule suggested by Sir Henry, the Commission weakly suggested that the jury be directed to 'look for independent support' before relying on the illegally obtained statement.

The Commission looked instead to Northern Ireland for its proposals. Under the 1976 Emergency Provisions Act, evidence will be excluded automatically only if the defence can establish that it was obtained by means of torture or inhuman or degrading treatment. In its desire to ensure that convictions could be obtained on the basis of 'confessions' which would normally have been ruled inadmissible, the Government apparently intended that only statements obtained through the outlawed methods should be excluded. The Northern Ireland judiciary has, however, asserted its overriding 'discretion' to exclude other statements which, although not obtained through torture or similar methods, are nonetheless considered unreliable.[36]

The problem, however, with any reliance on judicial discretion to deal with illegally obtained evidence is that the police may continue to flout the rules in the expectation that, nonetheless, 'confessions' so obtained will form the basis of convictions, however unsafe. Only a strict rule excluding any evidence obtained in breach of the prescribed standards will provide the suspect with a guarantee of his rights. In response, it is argued that it would be absurd to exclude evidence simply because there has been a breach of a 'trivial' rule – for instance, one concerning the provision of refreshments at specified intervals. No one would seriously argue that a five- or ten-minute delay in providing tea should result in the exclusion of otherwise acceptable evidence. But the difficulty is hardly insuperable. If the strict exclusionary rule is to apply to all provisions for the treatment of suspects, then those provisions will be worded in such a way as to deal with small delays. But the strict exclusionary rule must be applied to those standards which are considered fundamental to the treatment of the suspect and, therefore, to the quality of any evidence obtained from him. Those standards must include: a time limit on the period of detention before charge; a time limit on each period of questioning; provision for rest and refreshment; the right of a suspect to see a solicitor; the right of a suspect to communicate his whereabouts to his family; and, for the young and the mentally handicapped, a provision ensuring that no statement will be taken except in the presence of an independent adult known to the suspect. Furthermore, the full tape recording of interviews at police stations should be introduced as soon as necessary training and the installation of equipment has been completed.

Bail or custody?

The argument against detention in police custody – that it is a punishment inflicted on someone whose guilt has not yet been tried – applies as strongly to detention in prison before trial. It is true that by this stage the suspect has been charged with a criminal offence, but the presumption of innocence remains as strong, and with it must go a presumption of bail. Pre-trial detention is a punishment inflicted before conviction, which not only makes it more difficult for the defendant to arrange for his defence but may also jeopardize his home and his livelihood.[37] Of people remanded in custody during 1980, about 3 per cent were acquitted at their subsequent trial, and about 40 per cent, although convicted, were awarded non-custodial sentences. The Bail Act 1976 was designed to place the presumption of bail on a statutory basis, allowing magistrates to refuse bail only if certain specific criteria were fulfilled. In practice, however, the Act allows magistrates very considerable discretion. In the immediate aftermath of the rioting in July 1981 it became apparent that magistrates in some cities were using their power to impose curfews as a condition of bail, and to deny bail altogether even to defendants charged with a first offence.[38] And it is by no means uncommon for people to be acquitted at trial who have spent months in custody beforehand. The police argue, of course, that it is quite usual for someone who has been released on bail subsequently to be arrested for a serious offence. Nonetheless, a research study initiated by the Metropolitan Police into absconding on bail and arrests of bailees found it impossible to obtain an estimate of the numbers arrested while on bail.[39] And the suggestion that bail should be denied in case the defendant commits another (sic) offence not only makes a nonsense of the presumption of innocence but is tantamount to a system of preventive detention.

In 1980 the High Court sanctioned a serious erosion of the defendant's rights when it upheld the practice introduced by the Nottingham magistrates and their clerks of refusing to hear subsequent applications for bail by a defendant who had already been remanded in custody unless there had been a change in the defendant's circumstances.[40] In other words, the seven-day remand in custody, which at least ensured that the defendant was regularly brought before the court, had been transformed into an indefinite remand – an expedient similar to the one that was adopted under the emergency legislation introduced during the 1981 prison officers' strike.[41]

Amending legislation is clearly now required, not only in order to place a heavier burden on those challenging an application for bail and to reverse the decision in the Nottingham magistrates' case, but also to provide a system of appeal against a magistrate's refusal of bail. It is well established that an application for bail made to a judge in chambers on behalf of a legally represented defendant has a reasonable chance of success, whereas an application made 'on the papers' through the Official Solicitor has very little. But the majority of defendants appealing to a judge against refusal of bail are compelled to use the Official Solicitor procedure, not because legal aid is not available for such an application but because, as the Legal Action Group has repeatedly pointed out,[42] the Law Society refuses to grant legal aid for such cases as a matter of policy. The Law Society should be required to implement the statutory provisions concerning legal aid for bail applications, and additional provision should be made for an appeal, with legal aid, to a Crown Court judge.

The right to legal representation

The International Commission of Jurists, in its conference in 1959 on the rule of law, held that 'equal access to law for the rich and poor alike is essential to the maintenance of the rule of law' and that all defendants should be entitled to the assistance of their chosen legal adviser. Twenty-two years later that ideal has not been realized in this country. Although the majority of those tried by jury in the Crown Courts are legally represented,[43] they constitute only a small proportion of the total numbers of people facing criminal charges each year. And in the magistrates' courts, where the majority of defendants are tried and, if convicted, sentenced, nearly 33 per cent have no legal representation at their trial. The cause is partly ignorance, but the absence of legal advice is also due to the extraordinary discretion granted magistrates in deciding applications for legal aid. Since there is no absolute financial qualification for legal aid, every defendant is able to qualify on financial grounds. But the magistrates have complete discretion to decide whether or not a case 'merits' legal aid. The consequence is appalling discrepancies between different magistrates' courts, against whose decision there is no right of appeal. Howard Levenson's research[44] has shown that although the overall rate of *refusals* of legal aid in magistrates' courts was just over 13 per cent, the refusal rate was one-third in the Ormskirk court and nearly half in Highgate magistrates' court. Among the Inner London courts the refusal rate to defendants being summarily tried for non-indictable offences was a staggering 76.5 per cent in Woolwich, 46.7 per cent in Bow Street and 45.5 per cent in Tower Bridge.

An extension of duty solicitor schemes and improvements in the quality of the service provided would be of particular help to the inarticulate defendant appearing in court for the first time after charge. But it is also essential either to make legal aid mandatory at least for any offence carrying a sentence of imprisonment or to provide for the right of appeal against a magistrates' court which refuses legal aid.

The appeal system

Even if a public prosecutor took over responsibility for criminal cases for the police, and even if safeguards for suspects were strengthened in the ways I have suggested, the occasional wrongful conviction of an innocent person would still be inevitable. But the system for dealing with criminal appeals seems to be incapable of providing redress for the victim of injustice.

In June 1979 the Court of Appeal quashed the conviction of George Lindo, an innocent man of previous good character who had spent over twelve months in prison after being convicted of a robbery charge. The case against Mr Lindo consisted of a 'confession' statement – disputed by the defence – and verbal statements which the police officers in the case claimed that the defendant had made. Mr Lindo was convicted in February 1978. A few days later the defence learned that charges in a different case altogether had been dropped because, despite a 'confession' from the original defendant, another man had himself pleaded guilty to the crime: the officer in the case was one of those who had given evidence against Lindo. In September of the same year another officer concerned admitted that he had forged witness statements during the Yorkshire Ripper investigation. By December at the latest, and possibly earlier, the office of the Registrar of Criminal Appeals knew of the suspicions against the policeman involved in Lindo's case. But in January 1979 Lindo was refused bail pending his appeal, and by the time he was released, he had only two weeks to go before he was due to be paroled.[45]

This case underlines the need for the proposal made elsewhere (see page 77) that the defendant and his lawyers should have right of access to the report of a police investigation that bears directly on the safety of the defendant's conviction. It also indicates the need for a far stronger presumption in favour of bail to apply even in cases in which the defendant has been convicted but leave to appeal has been granted. And, perhaps most important, it illustrates the case for a statutory system of compensation, so that those who have been imprisoned for a crime of which they are innocent are entitled to redress and are not dependent on the grudging hand-outs of the Home Office.[46]

The rights of prisoners

Discussion of the administration of justice too often stops at the prison gate. But then so do all the safeguards provided before conviction in an attempt to ensure that justice is done. Until recently, the administration of the law inside prisons was secretive, arbitrary and absolute, and even now the courts have only begun, tentatively, to develop a system of judicial supervision over the administration of British prisons.

An early attempt to challenge Home Office practice was made in 1971 by Golder, a prisoner who had attempted to sue a prison officer for defamation but had been prevented from communicating with his lawyers. Despite Golder's success in the Human Rights Court in 1975, the Home Office amended the Prison Rules only to the extent that a prisoner could freely communicate with a solicitor about possible civil proceedings and, even then, could not communicate on any matter relating to the prison administration – which, after all, was exactly what Golder was trying to discuss with his solicitor – unless the internal complaints machinery had been exhausted. In other words, prisoners continued to be faced with the choice of abandoning their right to seek redress in the civil courts or disclosing their entire case to the authorities protracted internal investigations.[47]

But the precedent established by Golder has been employed more successfully by a group of prisoners who complained to the Human Rights Commission in 1972 against the censorship of their correspondence. In August 1981, while a decision from the Court was awaited, the Home Office announced that the secret standing orders governing the detailed administration of prisons would be amended to allow prisoners unfettered correspondence with outside organizations and individuals (this freedom extended to matters relating to prison administration) and even, in some circumstances, with the press. The new circular, apparently prompted by the knowledge that the Court would rule against the United Kingdom Government on the prisoners' applications, would also be made public, although the Home Office warned that it would take some years before all the existing circulars were revised and published.[48]

The landmark case in judicial review of prison administration concerned an adjudication by the Board of Visitors of Hull Prison following prison riots in 1976. Disciplinary proceedings were taken against a number of prisoners. Despite the fact that they were not represented at the disciplinary hearing, often knew of the charges against them only hours beforehand and had no opportunity to cross-examine witnesses, many of the prisoners were 'awarded' sentences of loss of remission equivalent to an original sentence of up to one year's imprisonment. In 1979 the Court of Appeal over-turned the High Court decision rejecting the prisoners' application against the Board of Visitors and decided that Boards of Visitors conducting disciplinary hearings must apply the rules of natural justice.[49] In the subsequent hearing of the prisoners' substantive applications the High Court ruled that the Board had, in fact, breached the requirements of natural justice in some cases and therefore overruled the sentences imposed by the Board. Thus the case opens up the prospect that Board disciplinary awards will in future be overturned unless the Board behaves fairly. But the standards of fairness required by the Court of Appeal are not particularly rigorous. Clearly, the prisoner must be granted an opportunity to cross-examine the prison officers who are giving evidence against him and, presumably, to call his own witnesses. But a failure to provide a prisoner with full and early notification of the charges against him or a refusal to allow him legal repre-sentation would apparently be considered acceptable.[50] And the Court's decision applies only to the minority of cases (albeit the more serious ones) heard by a Board of Visitors: the majority, which are dealt with by the prison governor, are not affected at all. Nonetheless, in a dissenting judgment Shaw, LJ, argued that there was no difference in principle between disciplinary proceedings carried out by the Board and those carried out by the governor; both implemented the same regulations, and the consequences were 'in nature if not in degree' the same for the prisoner.

In late 1981 the Court of Appeal will have another opportunity to extend judicial review of decisions affecting prisoners when they consider the case of *Williams* v. *the Home Office*.[51] The case arose from Michael Williams's confinement in the control unit at Wakefield Prison in 1974, under a regime which was designed to impose an initial ninety days' solitary confinement on 'trouble-makers' followed by a further ninety days' restricted association with others in the unit, any slight misbehaviour condemning the prisoner to start the regime all over again. A public campaign following revelations by the *Sunday Times* of the nature of the regime led to the abandonment of the units soon after they were opened. But their legality was not tested until 1981, when, after a five-week hearing, the High Court held that although Williams's confinement had, of necessity, been in breach of the Prison Rules (which impose a maximum of fifty-six days on any one award of solitary confinement), the Rules were 'regulatory and not mandatory' and their breach had no legal effect. Although similar regimes had been held unconstitutional in the USA and in Canada, the court held that the control unit system did not breach the ban on 'cruel and unusual punishment' imposed by the Bill of Rights of 1689, and that the Prison Act 1952 in effect allowed the Home Secretary to impose whatever regime he chose on those in his lawful custody. If necessary, however, Williams is likely to pursue his case to the European Commission on Human Rights, which recently achieved a settlement with the United Kingdom Government in the case of a patient at Broadmoor Hospital, who claimed that the conditions of his 'seclusion' violated the prohibition of Article 3 of the Human Rights Convention against inhuman or degrading treatment or punishment.[52]

The *Williams* case may yet open up the courts to prisoners, as the Hull cases did. But regardless of the final outcome, the *Williams* case has also offered a major challenge to the secrecy of the Home Office Prison Department. In two preliminary hearings the Home Office's claim to public-interest immunity with respect to a number of documents requested on discovery was overruled by the court; the result was that, for the first time, a prison litigant was able to obtain extensive information about how policy had actually been made – and, in this particular case, to learn that the control unit regime which was actually introduced was far harsher than the system which had been offered to, and approved by, the then Home Secretary, Roy Jenkins. But the Home Office's use of the contempt of court laws to prevent Michael Williams's solicitor from disclosing the papers even after they had been read out in open court (see page 93) has so far censored full public and Parliamentary debate of the conduct of the Prisons Department.

The slow, uncertain process of establishing prisoners' rights through the courts should now be taken over by Parliament. In 1981 Alf Dubs, MP, failed, although by only a narrow majority, to secure a second reading for his Rights of Prisoners Bill, which would have given prisoners the vote (a sure way of securing the interest of more MPs in their conditions), would have ensured that prisoners facing disciplinary charges knew of those charges in advance and were entitled to legal representation at the hearing and would have made the Prison Rules justiciable. Until legislation along these lines is passed, or unless the courts build rapidly on the foundation of the Hull cases, prisoners will remain subject to arbitrary, secret and unchallengeable decisions on matters which directly affect the length and conditions of their confinement.

2

Causing Problems for the State

The British police have come to see their task not so much as the enforcement of the law but as the defence of the state. The classic view of the police as responsible for and to the community as a whole – in the words of Sir Robert Mark, formerly Chief Commissioner of the Metropolitan Police, as discharging 'the communal will, not that of any government minister, mayor or other public official, or that of any political party'[1] – is, of course, highly political. Implicit in it is the view that the police alone truly know what constitutes 'the communal will'. Astonishingly for a 'non-political' police officer, Sir Robert firmly placed the role of the police in the context of opposing socialism:

> The police are very much on their own in attempting to preserve order in an increasingly turbulent society in which socialist philosophy has changed from raising the standards of the poor and deprived to reducing the standards of the wealthy, the skilled and the deserving to the lowest common denominator.[2]

In chapter 3 I explore the implications which Sir Robert's view of policing has for structures of police accountability. What needs to be stressed here is that over the last two decades there has been no force to counterbalance the growing use of the police for political purposes. The police themselves have relished the job of identifying and watching the 'enemies of the people'; Governments have demanded it of them; Members of Parliament, along with police authorities and the press, have proved unwilling or unable even to find out exactly what is going on, let alone to call a halt.

In his report on the Profumo affair in 1963 Lord Denning defined a subversive as one 'who would overthrow or contemplate the overthrow of government by unlawful means'. By 1978 the then Home Secretary, Merlyn Rees, was able to tell the House of

30

Commons that subversive activities were those 'which threaten the safety or wellbeing of the State, and are intended to *undermine* or overthrow parliamentary democracy by *political, industrial* or violent means' (my emphasis).[3] If such a definition could be accepted by a Minister in a Labour Government, who presumably retained some suspicion that the police might go too far in their surveillance of politicians or trade unionists, it seems likely that it had been accepted earlier by the Heath administration of 1970–4. The uncertainty about how and when the definition became part of official policy underlines the crucial fact that a central element of constitutional law, the definition of the enemies of the state and therefore the identification of the legitimate targets of police surveillance, had been fundamentally changed not by Parliament, not even by the courts, but secretly by the security services, the police, civil servants and Ministers. From Lord Denning's definition, capable of 'clear, precise and narrow interpretation based on statute and common law', encompassing those who would attempt insurrection or assist foreign powers against the government of this country, we have moved to Rees's impossibly vague notion of 'those who I think cause problems for the State' – a revealing formulation of arbitrary and unchecked executive power.

The role of the Special Branch

The task of dealing with 'those who cause problems for the State' belongs to the Special Branches of each police force and to the security service, MI5. Founded in 1883 to deal with problems among the Irish community in London, the Metropolitan Police Special Branch remains the largest in the country. The official definition of its task was given by the Inspector of Constabularies:

> Special Branch duties are concerned mainly with criminal offences against the security of the state, with terrorist or subversive organizations, with certain protection duties, with keeping watch on seaports and airports, and with making inquiries about aliens.[4]

Special Branch operations are largely secret. In 1968 Peter Jackson, MP, sought unsuccessfully to obtain Special Branch budget estimates, which remain undisclosed today. In 1978, after considerable pressure from Robin Cook, MP, and others, the Home Secretary disclosed for the first time that a total of 1259 Special Branch officers worked in England and Wales, including 409 in the

Metropolitan Police force. The Special Branch of the Royal Ulster Constabulary (RUC) consisted of 279 officers. Figures for Scotland were not given, but State Research have estimated that a further 100 Special Branch officers work there.[5] In the same year, for the first time and apparently in response to a central request, about half of the annual reports published by Chief Constables included some reference to the Special Branch. But Parliamentary questioning about the extent of Special Branch records, the nature of the targets, the information held and the use to which it is put has proved fruitless. Chief Constables are fond of stressing that Special Branch work is part of normal 'operational' activity and therefore not a matter for inquisitive Police Authorities or MPs.

When it comes to public order, as we shall see in chapter 5, the police have an extensive and often abused discretion. But as far as political surveillance is concerned, the police and the security services operate almost entirely outside the law. That is not to say that they *break* the law: quite simply, there are hardly any laws for them to break. The methods of surveillance – the collection of personal information, the use of informers, telephone tapping, the interception of letters and so on – are effectively uncontrolled by law. The terms within which the political police operate are a matter of executive, not Parliamentary or judicial, decision making. In no sense can they be said to be accountable to the Police Authorities or to Parliament. And what is true of the Special Branch is true to an even greater degree of the security services themselves.

The central function of the Special Branch is surveillance. The number and selection of their targets is a matter of almost complete official secrecy. Sir Robert Mark indicated the general area of activity when he wrote: 'Fascists, communists, Trotskyites, anarchists *et al.* are committed to the overthrow of democracy and to the principle that the end justifies the means.'[6] A more detailed picture of those whom the authorities consider 'subversive' may, however, be pieced together from other sources.

In November 1977 the then Premier of South Australia, Don Dunstan, MP, appointed Judge White to investigate the activities of the state Special Branch. The investigation revealed that records were held on alleged communists; alleged terrorists; all politicians of the Australian Labour Party at state and federal level; all current and former State Governors; half of the judges of the Supreme Court; magistrates; all university personalities whose views could be classed as 'left' or 'radical'; all prominent demonstrators; most prominent trade union officials; most prominent clergymen in peace movements; homosexuals; supporters of the women's movement; divorce-law reform campaigners; anti-race discrimination campaigners; all members of the National Council for Civil Liberties; most prominent socialists; and others who 'came under notice'.[7] Clearly, the 'enemies' of the people of South Australia were in the majority! The premier ordered the destruction of over 80 per cent of the records and a tightening up of the rules governing police surveillance.

The South Australian experience cannot be dismissed as an Antipodean extravagance. The Chief Constable of the South Australian police force who directed the Special Branch's operations was a former Chief Constable of the York, North Riding and East Riding police forces, Harold Salisbury. In March 1981 he explained to the BBC TV programme *Panorama* that he would consider as 'subversive' anyone with communist or 'extremist' political views, homosexuals and anyone else who undermined 'marriage and the family', those who campaigned for shorter prison sentences for antisocial crime, people who tried to undermine discipline in schools and people who 'advocated the acceptance of certain drugs'. He made it clear that he believed that the British police used exactly the same criteria as those he had adopted in South Australia.[8]

Reports from people who have been approached to act as police informers, complaints from victims of police surveillance, evidence given in certain court cases, information about computer systems and leaks to journalists make it possible to compile a minimum list of the targets of official surveillance in this country. They include left-wing political organizations and their activists; left-wing members of the Labour Party, inside and outside Parliament; trade union officials and activists; radical and left-wing newspapers, their editors and journalists; the organizations, activists and journals of the extreme right; student activists; politically active foreigners and aliens who apply for naturalization; those involved in Irish issues (including members of the Troops Out Movement, the British Withdrawal from Northern Ireland Campaign, Clann n'ha Eireann and the Hands Off Ireland Campaign); gay organizations, their members and activists; squatters; publicly known members of organizations like NCCL and Release; Friends of the Earth and anti-nuclear power groups (on the grounds that such organizations are either subversive in themselves or at any rate ripe for infiltration by subversives;[9]) and journalists writing about national security, policing policy and defence.

Much Special Branch surveillance is of a routine nature – although its pedestrian qualities do not render it acceptable or harmless. Special Branch officers apparently spend a considerable part of their time on duty attending political meetings; reading political literature; checking signatures on petitions; attending and photographing demonstrations; watching 'gay' pubs and noting down the numbers of cars parked outside; visiting squats, political bookshops and other known subversive haunts; infiltrating defence committees and political campaigns. The methods differ little from those used by the Special Branch in the nineteenth century, but the scope for storing, analysing and disseminating vast quantities of information has been revolutionized by computer technology.

The technology of surveillance

The British police now have available to them some of the most sophisticated police computers in the world, and they are acquiring new systems rapidly. Excellent reviews of police information storage and retrieval systems are available elsewhere;[10] a brief summary will suffice here.

The largest police databank in this country is the Police National Computer (PNC) at Hendon in North London, which handles six major applications: vehicle owners, stolen or suspect vehicles, fingerprints, an index to criminal records, wanted and missing persons and disqualified drivers. By far the largest application is the file of registered keepers and owners of vehicles, covering 23.25 million adults. These records originate with the Department of the Environment's Driver and Vehicle Licensing Centre (DVLC) at Swansea, which provides a daily update of its records to Hendon. As Duncan Campbell (the *New Statesman* journalist and defendant in a notorious official secrets trial) has pointed out, the simple device of copying DVLC records to Hendon has ensured that every vehicle owner or keeper who moves home is unwittingly required to notify the police of his or her new whereabouts.[11] The PNC also holds a file of some 100,000 stolen or suspect vehicles. Although the stolen vehicles index is often quoted by the police to demonstrate the PNC's value, and despite its undoubted usefulness in tracing stolen cars, only about a quarter of the stolen vehicles index actually relates to stolen vehicles. Another quarter of the entries relate to cars used by the police themselves; and about a third are estimated to involve vehicles which are regarded as 'suspect' or of 'long-term interest' to the police.

Although Government Ministers for many years denied that the PNC contained political intelligence, the vehicle files provide the police with a handy base for such information. In January 1977 it was revealed that the PNC record on a particular vehicle included the fact that its owner 'was a prominent member of the Anti-Blood Sports League'.[12] The following year an Executive Committee member of the NCCL, Roland Jeffery, visited the local police station after an accident on his motorbike; there he overheard the police officer who had checked the details of his motorbike registration with the PNC telling another officer, 'Watch out, you've got a [inaudible] member of the NCCL.' On a similar occasion later that year a member of the Gay Activists Alliance found that details of his association were recorded on his vehicle file.[13] Parliamentary questioning by Jo Richardson, MP, after the Anti-Blood Sports League incident revealed, first, that 'information about political beliefs and activists is not held on the PNC' and, second, that 'information about association with an organization' is 'occasionally' held in the index of stolen and suspect vehicles! Duncan Campbell has also disclosed that both that index and the main file of vehicle owners can be 'flagged' to indicate that Special Branch have an interest in a particular vehicle, thus ensuring that the Special Branch is informed immediately if any query is made about that vehicle.[14]

The PNC includes an index to 2.5 million fingerprint records held at Scotland Yard (the fingerprints themselves have not yet been computerized). Although Roy Jenkins, then Home Secretary, told the House of Commons in May 1976 that the index covered those tried and convicted of 'serious' offences over the last forty years, together with those awaiting trial, in fact both the index and the fingerprints collection cover nearly 5000 people detained under the Prevention of Terrorism Acts but never charged with any criminal offence. An index to criminal records is similarly held on the PNC, allowing speedier access to the complete records at Scotland Yard. Again, the index of 'criminals' is not restricted to those with previous convictions, since it includes those who have been *charged*; an acquittal will not result in the name's being deleted if the person already has an entry or if the charge related to certain sexual offences or to crimes of dishonesty. According to the Data Protection Committee,[15] the criminal names index can be 'flagged' to indicate that the individual is of interest to the Special Branch, or that the person has made complaints against the police. The name of one person can also be linked with 'known associates'.

Police forces throughout Britain are linked to the PNC through visual display units (VDUs) situated in all headquarters buildings and, often, divisional or subdivisional buildings of each force. Each officer on the beat or in a patrol car has almost instant access to the PNC records via personal radio contact with the police VDU operator. The advantages to the police and the community in tracing stolen cars are obvious and frequently stressed. But the file of stolen cars is only a tiny part of the 30 million records which the PNC now handles and the 40 million for which it is equipped. Police apologists claim that the information handled by the PNC was all available previously through less efficient, manual systems. But they draw a veil over the ability of the PNC to analyse and combine the information in new ways now and to make it available in a matter of a few minutes to police officers throughout the country. The PNC generates a staggering amount of traffic – a level which no manual system could ever have dealt with. In 1979 the PNC was said to be handling 160,000 messages a day (about 58.4 million a year). [16] The West Midlands police have said that in one month of 1979 alone they made 100,000 enquiries of the PNC.

Unlike the PNC, the Metropolitan police force's new computer system will be used by that force alone. Since the Met. is not only the largest police force in the country but also the one which handles the most sensitive and controversial policing operations, its information system is of particular importance. But the refusal of both the Met. and the Home Office to provide more than minimum information makes it impossible for Parliament, the press or the public generally to assess the operation fully. The new system, which will be fully operational by 1985, is designed for the intelligence sections of the Metropolitan police: the Criminal Intelligence Division, the Central Drugs Intelligence Unit, the National Immigration Intelligence Unit, the Fraud Squad and the Special Branch. Of the 2 million names which the system will apparently contain by 1985, over half will come from the Special Branch alone. [17] According to *The Times*, which first produced information about the new system, all records would include 'details of convictions, addresses, telephone numbers, places frequented, passport details, cars used and physical descriptions'. But only a minority of the files would cover people with previous criminal records.

Some of the Special Branch entries on the new system would

come from the monitoring of 'political meetings', which is now standard practice for the Metropolitan police. In 1980, during the dispute between the Musicians' Union and the BBC over the dismissal of some BBC orchestras, those attending a small meeting outside Broadcasting House were approached by a police inspector equipped with a standard form on which to note down the names of organizers, speakers and chairperson, numbers attending, the subject of the meeting and so on. After a similar complaint had been received by NCCL in 1979 Jo Richardson tabled a Parliamentary Question about why such meetings were attended by the police and under what authority, but received the stock reply that this was an 'operational' matter for the Commissioner of Police.[18]

The Data Protection Committee (DPC), which was established by the Home Secretary at the end of 1975 to make recommendations about a data protection law, attempted to discover the purpose of Scotland Yard's new intelligence system. They were rebuffed. They learned no more than had been admitted in response to press inquiries – that the information to be computerized was that already held by the departments involved, and that the computer records would not be available outside the originating departments. But police witnesses did confirm to the Committee that the new system would have a 'multi-factor searching capability'. In other words, it would be possible to search the records held in the computer by means of checking a combination of details about vehicle registration, political affiliation, nationality, year of birth and so on. As the police said, the computer would be able, in a few seconds, to provide a list of names and addresses in response to the question: 'Which red-haired Irishmen on record drive white Cortinas with MR and 6 in the registration?' The example was no doubt chosen to illustrate the possible value of such a system in dealing with terrorist crime. But the same system could also provide for Special Branch a list of the names and addresses of 'subversives' involved in, for instance, protest against nuclear developments. It is disingenuous for the police to argue, as they did to the DPC, that the same task can be performed with manual records. Searching for the required red-haired Irishman in a card-index system would take weeks or months, not seconds. The DPC was extremely concerned about the scope for abuse: the records, it claimed, 'provide an easy method of browsing through such collections of information [and] are well suited to surveillance requirements'.[19] The Committee was unable to give any reassurance to the public about the legitimacy or acceptability of Scotland Yard's new intelligence system.

A computer system with the 'multi-factor searching capability' described by the DPC can also be used to build up profiles of individuals who have come to police attention. In other words, a request for information about one individual could produce not only the record of a previous criminal conviction, if applicable, and details of car ownership, but also every entry made for, say, a signature on a petition, appearance at a demonstration, a speech at a 'political' meeting, offices held in organizations, authorship of letters to the press and articles or pamphlets, together with a list of 'associates', organizations of which the individual was believed to be a member and any 'special characteristics', such as political views, homosexuality, the fact that he had made a complaint against the police or lived in a squat and so on. There is a double danger in such 'profiles': first, items of information may be entirely inaccurate and, second, the combination of items (whether accurate or inaccurate) may produce an entirely misleading profile. There are aspects of the history and biography of almost every one of us which, if presented and juxtaposed in particular ways, may lead to an entirely improper conclusion about our ideology or disposition.[20] Even criminal records, which are based on 'hard' data, all too frequently prove to be inaccurate (see below, page 50); suspicion, hearsay and the unverified reports of informers or police observers are far more likely to be wrong than right.

Surprisingly, the DPC did not investigate the experimental 'police notebook' system adopted by the Thames Valley police force. Designed to establish whether or not a computerized intelligence system could assist in the detection and prevention of crime, the system was introduced under Home Office auspices and amid considerable secrecy in 1974. As its title suggests, the Thames Valley databank is fed with all the items of information, however trivial, unsubstantiated or unconnected, that would find their way into a policeman's notebook or memory. (Once again, we are assured, the computer does no more than the previous manual systems did.) The databank is, in fact, a computerized version of the job of the police collator, who brings together within one force items of information, details of arrests, charges and convictions and so on supplied by other force members. The system has a capacity for records on 150,000 people, or 10 per cent of the population in the Thames Valley area. Indeed, since most police records deal with adult men, it is likely that between a quarter and a third of all adult men in the area would be covered by a computer dossier. In addition, the system can hold records on up to 300,000 vehicles, 300,000 addresses, 250,000 'occurrences' (including, it seems, complaints against the police) and 120,000 crimes.[21]

American Federal Bureau of Investigation (FBI) visitors who came to assess the Thames Valley system in 1978 were apparently dismayed by what they saw. They were shown a printout on a local resident stating that this man 'fancied small boys'. The item had apparently come from an officer whose wife had overheard some gossip in the village shop. *Police Review*, the Police Federation journal to whom the incident was reported, rightly criticized the practice of feeding 'unchecked bunkum' into the system – particularly in view of the possibility that the resident named in the report might find himself included in a list of suspects generated by the databank after a sexual crime.[22]

The Home Office has refused to publish the terms of reference governing the Thames Valley experiment or the conclusions of the working party which evaluated it.[23] Nonetheless, the system has now been bought from the Home Office by the Thames Valley police force itself, whose Police Authority has authorized the expenditure on its continuing operation. And the Metropolitan police intelligence system outlined earlier is a comparable but considerably more sophisticated version of the Thames Valley system – and one which may well be copied by regional forces.

Metropolitan police collator files which were passed to journalists in 1979 demonstrated the startling extensiveness of police information gathering. As Duncan Campbell reported:

> A file on a middle-aged mother of three, 'Mrs Carol Wilson', who had no criminal convictions of any kind, was opened in 1975 when her car was 'seen parked outside' the address of a man with convictions for rape, burglary and grievous bodily harm. But it does not note whether she was the driver or, indeed, whether the car had anything to do with the house. (In fact, she had, on the day concerned, lent the car to a friend, and has never heard of the person concerned.) . . . Files on her sons provided examples of the recording of hearsay and gossip, and details of offences of which they were acquitted.[24]

The record on one of 'Mrs Wilson's' sons included details on five other people, three of whom had been entered in the file after being stopped in the street one day when walking with the son in question.

The regional police forces are also acquiring their own computer

facilities. Generally used for 'command and control' functions –
such as personal records, salaries and the tracking of police cars –
such systems also offer an opportunity for developing local
criminal records and intelligence systems. Successive Home
Secretaries have denied that the national Criminal Records Office
holds details of arrests which do not result in convictions. But
records of all arrests – regardless of whether they result in a charge
or a conviction – are kept by local police stations. In the USA there is
widespread concern about the effect that disclosure of an arrest
record can have on a person's employment prospects, even when
the arrest was not followed by a charge or led to an acquittal. There
is already evidence that arrest records are similarly abused in
Britain. In April 1978, during the trial of one of those arrested on the
Grunwick picket line, the prosecution attempted to discredit a
defence witness by telling the court that the witness had himself
been arrested on the picket. In fact, the witness – a photographer
who had not been picketing – had been caught up in a crowd of
people taken to the police station; he had not been charged, but his
arrival at the station had been noted in police records. As local
forces acquire or extend their computer systems, it is likely that
arrest records will be included in the new databanks and, as a
result, made far more easily available to police officers inside and
outside each force.

A new source of concern is the development of Home Office
databanks containing information about immigrants and other
travellers. I have already mentioned Scotland Yard's National
Immigration Intelligence Unit, which has been used in the passport
raids on firms employing black workers (see page 200). The Home
Office has also introduced a computerized system for recording
details of people entering and leaving the country. The system will
not only enable immigration officers and the police to check up
more promptly on those who have stayed beyond the period
specified on their entry permit, but will also provide extensive
information about the travel patterns of anyone whom the Home
Office, the police or the security services consider to be of interest.
It also appears that officials at the Home Office, with their
counterparts from the USA, West Germany and other countries,
has been involved in a feasibility study on a computerized passport
system. In March 1981 the Commission of the European Economic
Community (EEC) announced its detailed plans for the introduction
of a common-format national passport throughout the EEC. Public
and parliamentary debate about its colour and the prominence of

the coat of arms concealed a truly worrying development: in the EEC working-party discussions the United Kingdom Government had successfully pressed for the inclusion in the passport of a machine-readable page of coded personal information. It is not known what details will be included in the machine-readable section. In 1979 it was revealed that the Home Office employed a secret system of coded markings on passports, which conveyed to immigration officers both here and abroad that, for instance, a report had been sent by the immigration service to the Home Office; or that the immigration officer believed the passport to be false; or that a report was required for the Intelligence Unit; or that the passenger had been deported.[25] Until the nature of these endorsements was published, a passport holder had no way of establishing what messages were being conveyed about him or her, or whether they were, in fact, accurate. In 1980, when the French Government announced proposals for a new identity card which would include a machine-readable strip along one edge, the French Privacy Commission immediately instigated an expert examination of the proposed format of the new card to establish whether or not information other than the holder's name and card number could secretly be included on the coded strip.[26]

The interception of communications

Just as computer technology has transformed the scale on which the police and government departments can obtain, store and disseminate information, so other methods of surveillance are being revolutionized by developments in communications equipment.

Until April 1980 successive Governments had refused to update the figures given in the 1957 Birkett Report on telephone tapping and the interception of mail. Concern expressed by MPs, judges and the press finally persuaded the Home Secretary, William Whitelaw, to publish a White Paper, *The Interception of Communications in Great Britain*,[27] which gave fresh details about the numbers of telephone taps and the procedures by which they were issued. According to the White Paper, 467 phone-tapping warrants were issued in 1979, a figure considerably lower than previous estimates, which had ranged from 1200 to about 3000. But the White Paper omitted any discussion of interception by or on behalf of the Government Communications Headquarters, which is responsible for intercepting all overseas telegrams and telephone calls, as well as for the illegal surveillance of diplomatic communications. The White Paper admitted that a warrant for a 'target' organization, individual or activity may cover a number of lines, with no restriction on the total involved, and that the use of a warrant may be extended by a civil servant under delegated powers. Discrepancies between the number of warrants issued *during* each year and the number in force at the *end* of each year suggest that some 'permanent' warrants for MI5 and the Special Branch, which need to be reauthorized every six months, are listed only when first granted. It has been estimated[28] that about 75 per cent of all the warrants issued are for the security services.

Non-security telephone tapping is meant to be confined to serious offences (those for which a first offender would receive at least three years' imprisonment) where normal methods of investigation have been tried and failed and where evidence obtained by a phone tap would have a good chance of resulting in a conviction. But the White Paper also disclosed that the Home Secretary had added a significant new element to the definition of serious crime, which now includes 'lesser' offences where 'there is good reason to apprehend the use of violence'. The definition is, of course, vague enough to cover breaches of the peace on a picket line or in a demonstration. As far as security warrants are concerned, the White Paper makes it clear that the security services may tap telephones in order to obtain *information* and not to secure convictions. The same admission was made in the Birkett Report, but in the twenty years since the Birkett Committee investigated the matter, the definition of 'subversive' activity – one of the criteria for the justification of a security telephone tap – has, of course, been radically extended.

The warrant procedure for telephone taps does not extend to the monitoring of calls made from a particular line. Using a meter-check printer, the Post Office is able to obtain a list of all telephone numbers dialled from a number under observation. The device is mainly used where a customer complains about a bill, or in cases of suspected 'phone phreaking' (i.e., evasion of telephone charges), or nuisance calls. An internal Post Office memorandum obtained by NCCL in 1978 indicates that such information is also made available to the police, without a warrant, on the authority of a senior Post Office official. A full list of numbers dialled by someone under surveillance would be of obvious value to Special Branch and corresponds to the information about associates and friendship networks regularly obtained by the copying of address books of people arrested on drugs charges or under the Prevention of Terrorism Act or by the removal of membership lists during a search of an organization's premises.

Although a meter-check printer has to be attached to the telephone line about which information is required, the new 'System X' telephone exchange will provide such information far more simply. A modification to the programme governing the system will ensure that a list of all numbers dialled from a particular telephone is automatically produced. Such a facility will be available to customers, who will be billed for the information. But the same facility (without the give-away charge) will also be available to officials meeting an authorized request or simply providing a friendly service for a police contact.

The opening of letters, which requires no such sophisticated developments, can be traced back at least to the spy services of Tudor monarchs. The warrant procedure used for telephone tapping is also meant to apply to mail interception, and the White Paper cited above discloses that fifty-two mail-interception warrants were issued in 1979 (the high point being 1561 in 1940). No figures for Northern Ireland are given.[29]

No warrants at all are required for use by the police (or anyone else) of the variety of bugging and surveillance devices now available. Among those listed in the Younger Committee's Report[30] and on sale in the USA, if not openly in Britain, is the 'infinity bug', which allows a listener to dial the number of the telephone to which the bug has been connected and, by blowing a special frequency whistle into the machine, to bypass the telephone bell and to listen into all the conversations in the room containing the telephone. The effectiveness of such a device was demonstrated in 1975 by the *New Scientist*.[31] Wall microphones, laser-beam listening devices which translate vibrations on a window-pane generated by a speaker inside the room, night glasses and long-distance microphones are among the equipment now available to Special Branch and the security services, but the extent of their use is unknown.

Legal protections for privacy?

The citizen in the United Kingdom is completely unprotected by law against the collection and use of personal information. A number of attempts were made between 1967 and 1971 to introduce

Private Members' Bills, the latest of which (Brian Walden's Protection of Personal Information Bill) was withdrawn in return for a Government pledge to establish a Committee of Inquiry. But when the terms of reference of the Committee, chaired by Sir Kenneth Younger, were published, it was found that the Government had omitted the most important and most controversial issue – invasions of privacy by government departments, the police and other public authorities. In 1976 the Labour Government published two White Papers – *Computers and Privacy*[32] and *Computers: Safeguards for Privacy*[33] – which were followed by the establishment of the Data Protection Committee, chaired by Sir Norman Lindop.

The Lindop Committee's Report,[34] published in December 1978, disclosed the intense lobbying by the police and security services to keep their information systems out of the clutches of any watchdog proposed by the Committee. No action was taken on the Report before the May 1979 election, and it was not until March 1981 that the new Home Secretary announced that, in principle, the Government was committed to data-protection legislation. But the Government had rejected the previous Government's proposal for the creation of an independent Data Protection Authority – on which the work of the Lindop Committee had been premised – and offered no timetable whatsoever for legislation.

International developments may, however, force the Government's hand. In October 1980 the Organization for Economic Co-operation and Development (OECD) announced guidelines on data protection and privacy[35] which, it hoped, member states would follow. In January 1981 the Council of Europe opened for signature a new Convention for the Protection of Individuals with Regard to Automatic Processing of Personal Data,[36] which requires states ratifying the Convention to implement domestic legislation giving effect to its principles. And the Commission of the EEC has undertaken its own study of privacy laws following a resolution of the European Parliament in September 1979.[37] International guidelines of this kind are not pious exhortations. They have been motivated not merely by a laudable desire to protect individuals but also by the pressing need of multinational corporations and Governments themselves to be able to transfer computerized data across national boundaries. With electronic communications at the heart of future industrial development, businesses cannot afford restrictions of the kind imposed by, for instance, the Swedish Privacy Board on the processing of data concerning Swedish citizens in foreign countries. The Swedish Board takes the entirely sensible view that personal data which would be subject to stringent safeguards in Sweden itself cannot be processed on computer systems in countries which have no such safeguards. Thus the establishment of 'offshore data havens' poses a real threat to the free transfer of information and requires the establishment of an 'information common market' of countries with common data-protection standards.

The USA has had a federal Privacy Act since 1974; Sweden's Privacy Board has been in operation since 1973; West Germany introduced a new Data Protection Act in January 1978, and France a similar one in the same year.[38] It is because the United Kingdom has obstinately refused to comply with international standards that British businesses, as well as consumer groups and professional associations, have lobbied so hard for a data-protection law. In announcing its commitment 'in principle' to such legislation, the Government declared that the new legislation would enable the United Kingdom to ratify the new European Convention, which, in the meantime, the Government would sign.

The new Data Protection Act will, apparently, return to the principles of the Younger Committee's Report, published nine years ago. But if the European Convention is to be ratified, the Act will have to give statutory force to its more strongly worded principles: personal data to be processed automatically must be adequate, relevant, accurate and not excessive for the prescribed purposes, and any data subject must be able to establish the existence of, and obtain a copy of, his records. It is essential that exceptions to the principle of individual access to personal records be kept to a minimum. Criminal investigation records, whose usefulness would be entirely destroyed by individual access, should be exempt. But there is no reason why criminal conviction records, which are often inaccurate, should not be open to individual access and correction.

The Convention requires Governments to name a single national authority responsible for co-ordinating the operation of data-protection legislation. Because the Conservative Government has refused to establish a data-protection authority, it is possible that the Home Office itself will be named as the supervising authority. Any such proposal must be strongly resisted. Not only has the Home Office done everything to hinder and to delay privacy legislation, but it is also directly responsible for some of this country's most sensitive databanks. An extension of the powers and terms of reference of the Ombudsman that would allow him to supervise data-protection legislation would at least provide a real measure of independence; but in the end a data protection authority that is able to employ expert investigators will be essential if any proper supervision of personal records is to be achieved.

Unfortunately, both the Lindop Committee's Report and the European Convention are restricted to computerized data, although the Convention does invite Governments to extend legislation to manual systems. Although, as I have argued in this chapter, automatic processing entirely changes the scale on which personal information can be collected, analysed and made available, the essential dangers of the unsupervised use of information which may be irrelevant, inaccurate or out-of-date are present equally in personal records stored in card indexes or filing cabinets. The new Data Protection Act must extend to manual systems in order to ensure that its principles are not circumvented.

But until a Data Protection Act is implemented, and unless it extends to the operations of the police and the security services, the selection of targets for surveillance, the nature of the information collected, the methods of maintaining information and the decision about whom the information is shared with will remain entirely a matter for the unchecked discretion of the police and the secret services themselves.

The Data Protection Act would probably not extend to telephone tapping and mail interception, however. The Birkett Committee itself stressed that it could find no legal authority for the power of interception claimed by Governments. The claims made for the royal prerogative and ancient common law right are not supported by any legal authority or statute. In 1979 the High Court held in the case of *Malone* (who had discovered, during his trial on charges of handling stolen goods, that the police had a transcript of his telephone calls) that there was no law to prevent anyone in the United Kindom – whether police officer, security agent or private detective – from tapping a telephone. The judge observed that the absence of controls left the United Kingdom in breach of the European Human Rights Convention, and that the situation cried out for legislation.[34] Malone is now bringing a complaint to the European Human Rights Commission, which has already held, in the West German case of *Klass*, that 'powers of secret surveillance of citizens, characterizing as they do the police state, are tolerable under the Convention only in so far as strictly necessary for safeguarding the democratic institutions', and that the Convention requires 'adequate and effective guarantees against abuse'.[40] It is unlikely that the investigation of handling stolen goods falls within the Government's own criterion of 'serious crime', let alone within the Commission's definition of 'safeguarding the democratic institutions'.

Instead of anticipating a European Commission case and importing the *Klass* standards, the Government has flatly refused to provide a statutory basis for phone tapping and mail interception warrants. The Home Secretary announced at the time of publication of the White Paper that Lord Diplock would carry out a 'continuing review' of the exercise of the warrant power. Since Lord Diplock was the architect of the non-jury courts in Northern Ireland (see page 159) and is a member of the Security Commission, his appointment reassured none of the critics of arbitrary executive power. His six-page report, published in March 1981,[41] concluded that 'the procedures for the interception of communications . . . are working satisfactorily and with the minimum interference with the individual's rights of privacy in the interests of the public weal.'

An amendment to the 1981 British Telecommunications Bill, achieved through an unexpected alliance in Committee of Labour MPs with Conservative backbencher John Gorst, MP, would have provided statutory force for the criteria which, according to the Home Secretary, already govern telephone tapping. But the Government refused to allow even this provision to obtain a majority when the Committee's amendments were debated by the full House.

But other controls over *methods* of information gathering are also needed. Although the criminal offence of conspiracy to effect a public mischief was used in the late 1960s and early 1970s (for instance, in the case of a credit reference agency whose employees impersonated officials in order to obtain information), the House of Lords held, in a case involving the use of bugging devices by private detectives, that the offence did not exist![42] Together with telephone tapping and mail interception, the use of specified surveillance devices should be made illegal unless a warrant has been obtained either from a High Court judge or from a committee of MPs and judges. Warrants should be restricted to cases of extremely grave offences, when there is a likelihood that evidence would be obtained that would lead to a conviction. In national security cases a warrant should be granted only if it is likely to produce evidence that will either result in a conviction or form the basis for other appropriate action. (Such action would, in the case of an alien, include deportation, but subject to an improved right of appeal.) As in West Germany, the victim of interception should be informed (except possibly in exceptional national security cases) when surveillance ceases.

Finally, Parliament should lay down a statutory definition of the criteria with which the police and secret services should operate in dealing with crimes against the state. Even Lord Denning's definition of subersives, quoted at the beginning of this chapter, includes people who might be thought to 'contemplate the overthrow of government by unlawful means' – thus giving wide scope for the political naivety or prejudice of the security services. The operations of the police and MI5 against this country's own citizens should be restricted to cases in which the individual is suspected, on reasonable grounds, of involvement in criminal activities. A proper definition of their legitimate targets, together with a reform of the criminal law relating to national security (primarily, the rewriting of the Official Secrets Act, as proposed in chapter 5), would abolish the need for at least most of the Special Branch's surveillance activities. But the Parliamentary Select Committee which would have special responsibility for overseeing police matters (see page 69) should also be charged with the surveillance of those who, until now, have proceeded with surveillance of the citizen unchecked.

Nothing to fear?

The usual answer to complaints about unregulated surveillance is that none of it matters to the innocent ('If you've nothing to hide, you've nothing to fear'). It takes little reflection to expose the fallacy. Six quite specific and objectionable consequences of the uncontrolled collection and use of personal information can be identified.

First, the information obtained may be inaccurate or irrelevant. Nonetheless, the information may be used as the basis for a decision crucially affecting someone's life; and if the person concerned does not even know that a record of the 'information' exists, its accuracy can never be challenged. The experience of Jan Martin, reported on a BBC TV *Panorama* programme in March 1981,[43] illustrates the dangers that may threaten an entirely innocent person as a result of uncontrolled information gathering. When Jan

Martin applied for a job with a former BBC broadcaster, Michael Barrett, to assist with the production of industrial films, Barrett was told by one of his clients, Taylor Woodrow, that Ms Martin would 'not be welcome' on their premises. They said she had a connection 'with terrorists in Europe' and mentioned the name of Baader–Meinhoff. Ms Martin's father, a former Detective Chief Superintendent at the fingerprints division of Scotland Yard, was able to establish that the accusation had been leaked to Taylor Woodrow from Special Branch. Its origin? The Dutch police, who had received a phone call from the owner of a café where Ms Martin and her husband had stopped during a holiday. It was apparently the day after a shooting in Amsterdam involving the Baader–Meinhoff, and the café keeper thought that Mrs Martin's husband looked like one of the terrorists, Willie Stoller, later shot dead by the German police. Neither she nor her husband was interviewed by the police: but the café owner's suspicion stayed on file, not only (presumably) in Holland, but also in the records of the Metropolitan police Special Branch, which apparently passed the item on to a private company as fact.

Second, 'confidential' information may be quite carelessly transferred to others. The police are required by a Home Office directive to pass on information about convictions to a wide range of employers and professional associations, covering all civil servants, medical practitioners, lawyers, chartered or certified accountants, dentists, nurses and midwives, vets, opticians, court employees, prison officers, teachers and police officers themselves. Applicants for a public-service vehicle driver's licence and for casual Post Office work are also checked with the police. Although the directive specifies that only *convictions* should be notified, there is nothing to prevent the police from passing on information about arrests or even suspicions. In 1972, for instance, the Chief Constable of the Yorkshire police wrote to the Central Midwives' Board about a midwife who was dismissed after the theft of some drugs. The midwife was not charged with the offence. But the Chief Constable wrote, 'it is known that she has a tumour on her spine; that she has some domestic troubles; and that she has an inferiority complex.'[44] Despite a review of the Home Office circular, complaints continue to arise about police information going to unauthorized recipients.

In theory, criminal records and other information held by the police is confidential to the police unless a specific requirement directs them to make it available. In practice, private detectives boast of their ability to check people out with the police, and employers often obtain information about criminal records which, in many cases, must originate with the police. In 1978 a sergeant in the Nottingham police force was suspended for obtaining names and addresses of the keepers of cars which had been seen outside certain gaming clubs and for passing the information, at 50p an item, to the owners of a rival gaming club. Up to 10,000 names and addresses were obtained in this way.[45] Although the police announced that steps had been taken to prevent a recurrence of such abuse, in 1980 two officers in a different force were dismissed after visiting and propositioning women whose names and addresses they had obtained by noting down their car numbers. The amount of traffic generated by the PNC and the ability of any officer to obtain information held there makes it impossible to prevent some officers from selling the information for money or other favours.

Nor are criminal records necessarily accurate. One man wrote to NCCL in 1980, having discovered during an appearance in court that he had a previous conviction for taking and driving away – although, in fact, his only previous conviction was not for an offence of dishonesty but for drunken driving. After some correspondence with the court, the PNC and the DVLC, the error was corrected. But it was impossible to correct the error in a case brought to the attention of Northumberland and Durham NCCL in 1979, in which someone who had been convicted of a minor offence heard the police officer inform the magistrates' court that there was one previous conviction arising out of an Aldermaston march in the early 1960s (which was accurate) and a second conviction 'which wasn't relevant'. When he asked the police officer about this second conviction, he was appalled to hear that he had apparently been convicted of gross indecency. In fact, the record of that conviction belonged to a different person with a similar name and birth date.

Third, police surveillance inevitably invades the privacy of innocent people. It is almost inconceivable that Parliament would have enacted a law requiring all citizens to notify a change of address to the police. But such a requirement has now been introduced for most adults, without any legislation whatsoever, by requiring keepers of vehicles to notify the DVLC at Swansea, which transfers the information immediately to the PNC. The consequences of police surveillance may be devastating. In Bradford in 1977, during a murder investigation, the police visited the homes of owners of cars which had been spotted outside gay pubs. One of the owners visited was the father of a boy who had borrowed the car to drive to the pub: the police visit was the first indication to the parents that their son was homosexual.[46]

The fourth consequence of unchecked surveillance is even more serious. The extensive availability of laws relating to political activity makes it easy for the Special Branch, acting on its own behalf or for the security service, to prosecute, and possibly secure a conviction against, the targets of their surveillance. The most notorious recent example of such a prosecution was that of two journalists, Crispin Aubrey and Duncan Campbell, and a former soldier, John Berry, under the Official Secrets Act. Berry had written to the Agee–Hosenball Defence Committee, which organized the protest about the deportations of two American journalists in 1977 and which was housed at the NCCL offices, offering information about Sigint (Signals Intelligence), in which he had worked many years previously. (A *Time Out* article by Hosenball and Campbell concerning Sigint and GCHQ was a major factor in the decision to deport Hosenball.) Police information about the meeting between Aubrey, Berry and Campbell, which was arranged as a result of Berry's letter, could only have come from a telephone tap of the NCCL office, *Time Out* (where Aubrey worked) and/or Campbell's home, although it is also likely that mail to the defence committee and NCCL was being intercepted at the time. Campbell, a journalist of considerable scientific expertise who researched sensitive areas of defence and policing activity, had apparently been under surveillance for some time. After his arrest at Berry's house, the police used an Official Secrets warrant to search his Brighton flat, removing virtually the entire contents, down to the filing cabinets, wastepaper baskets and books. The determination of the police, the security services, the Director of Public Prosecutions and prosecuting counsel to put an end to Campbell's activities was vividly revealed by the decision to prosecute him under Section 1 of the Act, the section intended for foreign spies. In addition, all three were charged under Section 2 with communicating or receiving 'unauthorized' information.

The Section 1 charges against Campbell were eventually abandoned by the prosecution after strong criticism from the trial judge. That, together with acquittal on some other charges and light penalties on the remainder, represented a real victory for the independence of judge and jury against the state. But the very fact of the prosecution – the original arrest and detention, the confiscation of belongings, the restrictions on bail, the cost of the case and the eighteen months' preparation for a trial which the authorities fully intended to result in imprisonment for the defendants – was in itself a severe punishment.

The conspiracy laws offer an even more useful weapon against those who 'cause problems for the state', as was illustrated by the succession of trials for conspiracy to corrupt public morals (see page 97) and the conspiracy trial of the Shrewsbury pickets in 1973. In 1972 the Incitement to Disaffection Act – unused since its passage in 1936 – was dusted off for use against Michael Tobin, an Irish worker who was sentenced to two years' imprisonment for *possessing* (not even distributing) letters which attempted to persuade soldiers to desert from the Army in Northern Ireland.[47] Two years later the Act was used again against fourteen members of the British Withdrawal from Northern Ireland Campaign – the acquittals in that case representing another victory for independently minded jurors. But the cost to the defendants in such cases is not redressed even by acquittal, and the wider damage – the restriction on expression and the intimidation of others engaged in peaceful political activity – is incalculable.

The risks of criminal prosecutions, which so often end in an acquittal in these political cases, may be avoided by resort to purely administrative methods of punishment, the encouragement of which is the fifth consequence of unchecked surveillance. Since the end of 1974 over 5000 people have been arrested and detained under the Prevention of Terrorism Acts; 94 per cent of them were released without being charged with *any* criminal offence. But the very fact of detention in a police station for up to seven days without access to solicitor or friends, subject to interrogation and in the knowledge that the police will extend their attentions to one's family, friends and acquaintances is a punishment unpleasant enough in itself and one which may have further consequences, such as the loss of a job or publicity, which, given the situation in Northern Ireland, may even endanger life. The record of detention makes someone who has once been held under the Act an obvious target for future surveillance or further detention. Arrests of this kind are at one and the same time a consequence of the political surveillance of organizations and activists; a source of further information (for instance, through the copying of the address books of those detained); a punishment for those arrested; and a warning to others involved, however remotely, in Irish affairs.

The system of 'exclusion orders' created by the Prevention of

Terrorism Acts (of which a full account will be found on page 165) is paralleled by the system of deportations and removals under the 1971 Immigration Act. In 1980 669 people were detained in custody for an indefinite period under suspicion of being 'illegal entrants', and 908 people were 'removed' from the country under an administrative procedure which carries no right of appeal (see page 199). Furthermore, the 1971 Act provides for a special system of deportation in 'national security' cases, in which the appeal against deportation is heard *in camera* and the deportee has no right to know the evidence against him or to cross-examine witnesses. A similar deportation power had been used against Rudi Dutschke, the German student activist who had come to Britain to study in 1969, while the 1971 Act powers were used, despite widespread international protest, against Mark Hosenball and Philip Agee in 1977.

A refusal to naturalize a foreigner living in this country constitutes another form of administrative punishment which leaves the individual at the mercy of the Special Branch and the Home Secretary. A citizen of a foreign country who has lived in Britain for at least five years and who is free of immigration restrictions may apply to be naturalized as a citizen of the United Kingdom and Colonies (or, under the new British Nationality Act, as a British citizen). All such applicants are investigated by the Special Branch. On the advice of police and officials, the Home Secretary decides whether to accept or reject the application. But he gives *no reasons for his decision*. An applicant has no right to know what information has influenced the decision to reject his application and no right of appeal to a court or tribunal. The refusal may entail deportation if the Minister believes that deportation would be 'conducive to the public good'. In any case, refusal of naturalization makes it impossible for the applicant to take up any job in the public service, nationalized industries or any firm involved in defence contract work; nor can he vote or stand for elected office. In 1978, for instance, I represented an Iranian man in his application for naturalization. He was married to an English-born woman, and their daughter had been born in this country. On the basis of his excellent qualifications as an engineer, the man had attempted to obtain a post with a private company doing government contract work and had been refused because of his foreign citizenship. His application for citizenship was rejected. Unusually, the Minister of State involved stated that a past irregularity concerning his passport had *not* counted against him. The only black mark against him the Iranian could think of was his involvement in Iranian student protest years previously, in connection with which he had been interviewed by the police but never arrested or charged with a criminal offence. Whatever information formed the basis of the Minister's decision may well have been false; the Iranian applicant may have been denied citizenship and an adequate livelihood because of his association with others, or because of political activities which, although entirely lawful, were disliked by the authorities.

The 1981 British Nationality Act, by withdrawing the right of Commonwealth citizens settled here to register automatically as citizens, will substantially increase the numbers of people required to apply for naturalization. More people will suffer from the effects of the Minister's arbitrary discretion and the Government's refusal to accede to requests for an independent system of appeals against refusals of naturalization.

The sixth consequence of the use of Special Branch and other police information has been the corruption of the process of justice itself. In 1974 the then Home Secretary, Roy Jenkins, and the Attorney-General, Sam Silkin, discovered that a practice had grown up among prosecutors, mainly at the Old Bailey, of asking the police officers in charge of certain cases to check police records for information concerning potential jurors. Instead of putting an end to the practice – which undermined the principle repeated in a Lord Chancellor's Practice Direction of 1973 that a jury should be chosen at *random* – or asking Parliament to authorize jury vetting, the Home Secretary and the Attorney-General in the following year secretly issued guidelines to the police and the Director of Public Prosecutions requesting them to vet juries in serious criminal cases involving professional gangs and other serious cases with 'strong political motives' and to use the prosecution's power to stand by jurors with 'extreme political motives' or 'undesirable' connections.[48]

The deplorable practice of jury vetting came to light almost by accident at the beginning of the Aubrey–Berry–Campbell Official Secrets trial, when defence counsel Lord Hutchinson, QC, asked the court why the prosecution had obtained the panel of potential jurors some weeks before. Prosecuting counsel replied that they had conducted the 'normal' check of jurors and that anyone 'known to be disloyal' would 'obviously be disqualified' – adding, reassuringly, that the Crown had found no one to object to! The public outcry which followed this revelation of McCarthyite loyalty checks persuaded the Attorney-General to publish his guidelines.

The kind of information available to police and prosecuting counsel in assessing 'loyalty' or 'extremist political beliefs' was revealed by the *Guardian*, which obtained a copy of the results of the vetting of the jurors before the trial of a number of anarchists in 1979 (known as the Persons Unknown trial, after the charge of 'conspiring with persons unknown . . .'). A check of police records had revealed that one potential juror lived at an address believed to be that of a squat. Others were related to people who had been charged with, or convicted of, criminal offences. One person had made a complaint against the police.[49] A Private Member's Bill to outlaw jury vetting, introduced by Alf Dubs, MP, failed, but in 1980 the new Attorney-General, Sir Michael Havers, announced new guidelines which restricted vetting to two 'certain exceptional types of cases of public importance': national security cases where part of the evidence would be heard *in camera*, and cases involving terrorism. The new guidelines are, however, entirely academic, since the Court of Appeal has ruled[50] that there is no law to prevent vetting and, therefore, no requirement on the police or prosecution to observe the guidelines. Indeed, it was revealed in early 1980[51] that in Northampton the jurors in *all* criminal cases were routinely vetted. There is no guarantee whatsoever, therefore, that the Special Branch will not continue to ensure that, particularly in trials where it has a direct involvement, the jury is composed of people likely to be sympathetic to the prosecution.

Finally, it is essential to consider the general effects of un-controlled police surveillance. Americans speak graphically of the 'chilling' effect of such surveillance on democratic activity. Quite apart from the particular uses made of the fruits of surveillance, if it is widely known or believed that the Special Branch routinely keeps tabs on people attending public meetings, joining certain political parties or organizations, protesting about Government activities in Northern Ireland, opposing the development of nuclear power or other Government policies, attending demon-strations, becoming active in trade unions, participating in defence committees, writing for minority newspapers, handing out leaflets and so on, then fewer people will feel free to participate in such activities – which are the very essence of democratic freedom. Thus without resorting to censorship, without generally banning organizations, without openly prohibiting the expression of particular views, the authorities achieve their object: to confine the use of the democratic process to the expression of views acceptable to those in power.

3

Policing the Police

The 1929 Royal Commission on the Police and much subsequent discussion of the relationship between the police and the community started from the belief that

> The police in this country have never been recognized either in law or by tradition as a force distinct from the general body of citizens . . . the principle remains that a policeman, in the view of the common law, is only a person paid to perform, as a matter of duty, acts which if he were so minded he might have done voluntarily.[1]

The description was inaccurate even then. It ignored, for instance, the intense opposition to the establishment of modern police forces in the nineteenth century, when groups as disparate as shire Tories, radical Liberals and the Chartists all recognized that the new arrangements would serve interests other than their own.[2] But the myth helped to conceal the essentially political nature of policing. By presenting the police officer as an ordinary citizen, part of the community as a whole, answerable only to 'the law', it obscured the need to make the police answerable, in fact, to the community's representatives.

It is hard to believe that the notion of the police officer as citizen in uniform is widely accepted today. The professionalization of the police, the radical increase in their coercive powers which are *not* available to other citizens and the growing use of the police against 'subversives' have all intensified the separation of the police from the rest of the community. The problems of ensuring that police forces are answerable for their actions and that the law enforcers are not above the law have assumed a new and pressing importance.

Many senior police officers have been exasperated by proposals for greater police accountability and the publicity gained recently, for instance, by Michael Meacher, MP, in his campaign to expose deaths in police custody and by Jack Straw, MP, for his Police Authorities Bill. In June 1980 the Metropolitan Police Commissioner, Sir David McNee, assured the Association of Chief Police Officers that 'the police are accountable up to their eyeballs' – accountable to the law, the courts, the police authorities, the Police Complaints Board, the Home Secretary. But a close examination of all the mechanisms he cites suggests that none comes close to providing even a minimally acceptable system of supervision.

In 1968 Lord Denning, MR, restated in a leading case the principle that the police are answerable to the law. The Chief Constable, he said,

> is not the servant of anyone save of the law itself. No Minister of the Crown can tell him that he must, or must not, keep observation on this place or that; or that he must, or must not, prosecute this man or that one. Nor can any police authority tell him so. The responsibility for law enforcement lies on him. He is answerable to the law and to the law alone. . . .[3]

But the court would, in fact, only intervene in an extreme case of dereliction of duty.[4] The central duty of the Chief Constable – to enforce the law of the land – insofar as it involves the prosecution of offenders in the court is, increasingly, the responsibility of others. The Director of Public Prosecutions already has charge of the most serious cases, while the Royal Commission on Criminal Procedure has proposed the creation of a Crown Prosecutors' Service to take over all other police prosecutions.[5] One might expect that answerability 'to the law' would mean that the conduct of the police, as revealed in a criminal prosecution brought by them, would be scrutinized and, if necessary, checked by the courts. But the House of Lords has firmly rejected the notion that it is 'part of a judge's function to exercise disciplinary powers over the police or prosecution as respects the way in which evidence . . . is obtained by them'.[6] As I shall argue later (see below, page 71), other arrangements for dealing with police misconduct or even criminal offences by the police are woefully inadequate. Accountability to the law means only that the powers and the duties of the Chief Constable are circumscribed by statutory and common law provision – and that means in practice, that he enjoys an extensive discretion.

In 1962 a second Royal Commission on the Police was established to review arrangements for police accountability. The Commission stressed that the Chief Constable

> *is accountable to no one and subject to no one's orders* for the way in
> which, for example, he settles his general policies in regard to law
> enforcement over the area covered by his force, the disposition of
> his force, the concentration of his resources on any particular type of
> crime or area, the manner in which he handles political demonstra-
> tions or processions and allocates and instructs his men when
> preventing breaches of the peace arising from industrial disputes.
> (My emphasis.)

It concluded: 'The problem of controlling the police can therefore
be restated as the problem of controlling Chief Constables'.[7] The
problem has still not been resolved.

The Royal Commission left untouched the independent legal
status of the Chief Constable. But they proposed that he should
become more accountable to the community through the establishment of Police Authorities, which would be given the duty of
maintaining 'an adequate and efficient police force'. The
Authority's chief weapon for achieving this end was to be the
power to call for reports from the Chief Constable. As one doubting
member of the Commission later commented: 'This novel method
of government through reports without power to do anything is a
new development in the science of politics.'[8] But the limited
powers of the new Authorities are only one reason why they have
been irrelevant to the development of policing policies and techniques in the last two decades. There is a fundamental ambivalence
in the attitude of the police towards the whole notion of accountability to the community. Senior officers are fond of stressing that
the police are indeed accountable, that they can only police 'with
the consent' of the community. But when this platonic 'community' takes on a real shape through its elected representatives,
accountability is condemned as 'political interference'. The Chief
Inspector of Constabulary reported:[9] 'A particular concern of many
forces in 1979 . . . has been to get as many men as possible back on
the beat, on foot patrol, where they can get to know, and be known
by, the community they serve, and thereby come to grips with its
problems.' But in 1980, when the London borough of Hackney's
local council objected to saturation policing by the Special Patrol
Group (SPG), the local police Commander went on television to say
that he would not hesitate to bring the SPG back: 'I don't feel obliged
to tell anyone about my policing activities . . . we have got to be
totally cut off from the politics of it.'[10]

The Chief Inspector of Constabulary himself indicates the alien-
ation of police from public. 'The community', were told, is 'a major
crime prevention resource' – and police efforts 'are increasingly
taking account of this'! In discussing relations with the black communities, the Inspector manages, no doubt inadvertently, to make
the police sound like an occupying force: 'These events [in Southall
in 1979] undoubtely constituted a major setback for the police, not
only in London but in other parts of the country, in their efforts to
win over the hearts and minds of the ethnic minorities.'[11]

The Police Authorities

The modern Police Authorities are the feeble descendants of the
nineteenth-century watch committees. As Geoffrey Marshall has
pointed out,[12] the legal theory of an independent sphere of
constabulary authority is quite new and played no part in the
authority exercised by borough watch committees over their Chief
Constables. Marshall quotes a disagreement which arose in the
1880s between the Head Constable of Liverpool, Sir William Nott-
Bower, and his watch committee. In his report to the committee Sir
William recommended that only the more serious cases of brothel
keeping be prosecuted but stessed that 'if the Watch Committee
desired a change, I would of course spare no effort to give effect to
their decision.' Indeed, in 1890, after the municipal elections, the
new watch committee instructed Sir William 'to proceed against all
brothels at present known to the police without any undue delay
and *such proceedings shall be by way of prosecution*' (my
emphasis).[13]

The watch committee system continued until 1964, with officers
like Sir Robert Mark deploring the 'subservience' of the Chief
Constable. The 1964 Police Act, giving effect to the Royal Commission's recommendations, established new Police Authorities
throughout England and Wales, which, together with the Home
Secretary in the area of the Metropolitan police and the City of
London Common Council, are responsible for maintaining 'an
adequate and efficient police force for their area'. There are now
forty-one Police Authorities, two-thirds of their members
nominated by the local council or councils in the police force area,
the remaining third being appointed from among magistrates.
These police authorities are committees of the appropriate local
council, whose approval is required for the police budget.

In addition to its general responsibility, the Police Authority appoints the Chief Constable, his deputy and the assistant chief constables and, subject to the Home Secretary's approval, sets the size of the force establishment. The Authority deals with disciplinary complaints against the senior officers whom they appoint and, as a last resort, may call on the Chief Constable to retire 'in the interests of efficiency'. The Authority also has to approve the police budget (subject to the full council's consent), is responsible for providing and maintaining buildings, vehicles and equipment (again, with the Home Secretary's approval) and, finally, is meant to supervise the procedure for handling complaints against police officers. The Chief Constable is required to submit an annual report to the Authority, which may also call for a report on any matter connected with policing in the area.

The new structure has not met the need for effective supervision over policing policies. The Royal Commission failed adequately to distinguish between the need for independence from political interference when it comes to a decision to prosecute an individual suspect and the need for answerability to an elected body on general policing issues. In its desire not to compromise the former, it failed to specify the legitimate areas of Police Authority decision making or to equip the Authorities with adequate powers. Even then, the Authorities' responsibility for providing an 'adequate and efficient' force could legitimately have drawn them into active and rigorous participation in determining policy. But most Authority members have been only too willing to accept the official interpretation of their powers, restricting them to their housekeeping role. An examination of Police Authority minutes in Sussex revealed, for example, that discussion was almost entirely confined to matters such as alterations to police buildings, police travel allowances, poor rear lighting on foreign lorries and a grant to the local gun club.

Nor is a local Police Authority's control over the police force budget as crucial as it seems. The council's approval for the budget is not required for expenditure needed to give effect to regulations, including Home Office regulations on police pay, which, in Merseyside in 1979/80, for example, accounted for 73 per cent of the entire police budget.[14] Nor is the Authority's approval needed for expenditure directly funded by the Home Office. The Thames Valley force's experimental databank (see page 38) was financed by the Home Office and not the Police Authority, although local finance has recently been made available to maintain the system after the end of the experiment. In the West Midlands, where it was recently announced that the police had acquired a new fleet of helicopters equipped with high-precision cameras capable of identifying faces and car numbers from the air, it was discovered that the finance had again come from the Home Office and that the Police Authority had not been asked to approve the new equipment. [15]

The reduction in the number of police forces, from 123 just after the war to forty-one now, and the dramatic increase in the size of most forces has further removed the police from local supervision. Police Authority members are now drawn from a number of different local authority areas, of different political complexions and with very widely varying needs. In those areas where the police force area is not coterminous with a single local authority area, the members will be appointed by different councils; but even where all the elected members come from a single county council, the area may be too great for the Police Authority to feel a common identity with it or to assert an agreed view of local interests against that of a Chief Constable. Furthermore, the weakening of links between local police forces and the local community has been accompanied by strengthened contacts between Chief Constables, particularly through the Association of Chief Police Officers, which has become a major police pressure group at a national level. Specialist squads such as the regional crime squads, working together on an inter-force basis, have further developed the discretionary powers of Chief Constables at the expense of local accountability. And the growing professionalization of the police, through expanded training, specialist squads and increased reliance on communications technology, has led to a view that policing issues are 'technical' matters for police experts rather than policy issues for the community's representatives.

The trigger-point for Police Authorities' discussion of policing policy is supposed to be their power to call for and discuss reports by Chief Constables on any aspect of local policing. The limitations of his process were, perhaps unwittingly, revealed by the then Home Secretary during the passage of the 1964 Police Act:

> a Police Authority could *ask* the Chief Constable about the deploy-ment of the force. It could *ask* about the allocation of the force between crime prevention and traffic policing. It could *ask* about the state of crime generally or in particular parts of the area. It could *ask* about the extent of police protection provided in a certain district and it could call for a report and comment on it. (My emphasis)

No suggestion here that the Police Authority might debate or even *change* the allocation of police resources! But despite the Home Secretary's comment that a Police Authority which did not ask such questions could not possibly satisfy itself that the force was adequate and efficient, a survey in 1976 by the Association of County Councils (ACC) and the Association of Metropolitan Authorities (AMA) revealed that seven Police Authorities *never* asked for reports from their Chief Constable and twenty-four did so only infrequently. One county Police Authority *never* requested information on policing, received no regular reports from its Chief Constable, never gave advice on local problems and never had its advice sought on social issues![16] This is in striking contrast to earlier practice: in Swansea in 1844, for instance, the local chief police officer was required to report weekly to the local council sitting as a watch committee.[17] It is not surprising that many of those attending a seminar on police authorities organized in 1977 by the ACC and the AMA felt that they had little involvement in police affairs.[18]

A Chief Constable may indeed reject a request from the Authority for a report if he believes that such a report would contain information whose disclosure would not be in the public interest, or if he believes that the report is unnecessary for the discharge of the Authority's functions. The Authority may then refer the dispute to the Home Secretary for a final decision. It would appear that no request for a report has been referred to the Home Secretary under this provision. But individual Police Authority members, particularly if they are in the political minority, have found themselves frustrated by the majority's refusal to endorse a request for a report.

Although the thirty-one county Police Authorities in England and Wales (the remaining ten are combined Authorities) are committees of their local county councils, their functions are determined by statute and not by the councils themselves. Accountability of the Police Authority to the council is, in theory, provided by the power of any other councillor to question police committee members. In four counties, however, the AMA/ACC survey disclosed that the police committee makes no report at all to the council, and that in another two areas only infrequent reports are made. Only eleven county committees submit their full minutes to the council, often marking them 'for information only'. Excerpts from the minutes may be highly selective, usually relating to matters such as acquisition of land, for which full council approval is legally required. In Merseyside, for instance, the county solicitor rules on which items in the Police Authority minutes may be discussed by the full council.

Some Police Authorities have tried to assert their powers more forcefully. In South Yorkshire in July 1978 the Police Authority was strongly critical of the Chief Constable's refusal to man a school pedestrian crossing and of the controversial arrest of a young black man. The Authority cut the police budget but failed to change the mind of the Chief Constable, who later resigned – and joined the Police Inspectorate. The county council itself set up a working party to consider relationships between the community and the police but was forced to manage without the co-operation of the Chief Constable and of the police associations, all of which refused to give evidence. The working party's report[19] merits study, since it illustrates the thoughtful and practical attitudes of local councillors and community groups when invited to make proposals about policing policy. Far from being 'anti-police', most of those giving evidence wanted more police officers on the beat – a proposal strongly endorsed by the working party and accepted by the new Chief Constable, Brownlow. Although Brownlow said that the report, 'if used constructively', could strengthen community backing for the police, he also told a meeting of local councillors that he had been 'incensed' by the report, which, he claimed, was pervaded by 'a subtle bias against his police'. The police clearly resented the suggestion that police attitudes towards homosexuals and their policy of patrolling public lavatories needed reviewing. Some of the working party's proposals – such as the suggestion that photographs of those convicted of serious criminal offences be published – were rightly rejected by the police and might not have been made if the police had themselves been involved in the working party's study. But many of the conclusions were, in fact, accepted by the police or were claimed to reflect existing police practice.

In 1979 the West Yorkshire Police Authority requested a report from its Chief Constable on the financing of the publicity campaign which he had launched – without consultation with the Authority – to catch the Ripper. Authority members learnt of the contents of the report through the press, which received copies of the report before the Authority itself. In Merseyside some members of the Police Authority have tried to assert themselves, but when they asked the Chief Constable, Ken Oxford, to provide details about the police inquiry into the death of Jimmy Kelly (who was arrested for being drunk and disorderly and died from injuries received at that time), Oxford replied that he would add nothing to the press release he had already issued. In the same area Knowsley Borough Council found itself powerless to do anything about the policing of its local district, Huyton, apart from passing a resolution which called on the Home Secretary to hold a public inquiry.

In London the Police Authority is the Home Secretary himself. (The City of London Council is responsible for the small City police, an anomaly which should be abolished when a new Police Authority structure is established.) The Home Secretary cannot provide even that small element of local experience and advice which is offered by the other Police Authorities. His dealings with the Metropolitan Police Commissioner and any guidance which he may offer are completely shielded from public scrutiny. Successive Home Secretaries have shown themselves unwilling to provide Parliament with adequate information about the operation of the Metropolitan police – as instanced by Mr Whitelaw's refusal to answer a Parliamentary Question about police surveillance of political meetings.

The exceptional nature of the Police Authority in London reflects the exceptional role of the Metropolitan police as both a local police force responsible, as in any other, for policing a particular area and the single largest force responsible for certain national policing duties. The Metropolitan police are inevitably in the forefront of the policing of large national demonstrations, more of which take place in central London than anywhere else; they have special responsibility for guarding foreign embassies and visitors; they provide certain national services to other police forces, such as the Criminal Records Office at Scotland Yard and (in conjunction with the Home Office) the Police National Computer in Hendon; and they operate a series of specialist units, such as the Anti-Terrorist Squad (which operates nationally), the Special Branch (which works with Special Branch officers in other forces) and the National Drugs and Illegal Immigrants Intelligence Units. It has been suggested by Jack Straw, MP,[20] and by State Research[21] that the Metropolitan police should be divided into two forces. The first, accountable to a locally elected authority, should be responsible for policing Greater London; the other, accountable through the Home Secretary to Parliament, should be responsible for national policing functions and support services.

It is not clear that the proposed division of the Metropolitan police would deal with the problem of accountability or provide a better police service for London's citizens. The line between 'national' and 'London' policing functions is not easy to draw, and there is a real risk that the national police service would remain as unanswerable to higher authority as the Metropolitan police now is and would form the nucleus of an increasingly powerful and remote nationwide force. Other police forces and local Police Authorities would rightly resent the intrusion of members of a national police force, whose operations would not and could not be confined to the capital city. Many of these problems would, however, be avoided if the national police service were solely concerned with providing certain technical support facilities – in particular, criminal records and the national police computer – and had no executive functions itself.

A new structure of local accountability

The system of Police Authorities, established less than twenty years ago, has failed to give local communities an adequate voice in the development of police force policy. It reains generally true that, as the 1962 Royal Commission found, the Chief Constable 'is accountable to no one and subject to no one's orders'.

In 1979 Jack Straw, Labour MP for Blackburn, introduced a Private Member's Bill which would give the Police Authorities the power to determine the 'general policing policies' for their area and would require each Chief Constable to exercise his powers in accordance with those policies. The Authorities would also have the power, subject to consultation with the Chief Constable, to appoint chief superintendents and superintendents. In the event of a dispute between the Chief Constable and the Authority, the matter could be referred for a final decision to the Home Secretary, who would also be under an obligation to issue detailed guidance to Police Authorities. Like most Private Members' Bills, this one got no further than a debate, but it seems likely that a future Labour Government will accept the need for the strengthening of the Police Authorities' role.

In deciding how to improve procedures designed to ensure that the police are accountable to the communities they serve, it is essential to draw clear distinctions between the prosecution of individual offenders and the general powers and duties of the police, between general policing policies and the detailed implementation of those policies and between matters which should be decided nationally and those which are properly the responsibility of local bodies.

The police rightly argue that political interference with the decision to prosecute or not to prosecute an individual suspect is undesirable and could become corrupt, but they wrongly extend that argument to opposition to *all* 'political interference' with policing. There is now widespread support for the proposal of the Royal Commission on Criminal Procedure to establish a system of Crown Prosecutors, whose geographical area of responsibility would match those of local police forces. Unfortunately, however, the Commission also recommends the creation of joint Police and Prosecution Authorities to ensure local accountability to the Crown Prosecutor. Local control over prosecuting policy would reproduce the variations in prosecuting policy which exist at present; currently, a suspect's chances of being prosecuted for any particular offence depend on the part of the country in which he commits the offence. Giving responsibility for prosecuting policy to locally elected councillors, particularly at the same time as councillors are trying to exercise more vigorous supervision over policing policy, would lend credibility to police fears of political interference in individual prosecution decisions and would undermine the independence of the prosecutor from the police that the projected system is designed to achieve. Instead, prosecution policy should be a matter not for local but for national accountability, with the Crown Prosecutors responsible through the Attorney-General to a new, specialist Select Comittee of the House of Commons.

The transfer of the conduct of prosecutions from the police would remove any lingering justification for the appointment of non-elected magistrates to Police Authorities. These Authorities should be reconstituted as wholly elected bodies, their members coming from the appropriate local councils. A new Police Authority should be established for London, also consisting of elected local representatives (for instance, one Greater London Council and one borough councillor for each of the London boroughs, together with a county councillor from each of those counties with which the Metropolitan police area now overlaps). One problem would still remain: the size of the Police Authority area, with only one or two authority members coming from each district involved, would preclude the close involvement of the local community and the representation of detailed local needs. It would therefore be desirable to constitute district or borough council police committees under the aegis of the Police Authority itself. The local police commander should be under an obligation to attend local committee meetings and to report to them on local policing matters. Although the Police Authority would have statutory responsibility for formulating general policy, it would be required to take note of representations received from a district committee, which would also be able to express its views through the local members of the Authority.[22] The regional Inspectors of Constabulary, who at the moment report to the Chief Inspector at the Home Office, should in future also report annually to the Police Authorities in their region.

The 1962 Royal Commission identified the kind of policy issues which should be the proper preserve of a Police Authority. They referred, for instance, to the concentration of resources on any particular crime or area, the manner in which political demonstrations or processions are policed, the way in which breaches of the peace arising from industrial disputes are handled and so on. A current list of proper Police Authority concerns would also include the balance of resources between car and beat policing, the creation and use of specialist back-up units such as the controversial SPG and the use of local intelligence data systems such as the Thames Valley 'police notebook'. Arguably, the maintenance of an adequate and efficient police force already encompasses such issues, but the narrow view of Police Authorities' responsibilities which has developed in two decades, together with the difficulties encountered by those Authorities which have tried to extend their involvement in policing issues, suggests that a new statutory definition of the powers and duties of Police Authorities is required.

Commenting on Jack Straw's Bill, the then President of the Association of Chief Police Officers (ACPO), Alan Goodson, said:

> once you allow the political influence to play any part at all . . . you are changing the complete nature of policing in this country. I would see this particular Bill as beginning to be the start of a change in the relationship between the Police Authority and the Chief Constable, a greater encroachment upon his police function.[23]

He referred also to the 'politically instituted' nature of Police Authorities and to their 'political bias'. Similarly, a *Times* leader criticizing the London Labour Party's proposal in the 1981 Greater London Council election manifesto for the creation of a London Police Authority, said that such a degree of 'political control' would strike at the 'already precarious credit [of the police] as a body outside party politics'.[24] But policing is already a political matter. Decisions about how to enforce the law, what priority to give different kinds of crime, how to police controversial demonstrations and so on are all political decisions, which reflect views about how best conflicting interests may be reconciled. 'Political' activity, in the narrower sense, has itself become of particular interest to the police, whose decision to keep under surveillance large numbers of people involved in lawful and peaceful activity is, again, a highly political matter. And police spokesmen such as Sir Robert Mark and the Police Federation have taken up overtly political positions, even of a party nature. The 'nature of policing' in Britain today clearly does not exclude politics.

A more cogent objection has come from John Alderson, Chief Constable of Devon and Cornwall, who is himself responsible for the introduction of a highly publicized community policing scheme. Alderson has argued[25] that greater powers for the Police Authorities could lead to corrupt policing systems where the police operated in the interests only of a particular race or a particular religious group. An overtly sectarian police force did, of course, operate in Northern Ireland – without any elected Police Authority – and it is only recently that the Royal Ulster Constabulary, whose membership remains almost entirely Protestant, has begun to establish better relationships with Catholic working-class communities. Many black British communities feel strongly that the police already operate against their interests; direct representation of those communities on elected Police Authorities and smaller district police committees is essential if the police are to operate in the interests of the community as a whole – and are to be seen to do so. But it must also be stressed that fears of corruption through greater political supervision – coloured by the experience of corruption in many cities of the USA – are only really justified where the elected authority controls prosecution decisions. Under the scheme proposed neither the police nor the Police Authority could control prosecutions, which would be transferred to the new Crown Prosecutor. And no Police Authority could be given the power to direct the police to break, or not to implement, the law.

It could also be argued, with justification, that the majority who would dominate a particular Police Authority at any one time might wish to override the rights and interests of a particular minority group. For instance, a Police Authority's majority group might formulate a policy on demonstrations and processions which directed the police to keep such activities well away from busy shopping areas (in order to minimize the 'inconvenience' to traders and shoppers) and, wherever possible, to ban such activities. This risk is not met by leaving the decisions to the police, whose hostility to many demonstrations is detailed in chapter 5. But it is necessary to guarantee the rights of those who happen to be in the minority – for instance, by providing a statutory right to peaceful protest – in order to restrict both the discretion of the police and the power of the Police Authority. The Police Authority itself should be required not only to maintain an adequate and efficient police force and to formulate the general policy to be adopted by that force, but also to adopt policies which pay proper regard to the rights and interests of all sections of the community.

Exaggerated police fears of corruption or inefficiency have perhaps been mirrored by exaggerated expectations on the part of the supporters of stronger Police Authorities. Both the Labour Greater London Council manifesto and statements from the London Campaign for Police Accountability[26] bracket together the proposal for a new Police Authority with demands for the abolition of the SPG and an end to political surveillance. A Police Authority may indeed decide to disband, or not to create, a special squad like the SPG or to restrict surveillance and intelligence data systems to those with criminal records or those suspected of particular criminal offences. But the Authority might also decide that it wanted to devote more resources to 'saturation policing' in a particular area, and it would be entitled to do so. A Police Authority able to decide whether or not to devote resources to raids on sellers of 'obscene' literature might, for instance, decide to transfer its resources to beat patrols: but a different authority might decide that it wanted a moral crusader police chief like Manchester's James Anderton, bent on cleaning up pornography and prostitutes. Elected representatives will not always produce the decisions which those who are pressing most strongly for accountability would support.

However, there are issues which require a national view and on which the Police Authority for a particular area must work within national policy. Such issues are the criteria used to determine the circumstances in which a police officer may use firearms and the development of police technology. On such matters the Home Secretary should continue to formulate policy but should be answerable to the Home Affairs Select Committee of the House of Commons. Police information gathering should be supervised by the new Data Protection Authority (see page 44); the rights of individuals to see certain records held on themselves or to complain to the Authority about unjustified intrusion should be laid down by statute.

The debate about police accountability comes down to the issue of where decisions should be made. The police fear that if the political control of the local council and, therefore, of the Police Authority changed, the policy of the Police Authority would change too. But Police Authorities in Scotland are already made up entirely of elected representatives from the regional council, while prosecuting policy is already the responsibility of the Procurator Fiscal, who directs the police in the investigation of criminal offences. In England and Wales, however, as the system now stands, policing policy depends essentially on the views of the Chief Constable, and policies change not with an election of the Authority but with the appointment of a new Chief Constable. It is extremely rare for an Authority deliberately to seek out a Chief Constable who will support a general philosophy of policing on which the Authority has already decided.[27] And Alex Lyon, MP, a former Home Office Minister, had rightly pointed out that the Devon and Cornwall community policing scheme was entirely the initiative of the Chief Constable and not that of the Police Authority or other community groups, whose views and support were sought only after the policy decision had been made. It is surely preferable to recognize that policing involves political decisions; that those decisions should be a matter for debate within the community and during election campaigns; and that decisions on overall policy should be made not by the appointed Chief Constable but by the elected Police Authority.

The accountability of individual officers

So far, we have considered arrangements for ensuring that the police are more effectively answerable for general policing policy. But recent debate about accountability has also, rightly, concentrated on procedures designed to ensure that the individual police officer is answerable for his or her actions.

An investigation into the actions of an individual officer may be triggered off by a complaint from a member of the public or by a report from another officer, all officers being under an obligation (breach of which is itself a disciplinary offence) to report any incident involving themselves or other officers. It was not until

1976 that an independent element, the Police Complaints Board, was introduced into the internal investigation and disciplinary procedures, although reports on an alleged criminal offence by an officer had always been sent to the Director of Public Prosecutions (DPP), whose consent is required for the prosecution of an officer.

In the first instance, the complaint will be investigated by an officer from another division or, in the Metropolitan police force, another subdivision. A more serious complaint may be investigated by an officer from a different force, but the Police Complaints Board reported in 1978 and again in 1980 that deputy Chief Constables did not always consider with sufficient care the possibility of appointing an external investigator.[28] The investigator's report is submitted to the deputy Chief Constable; if it discloses evidence of a criminal offence, it is passed immediately to the DPP. If the DPP declines to prosecute, or if no criminal offence is revealed by the report, the deputy Chief Constable decides whether or not to bring disciplinary proceedings. If he does, the matter is heard by the Chief Constable, who decides whether or not to uphold the complaint and, if so, what punishment to award. If no disciplinary charge is brought, or if the officer contests the charge, the report is sent to the Police Complaints Board. At that extremely late stage, the Board may ask the investigating officer for more information or may order the deputy Chief Constable to bring a disciplinary charge. In exceptional cases, the Board may establish a disciplinary tribunal consisting of the Chief Constable and two Board members – but only one such tribunal was established in the first four years of the Board's operation.

This system is riddled with defects. First, any complaint against a police officer is investigated by another officer. The justification offered is that a police officer suspected of a criminal offence should be treated in the same way as any other suspect and that, in any case, no one will be as tough on police officers as the police themselves. The flaw in the system, however, is that even if the police investigation is as rigorous and as impartial as anyone could wish, the aggrieved complainant probably will not believe in it. Where relations are strained between the police and part of the community – whether young black people in Brixton, Asian families in Southall or working-class people in Merseyside – the spectacle of the police acting as investigators and judges in their own cause only deepens suspicion. Despite considerable evidence to support complaints of serious police misbehaviour in April 1979 in Southall, when Blair Peach was killed,[29] comparatively few complaints were made to the police, since many of those with complaints to make had no faith whatsoever in police investigation and disciplinary procedures.

Such suspicions are intensified by evidence that police investigations of police complaints are *not* always adequate. The West Midlands officer who investigated the death of Jimmy Kelly, following his arrest by Merseyside officers, did not interview witnesses who claimed to have seen Kelly manhandled by the arresting officers but relied instead on statements already taken by Merseyside officers. Justice has complained that

> some police officers will be motivated to disprove or minimize the complaint, particularly if it is made against a member of [their] own force, or of a neighbouring force. The letters and reports we receive tell far too often of investigating officers doing their best to persuade complainants to withdraw their complaints. . . . In cases involving allegation of actions designed to pervert the course of justice it is not uncommon for potential witnesses to make statements to solicitors or to Justice and then for investigating officers to report that the persons who made the complaints deny having made them or refuse to confirm them. In other cases, potentially important witnesses have not been interviewed.[30]

The Police Complaints Board is itself unhappy with the present position. Despite a membership drawn impeccably from the great and the good (until 1981 its chairman was Lord Plowden), the Board reported in its first three-yearly review: 'In some cases we have felt that the investigating officer might have uncovered more evidence if the interviewing of police witnesses had been more rigorous instead of being limited to a request for a statement by the witness, especially where he is a police officer.' The Board also said that although allegations of corruption, fraud or similar offences were vigorously pursued, in *assault* cases – which are those which have caused most public concern – 'the investigating officer is perhaps more likely to be influenced by early experience of his own and to be more ready to accept the policeman's account of what took place than that of the complainant.'[31]

The Board has recommended the creation of an independent team of investigators made up of police officers on secondment, but answerable to an experienced lawyer, preferably a former judge, who would be responsible for investigating any serious allegation of assault by a police officer. The recommendation is welcome, but there is no reason why the team of independent investigators should consist only of police officers or be restricted to assault cases. Complaints that a police officer has perjured himself or has fitted up evidence in order to convict an innocent person are at least as serious as allegations of assault and equally require independent investigation.

The second problem arises when the DPP considers complaints of possible criminal behaviour. As a general rule, in any case, the DPP will sanction a prosecution only if he believes that a 'reasonable jury' would be more likely to convict than to acquit. But in cases involving a police officer he also takes into account the apparent reluctance of juries to convict a police officer before making his estimate of the chances of a conviction.[32] In practice, therefore, the DPP requires a *higher* standard of evidence against a police officer than against a civilian. Some cases submitted to him would never justify prosecution, either because of the triviality of the matter or for lack of evidence. (For instance, the Police Complaints Board noted disapprovingly in 1979 that some deputy Chief Constables refer all complaints of swearing by a police officer to the DPP, even though a prosecution in such a case would be widely condemned.) But the operation of the '50 per cent rule' is an additional reason why so few cases result in a prosecution. In 1979, for instance, 4304 reports were referred to the DPP (excluding alleged traffic offences): in only 174 cases was a prosecution brought.[33]

The DPP's decision does not merely affect the question of criminal proceedings. During the passage of the Police Bill through Parliament in 1975 and 1976, the Home Office – faced with intense opposition from the Police Federation to the creation of the new Board – came to an agreement that no police officer would be disciplined on the basis of evidence which the DPP regarded as inadequate for a criminal charge. The rule is justified as avoiding 'double jeopardy'. But double jeopardy arises where an officer is 'tried' twice for the same offence, through both criminal proceedings and a disciplinary hearing. In some circumstances, a form of double jeopardy is inevitable and indeed desirable – if, for instance, an officer is convicted of a criminal offence which would make it intolerable for him to remain in the force. The Act itself states that if an officer is acquitted of a criminal offence, he shall not be disciplined on substantially the same charge. But the agreement between the Home Office and the Police Federation (contained in Home Office Circular 32/1980) treats the decision by the DPP not to prosecute as having the same effect as an acquittal. Thus the officer who has never been brought to court, but whose case has been considered and dismissed by the DPP, may not even be disciplined on evidence which has been held insufficient to warrant criminal proceedings. It may, nonetheless, be possible to bring disciplinary proceedings for a different matter. (For instance, an officer suspected of having misappropriated property found in a search, but against whom there is inadequate evidence for a charge of theft, may be disciplined for failing to account properly for the seized goods.) And the Police Federation has argued[34] that where the DPP's decision is based on the view that prosecution would not be in the public interest rather than on grounds of inadequate evidence, disciplinary proceedings equivalent to the criminal charge rejected by the DPP may still be brought. But the Board itself has pointed out that in many forces it is assumed that if the DPP has decided that there is insufficient evidence for criminal proceedings, there is no room for a disciplinary charge of any kind.[35] In a succession of cases of major public concern a decision by the DPP not to prosecute has been the end of the matter, with neither criminal nor disciplinary proceedings being brought despite evidence of serious police misconduct. The effect of treating a decision by the DPP as if it were identical to an acquittal by a court means that many officers suspected of the most serious misbehaviour escape all jeopardy entirely.

This third defect in the present procedure is perhaps the most serious. It means that neither the disciplinary system nor the Police Complaints Board can have any effect when a criminal offence has been alleged but the DPP has decided, for reasons of evidence, not to prosecute. But such complaints are, by definition, among the most serious ever made against police officers.

The fourth problem has been identified by Justice as the failure to connect a police investigation which bears on the conduct of a particular prosecution with the decision to uphold the conviction obtained. Some of the most serious complaints involve an allegation that a police officer has perjured himself in providing evidence which formed the basis for a conviction or has otherwise helped to secure a wrongful conviction. There may be good reasons for not instituting criminal proceedings against an officer, but there may also be sufficient evidence from the disciplinary investigation to cast doubt on the safety of the conviction. In such cases the defendant (who is usually also the complainant) must have access to the investigating officer's report, either so that he may use it as the basis for an appeal or (where an appeal has already been unsuccessful) in order to persuade the Home Office to reopen the case by referring it back to the Court of Appeal.

Finally, it will be clear from the description of the present procedure that the Police Complaints Board's involvement is so delayed as to be marginal. In 1980 out of 14,984 complaints dealt with, the Board asked for further information in 110 cases, established one tribunal (out of 107 cases in which the officer concerned denied the disciplinary charges made against him) and made recommendations for thirty-one disciplinary charges in eighteen cases (the deputy Chief Constable accepting fourteen of the recommendations, the Board itself dropping the other eighteen recommendations after discussions).[36]

The combination of these defects in the complaints and disciplinary system, together with the inadequacy of other procedures which are in theory available to deal with serious police misconduct, were vividly illustrated by the aftermath of the events in Southall in April 1979 (described on page 126). A senior Metropolitan police officer, Commander Cass, was appointed to investigate complaints relating to the death of Blair Peach who, according to a number of eye-witnesses, had been hit on the head by one or more officers. In fact, no formal complaint was ever made about Blair Peach's death, which should more properly have been treated as a death in suspicious circumstances. Cass's report to the DPP apparently recommended prosecutions not only for homicide but also for riot, affray and conspiracy to pervert the course of justice.[37] But no prosecutions were authorized. Under the double jeopardy rule no disciplinary proceedings could be brought on evidence which the DPP had rejected as insufficient and, although different disciplinary charges might have been brought, in fact it was reported in April 1981 that no disciplinary action would be taken in connection either with Blair Peach's death or with the other events in Southall on the same day.

Widespread demands for a public inquiry into the Southall events were rejected by the Home Secretary. Although the 1964 Police Act allows the establishment of an independent inquiry into any aspect of policing in any area, the power has been used only three times: in 1965, when a Metropolitan police officer, Challoner, was accused of planting bricks and similar items in the pockets of those arrested on demonstrations; in 1974, when Lord Scarman was appointed to investigate events in Red Lion Square during which a student demonstrator, Kevin Gateley, was killed; and in 1981, when Lord Scarman was again appointed to investigate the Brixton riots. The Home Office view that events such as those in Southall can be dealt with through the police investigations machinery and, where a death is involved, through an inquest, is simply inadequate. The failings of the police complaints procedure have already been noted; to those criticisms must be added the fact that the investigation of an individual complaint cannot and is not designed to deal with the wider policy issues which may be raised by the complaint. The function of an inquest, to establish who died, when and how, is also extremely limited. The inquest into Blair Peach's death did not fulfil even that limited purpose adequately. The report of the police investigator, which formed the basis of the coroner's decision about which witnesses to call, and which was used by both the coroner and the Metropolitan police lawyer to cross-examine witnesses appearing at the inquest, was withheld from the lawyers representing the dead man's family. Reforms in the inquest procedure designed to ensure that all parties have all the evidence available to them would also ensure a more thorough public scrutiny of the circumstances in which someone has died. But no inquest can act as a substitute for a wide-ranging inquiry into facts, law and policy which the circumstances of Southall clearly demanded.

Reforming the police complaints machinery

The Police Complaints Board, as we have noted, has itself proposed the appointment of a team of investigators to deal with serious assault cases. This proposal, by an independent body, was submitted to a Home Office working party, seven out of whose twelve members were themselves police association representatives. The Board's chairman, who also chaired the working party, and his own fellow member from the Board, were unable to persuade the police representatives, the DPP and the two Home Office representatives to accept the Board's recommendations. Instead the working party suggested[38] that greater use should be made of police investigators from different forces under the present procedures, and that the chairman or deputy chairman of the Board might supervise the investigation of serious complaints. Since those two officers would, of course, be too busy to exercise any effective supervision over many cases, they would be 'assisted' by, among others, a senior police officer. The working party's proposals were rightly condemned as inadequate by most of those who had pressed for an overhaul of the present machinery.

The Police Complaints Board is now the last port of call for the police investigator's report. It needs, instead, to be placed at the centre of the police complaints machinery. It should employ its own team of investigators to deal with any serious complaints, including allegations of assault, corruption and perjury. Although the investigators should include police officers on secondment, as recommended by the Board, they should also be drawn from among solicitors, barristers, former Customs and Excise officers and others with appropriate investigative experience. It has been suggested[39] that in particularly difficult and serious criminal investigations involving either the police or other people in positions of public trust, 'special prosecutor' teams should be created which combined the investigation with the preparation of the case for trial. It is clearly unsatisfactory that the DPP should continue to decide to pursue or reject a prosecution on the basis of written statements from witnesses, without any first-hand idea of whether a witness will 'come up to proof' in court. The Board's own team of investigators, if constituted in the way I have proposed, would be well equipped to make a judgment about the strength of a case, since those investigating a particular case would include lawyers with experience of defence and prosecution work.

It is also essential to change the present double jeopardy rule. The purpose of criminal proceedings is different from that of a disciplinary system designed to uphold the professional standards of a disciplined force. The rule against double jeopardy should continue to apply where an officer has been *prosecuted*, although a conviction will necessarily result, in most cases, in appropriate disciplinary action, which, in serious cases, would involve dismissal from the force. But the DPP's decision not to prosecute should not be allowed to substitute for an acquittal after a full trial; any case rejected by the DPP should be reconsidered afresh by the deputy Chief Constable and the Complaints Board for possible disciplinary proceedings.

Finally, the report of any disciplinary investigation which bears on the conduct of officers in a criminal prosecution should be made available to the defendant and his legal advisers for possible use in an appeal against conviction.

II

Freedom of Speech and Expression

4

Censorship and Secrecy

Until the early eighteenth century censorship in this country was almost entirely concerned with the protection of political and religious orthodoxy. It was not until then that the creation of a law against obscenity really got under way, although the attempt to restore sexual orthodoxy continues to flourish today. But with the notable exception of Government policy on Northern Ireland – where dissent still attracts prosecution – the criminal law is rarely used now for the direct suppression of political views. Instead, the Government and major commercial interests protect themselves by suppressing information: keeping secrets has taken over from punishing sedition.

But a stalemate has been reached between supporters of a freedom of information law which would require the Government to make most of its secrets available to press and public, and the Government's own desire to replace the thoroughly discredited Official Secrets Acts with a more restricted, but more effective, criminal law against disclosure. The failure of the Freedom of Information Bill introduced by Labour MP Frank Hooley in 1981 to gain its second reading suggests that such a measure is unlikely to succeed without a change of Government. On the other hand, the outcry from press and MPs of all parties which met the Government's own Official Information Bill in 1979 makes it equally clear that the Government will not secure a majority for a measure dealing only with official secrecy. The Government's desire for secrecy will be pursued through other means – most notably, the use of the Civil Service disciplinary system – but the growing frequency of leaks from within Whitehall suggests that this sanction is less effective than before.

The 1911 Official Secrets Act, introduced during a foreign policy crisis, was rushed through Parliament with little debate, all its stages in the House of Commons being completed in less than an hour. When its provisions were extended in 1920 the opposition proved bitter but ineffective, and it was not until 1939, after Duncan Sandys, MP, had been threatened with prosecution for asking Parliamentary Questions about the shortage of anti-aircraft guns, that the scope of the Acts was somewhat restricted. At every stage the Acts provide exceptions to normal criminal procedure: wider powers to arrest suspects and to obtain evidence; an extended jurisdiction for the courts, allowing the trial of a British subject for an offence under the Acts committed abroad; a lower burden of proof for the prosecution (under the more serious Section 1 of the 1911 Act the defence is required to prove that the defendant's actions were not for a purpose prejudicial to the safety or interest of the state); exceptions to the normal rules of evidence; and the power of the court to sit in secret. Such extraordinary provisions could only possibly be justified if they were directly related to the protection of national security and if they had been carefully and thoroughly scrutinized by Parliament. But, like most measures which most infringe civil liberties, the 1911 Act received almost no parliamentary scrutiny, and over and over again the Acts have been used when there has been no possible threat to national security. Indeed, the wording of the Acts makes such abuse inevitable.

Section 1 of the 1911 Act, although purporting to deal with spying, makes it an offence to obtain or to communicate any document or information which might be useful to an enemy, directly or indirectly, for any purpose prejudicial to the safety or interest of the state, or to make any sketch or note of a prohibited place which might be useful to an enemy for the same purpose. In 1964 members of the pacifist Committee of 100 were charged with conspiring to incite others to commit Section 1 offences after a demonstration at Wethersfield military airfield that was designed to ground all aircraft. The House of Lords held[1] that it was up to the Government itself to decide what was prejudicial to the interests of the state and that the defendants' own intentions – in this case, to reclaim the airfield for civilian use – were irrelevant. Referring to a 1916 case, the court held: 'Those who are responsible for the nation's security must be the *sole judges* of what the national security requires' (my emphasis). Exactly the same argument was used in 1977 by the Court of Appeal, when it dismissed Mark Hosenball's appeal against a deportation order made by the Home Secretary on national security grounds: according to the court, when 'the interests of national security demand', natural justice must give way.[2]

But it is Section 2 of the 1911 Act, carrying a maximum of two years' imprisonment, that is the broader, making it an offence to communicate *any* official information to any unauthorized person. In 1970 Jonathan Aitken, MP, Brian Roberts (editor of the *Sunday Telegraph*) and Colonel Douglas Cairns were prosecuted for the publication of a report on the war in Nigeria. Johann Wesler, a Foreign Office official, gave the game away when he told the court: 'It is no business of any official to try or allow the Government to be embarrassed. That is what we are working for. *Embarrassment and security are not really two different things*' (my emphasis).[3]

The trial judge in the *Sunday Telegraph* case was scathing about the prosecution:

> This case, if it does nothing more, may well alert those who govern us at least to consider . . . whether or not Section 2 of this Act has reached retirement age and should be pensioned off, being replaced by a section that will enable men like the defendants and other editors or journals to determine without any great difficulty whether a communication by any one of them or certain piece of information resulting from an official source, and not concerned in the slightest with national security, is going to put them in peril of being enclosed in a dock and facing a criminal charge.

The result was the establishment of the Franks Committee, which reported in 1972,[4] recommending the replacement of Section 2 by more tightly worded law covering, for instance, foreign affairs, defence, the currency and Cabinet secrets. But the Franks Committee Report joined the pile of official documents gathering dust in the Home Office; its limited recommendations have still not been implemented.

In 1977 the authorities again burned their fingers on the Official Secrets Acts when they brought Section 1 and Section 2 prosecutions against two journalists, Duncan Campbell and Crispin Aubrey, and a former soldier, John Berry (see page 51). Judicial criticism forced the abandonment of the more serious charges; convictions on lesser counts led only to a suspended sentence for Berry and conditional discharges for the other two defendants. Although the threat of prosecution is still available for use against recalcitrant journalists, it is unlikely that any Government would risk another such trial.

In July the following year the Labour Government proposed in a White Paper[5] to replace Section 2 with an Official Information Act covering four categories of information: defence and foreign relations, law and order, security and intelligence and confidential information about individuals. The proposals were seriously criticized, particularly because they made no reference to the need for a freedom of information law but were concerned only with making criminal sanctions more effective. The repeal of Section 2 would make no difference at all to the amount of Government information which would become available to MPs, the press and the public. The only effect of repeal would be to put disciplinary sanctions in place of criminal sanctions; a civil servant who was caught leaking information would face dismissal rather than imprisonment. The effect of the change would be slight.

The White Paper also failed to live up to the pledge of the then Home Secretary, Merlyn Rees, that 'mere receipt of official information' would no longer be a crime.[6] The Government's scheme left untouched Section 1 of the Act, although that section – as the charge against Duncan Campbell established – covered precisely the 'mere receipt' of official information. Furthermore, the new Official Information Act would exempt from Section 2 charges only passive recipients, those who had secrets stuffed into their letter boxes or were forced to hear the unwelcome confidences of a garrulous civil servant. Any journalist who actually questioned his source would still be open to prosecution for having solicited the material, regardless of whether or not use was ever made of it.

Following the Franks Committee, the Government also proposed that a decision by a Minister to classify a document as secret should effectively be final. (A proposal to have the Attorney-General review the classification was rightly dismissed as cosmetic, since the Attorney-General would in any case have to authorize the prosecution.) Thus, as at present, a Minister would make the final decision as to whether or not state interests would be harmed by publication of the contents of a particular document: the defendant would be unable to challenge the classification and the court unable to review it. Such a system would invite civil servants and Ministers to abuse the protection given to secrets properly deserving of protection by classifying documents whose disclosure would *not* be harmful but might be embarrassing. Finally, it would have been possible, under the White Paper scheme, to prosecute someone for communicating or publishing security and intelligence material even if the document were not classified at all – a proposal that directly contradicted the Franks Committee's recommendation that such information should be protected by criminal law only if such protection is deserved. According to the White Paper, intelligence is 'pre-eminently an area where the gradual accumulation of small items of information, apparently trivial in themselves, could eventually create a risk for the safety of an individual or constitute a serious threat to the interests of the nation as a whole'. It is precisely for collecting small items of often trivial information from public sources that Duncan Campbell was prosecuted, and the White Paper was clearly drawn up in the hope that a future Campbell would not escape conviction.

In 1979 Liberal MP Clement Freud secured an unopposed second reading for a Freedom of Information Bill drafted by a private research group, the Outer Circle Policy Unit. The Bill would have compelled Government to make most records public, while allowing for the discretionary disclosure of some information and providing criminal sanctions for the publication of certain secrets. Six categories of information would be exempt from the duty to disclose: defence and national security, foreign relations, law enforcement and legal proceedings, information protected from disclosure by other statutes, information about individuals (although the individual concerned would have been able to insist on a right of access) and Cabinet documents for up to five years. The Advisory Council on Public Records would advise government departments on the administration of the law, while an appeal against refusal to disclose would lie with the Ombudsman. Although the Labour Government, which had strongly opposed the Bill in Committee, eventually offered to let it through in return for Clement Freud's support for other Government measures, the Bill fell with the Government in April.

In the autumn of 1979, following a commitment in the Queen's Speech to 'reform' the Official Secrets law, the new Government introduced its Protection of Official Information Bill. Its provisions departed from the Franks recommendations in two crucial respects. First, as the previous Government had itself proposed, information relating to defence would be protected by criminal sanctions even if the documents concerned were not classified; it would therefore be impossible for any journalist to know whether or not publication of unclassified material might nonetheless risk prosecution. Second, the Bill proposed a new category of protected information relating to security and intelligence: *any* unauthorized publication would be criminal, regardless of whether or not it would cause serious injury to national security and regardless of whether the information had already been published elsewhere!

This section, had it been in force at the time, would have prohibited publication of Andrew Boyle's book *The Climate of Treason,* thereby preventing full discussion of the Prime Minister's statement about Anthony Blunt, a former intelligence officer and friend of Burgess and Maclean who had passed information to the Soviet Government during the war. This fortunate coincidence persuaded the Government to abandon the Bill even before its second reading.

Nonetheless, the Bill indicated the train of official thought under both the Conservatives and the previous Labour Government (the Bill had probably been originally drafted on the basis of the Labour Government's earlier White Paper). Any discussion of telephone tapping and mail interception would have been prohibited, and the definition of 'confidential' information would have been extended to cover almost any information received from foreign Governments, international organizations, commercial bodies and nationalized industries, as well as private individuals, without any test of whether publication of commercial information would, in fact, damage a company's competitiveness or whether publication of material from a foreign organization or Government would damage foreign relations. Oddly enough, Cabinet documents were omitted from the scope of the Bill, as was financial information relating, for instance, to the state of the reserves. But, as I have already stressed, such information is already protected by Civil Service disciplinary regulations, as is any official document whose publication has not been authorized.

The Bill aptly matched Merlyn Rees's unfortunate description of what was required by way of an Official Secrets law – that it should be 'an Armalite rifle, not a blunderbuss'. The desire of both the present and the previous Government to introduce such extensive criminal sanctions sits uneasily with their repeated expressions of commitment to more open government. Ministers of both Governments have referred in glowing terms to the 'Croham Directive' issued in 1977 by the head of the home Civil Service, which asked Departments to divide policy advice from factual material in internal documents, releasing the latter to the public wherever possible. The Directive itself only became known to the public through a leak to *The Times*! Its effect has been minimal. *The Times*'s Whitehall correspondent, Peter Hennessey, estimated that between May and October 1978 the Home Office, for instance, published nothing which would not have been made public anyway.[7]

It is only in the last few years that public debate has focused on the ill effects of Government secrecy. By definition, secrecy conceals its own consequences. But the information which has become available – either through leaks or because Ministers have chosen to publish – together with a comparison between what information is available in the USA and the policy of closed government which remains in Britain, has enabled MPs and journalists to begin to assess the damage done by Britain's structures of secrecy. When information is withheld neither MPs nor journalists (nor, indeed, voters) can do their jobs properly. Backbench MPs cannot effectively challenge or supervise Ministers and their Departments if they cannot establish the factual basis of a particular policy decision or the alternatives which were rejected. The Official Secrets Acts are only part of a system of secrecy, which includes not only Civil Service disciplinary regulations but also Parliamentary conventions which ban Parliamentary Questions on ninety-four different subjects[8] and which allow Ministers to withhold information from House of Commons Select Committees. Similarly, journalists cannot report or comment accurately and fully on matters of public interest if they depend on leaks or, worse perhaps, on official hand-outs. The *New Scientist* commented despairingly that in one issue alone there were 'at least four stories that do not tell the reader all there is to know about the subjects they cover'.[9] Thus the public is debarred from informing itself about, and properly judging, what is being done in its name – let alone challenging, with the power of full knowledge, developments of which it disapproves.

Although Ministers defend secrecy as essential to national security and to good government, the system is all too often self-defeating. In September 1980 the Ministry of Defence used the Civil Service regulations to stifle embarrassing critiicsm of safety standards at the Atomic Weapons Research establishment at Aldermaston. Trevor Brown, who is also a Liberal county councillor, had been brought to Aldermaston with the duty of improving safety standards after a succession of extremely disturbing, unpublicized accidents there. (One of the victims of these accidents, who later contacted NCCL, had attempted to bring civil proceedings against the Ministry for compensation, but was unable to do so after his doctor had been warned that an Official Secrets prosecution would follow if he provided expert evidence in the case.) After arguing for ten years that the establishment's monitoring of radioactivity in the air was inadequate, Brown finally succeeded, in 1977, in obtaining equipment which, when put into operation, revealed large sections of the plant to be unsafe. The radioactive sections of the plant were closed down, and a high-level inquiry confirmed his criticisms. In March 1980 Mr Brown agreed to speak as a county councillor in a BBC Newsnight pro-gramme, *Is Aldermaston Safe?*. Although he disclosed no secret information, he voiced his concern that safety standards remained lower than at other similar establishments and agreed that the secrecy surrounding the issue had actually contributed to the delay in improving matters. Mr Brown was severely reprimanded by the Ministry and, knowing that his chances of promotion had been irreparably damaged, he took early retirement from the Civil Service.

This structure of secrecy conceals law breaking, such as sanction busting in Zimbabwe, and inefficiency, such as the scandalous record of the Crown Agents Office, which was finally revealed in 1976 to have lost over £200 million, much of which might have been saved if a report on its dealings compiled in 1972 had been published then. The harsh and unjust treatment to which prisoners are often subject has generally been concealed from public view – for instance, by the rule which prohibits prison officers from speaking to the press.[10] Ironically, the present Home Secretary and the director of the Prison Department have recognized that the only way of generating public support for reforms in the prison system, particularly those designed to reduce overcrowding, is to publish more information about prison conditions.[11] And invasions of individual privacy – for instance, through the use of inaccurate, irrelevant or improperly obtained personal information – are almost always concealed from the individual concerned.

Perhaps the most difficult consequence of secrecy to identify accurately is the manipulation of information which such a system permits. The cloak of secrecy is not evenly woven. Ministers are only too willing to pass out to receptive journalists the official versions of policy or events, knowing that their versions cannot be set against the background studies, policy papers or committee minutes which provide a fuller story and knowing, too, that the publication of information gleaned from 'unattributable sources' will protect them from embarrassing questions. Journalists who should be at the forefront of the campaign for a freedom of information law may develop a personal interest in maintaining secrecy, which is the prerequisite for their 'exclusives'.

But the cloak is wearing threadbare. Certain journalists and journals have become increasingly ready to publish unauthorized material, the *New Statesman*'s series of revelations about telephone tapping and about the security services and *The Times*'s close attention to the official treatment of information being obvious examples. The ready availability of material from the USA not only offers new information but also points up the absurdity of the British Government's policy. For instance, a report from the Parliamentary Sub-Committee on Defence in 1976 was 'side-lined' – the Parliamentary euphemism for censorship – to delete references to the ranges of the Hawkswing and Dragon missile systems, ranges which had been routinely disclosed to the US Senate Armed Services Committee as, respectively, about 3000 metres and 60,000–61,000 metres. [12]

A threefold change is required. First, the Official Secrets Acts should be repealed, and criminal sanctions should be restricted to properly classified material in the realms of security, defence and foreign affairs whose disclosure would seriously affect national interests; information whose disclosure would assist in the committing of serious criminal offences or in facilitating an escape from prison or would otherwise seriously damage the enforcement of the criminal law; and confidential information relating to an individual (other than the person requesting sight of the material) or to a nationalized industry or private company when disclosure would damage commercial interests. If additional measures are thought necessary to deal with foreign spies, then a new Espionage Act should be introduced to replace Section 1 of the 1911 Act.

But a change of this kind would, of itself, do nothing to make more information available. The second requirement, therefore, is a Freedom of Information Act, placing a duty on government Departments and agencies to disclose documents in their possession. Exemption from the duty to disclose would, of course, include any document covered by the revised criminal sanctions. It would also be possible to exempt from disclosure documents whose unauthorized disclosure would *not* carry any criminal sanctions: for instance, Cabinet papers and minutes could be exempted for a limited, specified period. Any exemption should, however, be narrowly drawn, with a right of appeal to a court or a special Parliamentary Select Committee against refusal of access.

The first line of official defence against a freedom of information law is its alleged cost. For instance, in 1977 Sir Douglas Allen (later, Lord Croham) wrote to Arthur Lewis, MP, then chairman of the All-Party Committee for Freedom of Information, that the

American law had been 'formidably burdensome'. But no government department in either the USA or this country can be trusted to estimate accurately the costs of an access law to which they object. For instance, the US Office of Manpower and Budget (part of the President's Executive Office) estimated that the Privacy Act of 1974, which provides for access to personal information, would cost $200–300 million a year, with an additional $100 million in start-up costs – an estimate that proved three times too high for start-up costs and about nine times too high for annual operating costs. In June 1978 it was reported[13] that thirteen major agencies in the USA had spent between them less than $12 million a year between 1975 and 1978 in operating *both* the Privacy Act *and* the Freedom of Information Act. It has been suggested that similar laws in Britain would cost less than £2 million a year, a fraction of the amount lost by the Crown Agents and only a small proportion of the £25 million or more spent each year on official government information programmes.

In 1975 the then Labour Government looked to the civil law of breach of confidence in an attempt to prevent Jonathan Cape and the *Sunday Times* from publishing Richard Crossman's *Diaries of a Cabinet Minister*. The court refused the Attorney-General's application on the grounds that the 'secrets', then eleven years old, were too stale to merit protection. Nonetheless, the Lord Chief Justice made it clear that 'public secrets' could, in different circumstances, be protected from publication.[14]

The British Steel case in 1980[15] amply demonstrated the threat offered to investigative journalists by the breach of confidence law. A researcher with Granada Television had obtained confidential documents from an employee of British Steel, then involved in a major industrial dispute. After the documents had been used in a current affairs programme, British Steel sought and obtained an injunction against Granada to prevent their further use, together with an order for their return. The papers were returned, but the marks which would have identified the 'mole' who had supplied them had been removed. The House of Lords insisted that Granada disclose the name of its informant. The matter never came to a head, since the 'mole' disclosed himself in an interview with the press. But the case was disturbing, not only because of the decision but also because of the way in which it was argued. Dr Peter North has rightly pointed out[16] that it was quite unnecessary for Granada to admit, as it did, that it was in breach of a duty of confidence to British Steel, when it could have argued that in the disclosure of information about the mismanagement of a nationalized industry the public interest outweighed the claims of the British Steel management to preserve the secrecy of its deliberations. Lord Salmon, in a dissenting judgment, advanced the argument which Granada should have used when he said that if the documents 'exposed the faults and mistakes which were causing the immense losses made by British Steel, it would be Granada's public duty to disclose the contents of those papers to the public'.

The law of confidence was also used by Distillers in 1974, when the company prevented the *Sunday Times* from publishing documents which had been disclosed by the company to the families of thalidomide-damaged children following an order for pre-trial discovery. The House of Lords held[17] that the confidentiality of the discovery process should outweigh the public interest in the information disclosed, even on a matter of such seriousness. Fortunately, the European Human Rights Court, to which the case eventually went, held otherwise.[18]

The European Court decision led not only to the publication of the original *Sunday Times* articles, five years after they were written, but also to the introduction of the Government's Contempt of Court Bill, seven years after the Phillimore Committee had recommended major reforms of the law on contempt.[19] But the 1981 Contempt of Court Act signally fails to live up to the promise of reform made by its sponsor, the Lord Chancellor, Lord Hailsham, whose interpretation of the European Court decision is strikingly different from that of the *Sunday Times* lawyers who prepared and argued the case.[20] But it is clear that the Act would not protect the *Sunday Times* from an injunction against publication if circumstances similar to those of the thalidomide case recurred. Although the Act provides a defence that the publication was continuing the discussion of a matter of public interest, and that any prejudice to pending proceedings was only incidental, that defence applies only to cases in which the prejudice to proceedings is *unintentional*. But the House of Lords held that the *Sunday Times* intended, by means of its articles, to put pressure on Distillers to settle the case (with appropriate payment to the families) rather than allowing the matter to drag on through the courts. Because no defence is available in a case of deliberate prejudice to proceedings, the *Sunday Times* would be in the same position under the new law as it was under the old. Once again, the British Government has avoided implementing the provisions of the European Human Rights Convention.

As originally drafted, the Contempt of Court Bill would also have made it a contempt to publish material relating to criminal proceedings if there were any risk of serious prejudice to the trial; an amendment in Committee now makes it necessary to establish a serious risk of serious prejudice. But the Act has extended the operation of the *sub judice* rule by protecting cases in which an appeal is pending against sentence or conviction. The Act gives the court an ominous new power to order the postponement of reports on proceedings, while magistrates have been given a new power to punish for contempt a defendant, witness or member of the public who interrupts proceedings. Thus the magistrate who is offended will charge the contemnor, decide whether or not to grant legal aid, hear the case and decide sentence. Even more regrettably, the Government rejected the proposal made by, among others, Lord Salmon in his evidence to the Phillimore Committee, that civil proceedings (or at any rate the vast majority of civil cases heard by judge alone) should not be protected at all by contempt law.

The Government also took the opportunity offered by the Bill to reverse the decision of the Divisional Court in the *New Statesman* case in 1979, when it rejected the Attorney-General's argument that publication of an interview with a juror in the Thorpe case was contempt.[21] The trial had finished; no money had been paid to the juror; and the interview raised issues of considerable concern over the DPP's selection of charges in the case. In its original form, the Bill would have allowed publication of jury deliberations only if neither juror nor case were identified. But an amendment to the Bill, successfully moved by a Labour peer and QC, Lord Hutchinson, has imposed a complete ban on jury disclosures, whether during or after trial, whether paid for or not, whether anonymous or identified. Research interviews with jurors are prohibited, as are articles by journalists who have themselves served as jurors. Indeed, any juror who refers publicly to his jury-room experiences will be in contempt. It is, of course, necessary to protect jurors from press approaches before a verdict has been given, and it would seem inappropriate to allow researchers or journalists ever to pay jurors for an interview or to identify a juror without his or her consent. But the risk that a verdict will not be regarded as final if jurors may comment publicly on their decision or on how it was reached, or that the institution of the jury will itself be undermined if jurors' deliberations are open to public scrutiny and comment, seem to be exaggerated. Considerable publicity has been given in the past to jury-room disclosures, without consequent injustice to defendants or injury to the jury itself. Because the jury provides the only democratic element in the enforcement of the criminal law, there is considerable and legitimate public interest in its conduct and real public value in allowing jurors to discuss their experience, within certain limits, if they choose to do so. The institution of the jury is certainly threatened – not by researchers or journalists, but by Ministers who sanctioned jury vetting, who abolished the jury in serious cases in Northern Ireland and restricted their scope in Great Britain,[22] and by those who would do away with jury trial altogether. Publicity about the involvement of ordinary people in the administration of justice can only strengthen the institution of the jury, and it is much to be regretted that the ban on jury disclosures should come from a lawyer who is himself a staunch defender of the institution.

The ability of the courts to extend the law on contempt in unexpected, indeed absurd, directions, was amply illustrated by the *Harman* case. Harriet Harman, legal officer of NCCL, was representing a former prisoner, Michael Williams, in an action against the Home Office arising out of his incarceration in a special isolation cell, the Control Unit. An application for disclosure of Home Office documents relating to the establishment of the Unit was strongly resisted by the Home Office, which failed in its attempt to claim immunity from disclosure for many of the papers. Some 6800 pages of material, including advice to Roy Jenkins, the Home Secretary at the time the Unit was opened, minutes of departmental meetings and correspondence with prison officials, was made available to Ms Harman. Only 800 pages were selected for use in the case, with the agreement of the Home Office, and those papers were read out in open court during the course of the five-week hearing. After the hearing was completed the papers were shown to David Leigh of the *Guardian*, who had attended much of the hearing and who prepared a full-page feature article on the issues raised by the case. The Home Office then began proceedings against Ms Harman for contempt of court, arguing, as Distillers had done, that the papers were protected by the confidentiality attaching to discovered documents, which were to be used only for the case and not for any ancillary purposes. But whereas the Distillers documents had never come into open court, the Home Office papers had been read out in the course of an open hearing and could be bought, in the form of a court transcript, by anyone with the necessary cash. (There was no argument over the need to protect discovered documents *before* trial, nor to preserve the secrecy of discovered documents which were not used as evidence. Indeed, the remaining 6000 pages of the Home Office papers disclosed to Michael Williams's solicitor have never been shown to anyone not directly involved in preparing the case.) Nonetheless, the Divisional Court and the Court of Appeal both held[23] that Harriet Harman had committed a serious contempt of court, and that discovered documents, even after they had been openly read, could be shown to a journalist or anyone else only with the consent of their owners.

Baroness Wootton's comment in the case was apt: 'The law is often said to be an ass, but I do not think that it could be a greater ass than if it decreed that a document which had been read out in open court and listened to by any members of the public who happened to be there is still confidential and must not be reproduced in print.' But the court's willingness to reach such an absurd result was undoubtedly influenced by the nature of the *Guardian* article itself. Headline, 'How Ministry hardliners got their way over prison control units', the article analysed in depressing detail how civil servants had toughened up proposals for a special regime which had been authorized in a very different form by the Minister. The article was an important contribution to public understanding of how policy is made in one of the most powerful and the most secret Departments of State. That was precisely what troubled Lord Denning, who said in his judgment that the article was 'highly detrimental to the good ordering of our society'! The *Williams* case[24] had been brought in an attempt to open up government power to the scrutiny of the courts: the Court of Appeal decided instead to shield evidence given in open court from the scrutiny of the press.

Despite considerable lobbying from Labour, Liberal and Conservative MPs and from the press, the Government refused to accept an amendment to the Contempt of Court Bill to reverse the Harman decision. An appeal to the House of Lords is likely to be heard in early 1982 and will, if necessary, be pursued to the European Human Rights Commission.

The Commission was also invited, in 1975, to consider the use of the 1936 Incitement to Disaffection Act against critics of successive Governments' policy in Northern Ireland. This deplorably vague law makes it an offence (under Section 1) to attempt to seduce a member of the armed forces from his loyalty and duty to the Crown; it is also an offence to *possess* any document whose dissemination to members of the armed forces would be an offence, if the purpose of the possession is to commit or assist a Section 1 offence. In 1937 an 18-year-old student, Ronald Phillips, was sentenced to twelve months' imprisonment after a conversation and correspondence with a disillusioned Air Force corporal, who, Phillips had suggested, might care to fly to Madrid 'on the sly' if he really felt 'revolutionary'.[25]

The Act then remained unused until 1972, when Michael Tobin, an anarchist, was sentenced to two years' imprisonment for possessing two pamphlets urging soldiers in Northern Ireland to desert. Two years later Pat Arrowsmith was convicted for distributing and possessing a leaflet produced by the British Withdrawal from Northern Ireland Campaign. The Court of Appeal upheld her conviction,[26] and the European Commission rejected her complaint as inadmissible, on the grounds that the leaflets did not manifest a pacifist belief and were therefore not protected by Article 9's provisions on freedom of conscience; any interference with freedom of expression was justified.[27]

In 1975, however, fourteen members of the Withdrawal Campaign who were charged with distributing or conspiring to distribute a leaflet similar to that for which Pat Arrowsmith had been convicted were *acquitted* of all charges.[28] The result was a vindication of the campaign against the conspiracy laws as well as that against the 1936 Act. The Act has not been used since, and it is high time that it was repealed – before a future Attorney-General decides to dust it off for use against critics of the Government.

The laws against obscenity

It is only twenty-two years since the then Home Secretary, Roy Jenkins, tried with his Obscene Publications Act 1959 to make sense of the laws against obscenity. He failed. By the end of 1979 the Williams Committee on Obscenity and Film Censorship[29] had pronounced the law a mess and had recommended the scrapping of all restrictions on the written word, with a new system for control of the public display (but not, except in the case of pornography involving children or the commission of criminal offences, the sale) of pictorial material. The intervening period has witnessed extraordinary innovations and reversals in the law and in prosecuting policy. The common law offences of conspiring to corrupt public morals and to outrage public decency, revived with some success in the 1960s and early 1970s, are once again dormant. Since the middle of the last decade juries have generally acquitted books, and even some 'hard-core' pictorial pornography, of obscenity. But the police have turned instead to the mass destruction of magazines through the magistrates' courts, while the conviction of the editor of *Gay News* for blasphemous libel in 1977 was a startling reminder of the ability of the courts to resurrect common law offences long believed dead.

The 1959 Act created a dual system of control.[30] The Act made it an offence, punishable by up to three years' imprisonment, to publish for gain an obscene article, the defendant to such a charge having a right of jury trial. 'Obscene' was defined as tending to 'deprave or corrupt', but the defendant could bring expert evidence to show that, despite its corrupting tendencies, publication of the article was in the public good! Alternatively, the police could apply to a magistrates' court for a forfeiture order, the distributor being summonsed to show cause why the material should not be destroyed.

Although supposedly concerned with sexual material, the Act could nonetheless be used where the prosecution's motives were clearly political. In 1971 Richard Handyside was convicted by a magistrates' court in London for publishing *The Little Red Schoolbook*, a young people's guide primarily concerned with challenging authoritarian school regimes. The appeal court which upheld the conviction condemned the book not merely for the chapter on sex but generally

> as inimical to good teacher/child relationships . . . subversive, not only to the authority but to the influence of the trust between children and teachers . . . the influence of parents, the church, youth organizations and other adults with whom they come into casual contact will be very seriously affected in the face of a very considerable portion of the children who read this book.[31]

The *Schoolbook* case encapsulated the defects of the obscenity laws. First, under the 1959 Act the police have extensive powers to search for and seize not only articles believed to be obscene but also any other material relating to the publisher's or distributor's business. Handyside found that the police went through all his office files, seizing everything related to the book – and, typically, refused to give a receipt for what they took. Second, the case revealed the absurd discrepancies between one part of the country and another: although convicted in London, the *Schoolbook*'s publisher was acquitted by magistrates in both Edinburgh and Glasgow. It is hard to believe that London schoolchildren were so much more in need of protection than their Scottish contemporaries. Third, the book was convicted ostensibly on the basis of one chapter, although the Act specifically directs attention towards the article taken as a whole. Fourth, it became clear from the comments of officers in the case that the real intention was to put Handyside out of business. The fine itself was minimal (£50), but seizure of his stock, if implemented, would have bankrupted him. The police search, however, omitted to discover the main bulk of Handyside's stocks, which were smuggled out of the office before the second search, thus enabling Handyside to meet much of the demand for the book which the prosecution generated – the publicity given to allegedly obscene material being the fifth and particularly absurd effect of the present law.

Handyside's trial coincided with the use of the conspiracy laws against the editors of *IT* (*International Times*) and *Oz*, two of the underground newspapers whose mix of drugs, sex, music and revolutionary politics was too much for the authorities to stomach. The *IT* case was preceded by a police raid, the seizure of office equipment, subscription lists and private correspondence, and the interrogation of homosexual men who had planned to insert 'contact' advertisements in the magazine. The editors' conviction for conspiracy to corrupt public morals followed the precedent set in the 1961 *Ladies Directory* case,[32] when the House of Lords re-asserted judicial power to safeguard the nation's morality. The *IT* judgment revealed that although consenting homosexual acts between two adult men in private had been legalized, an advertisement designed to procure a legal act remained illegal. The editors, who were also convicted of conspiracy to outrage public decency, received a suspended sentence of eighteen months' imprisonment, in addition to the £1000 fine imposed on the news-paper itself.[33]

In July 1971 the editors of the 'schoolkids' issue of *Oz* were charged with offences under the 1959 Act, as well as with con-spiracy to corrupt public morals. They were acquitted of the conspiracy charge, since the jury was not satisfied of their intention to corrupt anybody, but convicted of the obscenity charges – with sentences being imposed of up to fifteen months' imprisonment and a deportation order against the Australian editor, Richard Neville. The most serious convictions were, however, quashed by the Court of Appeal.[34] Two years later the acquittal of the editors of *Nasty Tales*, another underground paper, on the same conspiracy charges marked the end of the DPP's attempt to silence the alternative society. The republished version of the *Little Red Schoolbook*, with an amended chapter on sex but with its anti-authoritarian sections uncut, has not been prosecuted; the charge of conspiring to outrage public decency has not been used since the *IT* trial; and conspiracy to corrupt public morals was charged only once between 1974 and 1979.[35]

But the resilience of common law offences was demonstrated once again in 1977, when the editor of *Gay News*, Denis Lemmon, was privately prosecuted for publishing a poem about a homosexual's conversion to Christianity. The poem, by James Kirkup, had attracted no particular attention when it was published. But the possibility of reviving the old offence of blasphemous libel was considered some months later, when the press ran a story about the possible importation into Britain of a pornographic film concerning the life of Christ. Never one to miss an opportunity, Mary Whitehouse sought and obtained permission from the High Court to prosecute both Lemmon and the publishers of *Gay News*. Their conviction was upheld by the Court of Appeal in a judgment which ended the requirement to prove an attack on the Christian religion or to establish the risk of a breach of the peace – a judgment which was, in turn, upheld in the House of Lords.[36] Any 'outrageously indecent or irreverent' comments about God, holy persons or articles of the Anglican faith may now constitute blasphemous libel; the defendant's intentions in publishing the words are irrelevant. As is so often the case with obscenity trials, the *Gay News* trial obtained for James Kirkup's poem a considerably wider audience than it had originally reached. But, unlike the subject matter of most obscenity trials, which involve productions of little or no value as art, the poem in this case, although shocking to many people, was also an extremely moving celebration of sacred and secular love. Its suppression did the courts little credit.

In any trial involving obscenity or public morals it is of the utmost importance that a jury, rather than a magistrate or judge, be left to decide the questions of what 'public morals' really are and whether ordinary people are indeed likely to be 'depraved and corrupted' by a particular publication. The prosecuting authorities were shaken by a series of jury acquittals in the mid-1970s in cases which suggested that the public was considerably more tolerant (or depraved) than the DPP had believed possible. In April and September 1975, in two trials at the Old Bailey, the juries failed to agree on whether American magazines showing bondage and sado-masochism were obscene, and in October of the same year a

Portsmouth jury acquitted much of the 'highly explicit' Danish pornography which they had been invited to condemn. As the Williams Committee wryly commented: 'Before that case, one of the certainties of life for the prosecuting authorities was that Scandinavian pornography was obscene.'[37] The acquittal in 1976 of the publishers of *Inside Linda Lovelace* (the circulation of which was considerably increased by the publicity surrounding the trial) means that written material is now unlikely to be successfully prosecuted.

The police and the DPP have instead turned to magistrates to protect a public which – judging from the juries – no longer wants protection. The number of forfeiture orders made by magistrates' courts jumped from thirty-one in 1969 to 550 in 1978, with the number of items seized by the Metropolitan police along rising from 35,390 in 1969 to a staggering 1,229,111 in 1978.[38] But forfeiture orders are a peculiarly arbitrary and unjust form of censorship. Because they depend on the initiative of the police in obtaining warrants to seize obscene material, they are especially likely to result in discrepancies in policy between different parts of the country. In 1976, for instance, the new Chief Constable of Greater Manchester, James Anderton, who views pornography as sinful, instructed his officers to take more energetic action against it – with the result that nearly 200,000 items were seized from retailers, including W.H. Smith, in a sixteen-month period.[39]

The magistrates' court which deals with a police application for the destruction of allegedly obscene material has already considered the matter in deciding to summons the distributor to show cause why the material should not be forfeited. It can hardly be considered an impartial judge of the matter. Its standards do not reflect those of the public at large – and, indeed, can hardly be expected to, since magistrates are not drawn from the public at large but continue to have in their ranks disproportionate numbers of older, middle-class men. In 1973, when a jury acquitted the editors of *Nasty Tales,* copies of *Men Only* were destroyed by magistrates in Watford. A year after the jury's acquittal of *Inside Linda Lovelace* a Liverpool stipendiary magistrate had to be prevented by the DPP from ordering the seizure from W.H. Smith of *The Joy of Sex.*[40] Despite appeal court rulings that allegedly obscene material must be properly examined by the magistrates, the speed with which some benches deal with thousands of items suggests that scrutiny is not very thorough. In 1972 the police seized 134,000 copies of thirty-four different books from Olympia Press. The six magistrates compared notes on the seized books, including one which the publisher claimed was an important Russian underground novel, during a ninety-minute lunch adjournment – and promptly declared the entire stock obscene.[41]

In theory, the author and publisher are entitled to be heard in forfeiture proceedings against a distributor. But since they are not entitled to be informed about pending proceedings, and since the distributor may have no wish to fight the case, it is not uncommon for material to be destroyed without either author or publisher having an opportunity to oppose the charge of obscenity. Worst of all, the use of the forfeiture order procedure enables the prosecution to avoid completely the need for jury trial. Neither the distributor, nor the publisher, nor the author has any right to insist on being charged with a criminal offence under the Act; the forfeiture order can be dealt with only by a magistrates' court; and an assurance given by the law officers to Parliament in 1964 that publishers would be given the option of jury trial if their books were in danger of destruction has not in fact been honoured.[42]

Powers parallel to those of the magistrates to order forfeiture and destruction of obscene material are given to the Customs officials who have the power to search for and seize any 'indecent' articles imported into this country. The most important difference between the controls on domestically produced and those on imported material is that the lower test of 'indecency' is applied to imports, thus relieving Customs officials of any need to consider contemporary standards as defined by juries. After the acquittal of *Inside Linda Lovelace*, for example, Customs officers were reminded by an internal directive that the acquittal had nothing to do with the law on imports and that any copies of the book commercially imported should be seized. Nor does the 'public good' defence apply in Customs legislation: in 1973 a sex education kit prepared by associates of Kinsey under the auspices of the Unitarian Church and imported by the BBC was confiscated by Customs and Excise officials. The importer of material seized by Customs officers is required to notify them should he wish to challenge their decision; if he does so, the case will be referred to a magistrates' court, and the burden of proof is on the importer, who has to establish that the material is not 'indecent'. If no notice is received or if the appeal fails, the material is destroyed. Customs officers appear to have relaxed their vigilance somewhat since 1969, when over two million items were seized. But in 1978 no fewer than 125,394 allegedly indecent books, magazines, photographs, films and other items were confiscated in accordance with a secret blacklist issued by the

Customs authorities. The June 1978 edition of this internal directive (which includes *Forum*, *Gay News*, *Penthouse* and the left-wing Compendium Bookshop in its list of suspect importers) engagingly admits that 'efforts to establish any universally acceptable legal definition of obscenity have been unsuccessful' and advises officers who find it hard to make their minds up to view the Department's collection of 'borderline' items.

Like Customs regulations, Post Office regulations apply to *solicited* material as well as to items which have not been ordered. It is an offence to send through the post any indecent or obscene 'print, painting, photograph, lithograph, engraving, cinematographic film, book and written communication, or any indecent or obscene article'[43] – even if the item has been ordered and paid for by the recipient. Among the transactions placed at risk are 'adult' magazines operating a subscription list, and in 1972 the publisher of allegedly indecent homosexual magazines was indeed prosecuted under these provisions. No evidence of 'public good' is admissible in such cases, and the lesser and extremely vague test of 'indecency' allows the courts to convict someone for posting material which could lawfully be sold across the counter.

In 1980 and 1981 a number of people involved in the Paedophile Information Exchange were prosecuted under the Post Office Act. But not everyone who had sent pornography through the post was prosecuted. Among those who escaped trial was a former British Ambassador, who had advertised through the Exchange under a pseudonym. In response to criticism that a public figure had been allowed to escape the embarrassment of a trial or even of being called as a prosecution witness, the DPP explained that it was his policy not to prosecute under the Post Office Act when material had been solicited and when no commercial interests were involved – in which case it is not clear why some of the other charges were brought. But it is high time that the law itself was amended to deal only with unsolicited material and to end the risk of prosecution for solicited material, regardless of whether or not payment is involved.

Proposals for reform

Because censorship is about the use of power, all censorship is, in the end, political. Those who wish to change the distribution of power within society, as well as those concerned with limiting any concentration of power, should be particularly alert to any extension of censorship. Restrictions or bans on published material, whether written or pictorial, should be accepted only if the restriction is directed specifically at avoiding an identifiable harm, the prevention of which overrides the general interest in the free communication and expression of ideas and if the restriction proposed is, in fact, likely to achieve the desired end. The protection of young people, the prevention of criminal activities which may be involved in the production of some obscene material (for instance, sex with a child) and the protection of adults from receiving unsolicited, highly offensive material – these aims are sufficiently clear, and capable of being translated into sufficiently precise legal provisions, to warrant some restriction or even exceptionally, a ban on the production or sale of certain kinds of material.

But it is also argued that some material, particularly pornography, is harmful generally to the community, or, more specifically, that it degrades women. The argument is an appealing one, particularly when in 1980 horror films about rape coexisted with the terror of the Yorkshire Ripper. Nonetheless, the alliance which has formed in some parts of the USA between feminist groups and extremely reactionary, pro-censorship and morality lobbies has warned the British women's movement of the dangers of supporting censorship in the name of feminism. The Williams Committee examined extremely thoroughly the evidence which was available on the connections between pornography and crime. They noted that the most comprehensive evidence available for the Danish experience revealed a 'very dramatic reduction in reported [sexual] offences against children which coincided with the sudden upsurge in the availability of pornography and which . . . cannot readily be explained by any other likely factor'.[44] In Britain the Committee found that the increase in sexual offences, which began years before pornography became more widely available, has been less rapid than the increase in criminal offences generally. Although it is still possible that there is some casual link between pornography and crime, there is no evidence that this is so. Nonetheless, even in the absence of evidence, the Committee accepted the possibility of a connection with crime in the case of films, which they regarded as particularly powerful; they therefore proposed that a film could be banned as being 'unfit for public exhibition' because of the manner in which it depicted violence, sexual activity or crime.[45]

Even in the absence of evidence which would justify a ban on certain kinds of pornography in the interests of reducing violent and sexual crime, it may be argued that the law should prohibit material which degrades women. Geoffrey Robertson has suggested that as long as the law punishes corrupting material, 'publishers placed at risk should be those who pander to sexist hypocrisy and discriminatory prejudice which demeans the dignity and threatens the happiness of any social, sexual or racial class.'[46] This very formulation shows that it would be impossible to frame a 'progressive' censorship law without running into exactly the same problems of vagueness, arbitrariness and absurdity encountered by the present laws on obscenity and public morals. A law which was wide enough to encompass material which degraded women (let alone all material which threatened 'the happiness of any social, sexual or racial class') would be wide enough to encompass almost any prejudice of the law enforcer. The degradation of women, which is a function of the relative economic, political and legal powerlessness of women, is unlikely to be altered by giving new powers of censorship to the powerful. As long as the magistrates and judges are involved in determining standards of acceptability, any new test applied to assess whether materials were 'degrading to women' would quickly be used to punish feminist images of sexually active and independent women, particularly if they were lesbian. And juries, by very virtue of the fact that they represent the standards of the general public, are unlikely to condemn images which are a problem precisely because they are so generally acceptable. There is a complex and inadequately understood interreaction between the ways in which we see ourselves and other people, the images through which we see ourselves and others portrayed and the ways in which we behave. Feminists are right to attack degrading images of women as part of the struggle against women's oppression: but that is not to say that the criminal law should be called in aid of a political and social campaign, or that the law would be of any use if the attempt were made.

We are therefore drawn back to the prevention of specific and identifiable harm as the only criterion for interfering with what adults choose to read or see. Furthermore, there is general agreement that some protection should be provided for those who do not choose to see pornographic displays. Adopting these two criteria – the prevention of specific harm and the protection of the unwilling – the Williams Committee proposed the abolition of all the present laws concerning obscenity, indecency, public morals and so on, along with all those terms incapable of proper definition which provide the basis of the present law. They recommend the lifting of any restriction or prohibition on the written word. Pictorial material would be restricted only if it were 'offensive to reasonable people by reason of the manner in which it portrays, deals with or relates to violence, cruelty or horror, or sexual, faecal or urinary functions or genital organs'; such material would be available on order through the post or in special premises to which under-18s would not be admitted and which would carry an appropriate warning sign. The only material to be completely prohibited would be images whose production involved the infliction of actual physical harm, or the involvement of someone aged under 16, for purposes of sexual exploitation. The Committee's definition is still too vague to provide adequate certainty about what does and what does not constitute a criminal offence. Such vagueness is inevitable in a law designed to cope with shifting public standards, which leaves newsagents and other distributors to choose between excessive self-censorship or the risk of prosecution. The alternative is to follow the example of two Australian states[17] and to establish a Classification Board with the task of licensing sexually explicit material, deciding what is to be generally available, what is to be sold only to adults and what is not to be publicly displayed. A classification-before-sale system avoids the risk inherent in the Williams Committee proposals but substitutes for a jury's determination of what is publicly acceptable the views of the classifiers. Despite the uncertainties and inconsistencies of jury censorship, the involvement of ordinary people seems preferable to the appointment of a licensing board.

Films

Films are at present subject to a fourfold censorship system. They are dealt with by the British Board of Film Censors, which certifies films for public showing; they are subject to licensing by local councils; if imported, they are subject to the powers of the Customs and Excise; and, since 1977, they have been subject to the 1959 Obscene Publications Act, which, unlike the licensing and certification systems, also applies to private cinema clubs.

The power of local councils to decide what adults should and should not view has, of course, led to absurd anomalies. In 1979, for instance, *Monty Python's Life of Brian*, on show throughout most of the country and passed by the Board for nationwide viewing, was banned in Doncaster. Other local councils have taken a more tolerant attitude, the Greater London Council deciding in 1967 to refuse a licence to sexually explicit films only if they were likely to 'deprave and corrupt'. In 1976, however, in a private prosecution brought by Raymond Blackburn, the Court of Appeal held[48] that the Greater London councillors would be guilty of aiding and abetting a criminal offence if they continued to license 'grossly indecent' films, and their licensing criteria were amended accordingly. By the mid-1970s it was common for some councils to refuse licences to films which the Board had approved for distribution, while other councils cheerfully licensed films which had been banned by the Board. The extension of the 1959 Act to films in 1977, which was intended only as an interim measure pending the report of the Williams Committee, has exacerbated the contradictions and uncertainties inherent in the 'depravity and corruption' test.

The Williams Committee, in addition to recommending the repeal of all the present laws on obscenity and indecency, has proposed an end to the system of local council licensing. It wishes to see the Board of Film Censors replaced by a statutory Film Examining Board whose brief would be to classify and censor films according to any restrictions thought necessary on the age of viewers. A particularly offensive film could be restricted to showings in licensed cinemas (the present exemption for private film clubs would be abolished), and a film could be prohibited altogether if it contained material prohibited by law or if, 'having regard to the importance of allowing the development of artistic expression and of not suppressing truth or reality, [it] is nonetheless unacceptable because of the manner in which it depicts violence or sexual activity or crime.'[49]

Thus the Committee proposes for films a censorship system far more severe than that proposed for other visual material and – in view of the proposal to bring private clubs within the licensing system – a system that is actually more severe than at present. The proposed criteria for restricted and prohibited films would leave extensive discretion with the Board itself. Worst of all, the Committee in effect suggests a new form of censorship by local councils by giving them an absolute power to grant or withhold a licence to a cinema to show 'restricted' films. Britain would be left with a film-censorship system considerably more restrictive than that which now operates in, for instance, France and Belgium, as well as in the Scandinavian countries. A better solution would be to combine the proposed new system for classifying films with the abolition of local council licensing powers. An amendment to the planning powers of local authorities would ensure adequate control over the location and number of private film clubs and sex shops.

The United Kingdom has rightly been described as one of the most secret countries in the Western world. The multiplicity of laws described in this chapter add up to a massive system of censorship which affects not only private reading and viewing material but also the decisions and operations of public officials. It will not be surprising if this system brings the United Kingdom Government into repeated conflict with the European Human Rights Court. The increasingly effective challenges which are being made by MPs, councillors, campaigners, journalists and officials themselves are not, as the Government would have us believe, a threat to democratic government: they are proof that our democracy has some health left in it.

5

Peaceful Protest and Public Assembly

The issue at stake in the current debate about public order is the claim of protesters to march and assemble in the streets and in other public places. Although presented as a discussion about the balance between peace and order on the streets on the one hand and freedom of assembly on the other, the very terms of the debate about public *order* suggest that, for the authorities at least, the balance is clearly tilted.

Even in the United States of America, where the Bill of Rights protects the right of citizens 'peacefully to assemble and to petition for the redress of grievances', the complex issues involved in defining the proper limits of the exercise of that right have not been systematically examined by the courts.[1] In this country there has been even less discussion of the theoretical issues underlining decisions about the common law and statutory powers of the police to control assemblies. Typically, the views of Government and the police are expressed in terms of the cost, the inconvenience and the violence of demonstrations, and not in terms of the social functions performed by assemblies. The main outlines of the issues may be summarized as follows.

Every community requires a certain level of peace and order, without which it cannot function. In the absence of laws which command general assent and are generally abided by and a system of law enforcement generally perceived to be fair, no structure of civil liberties is responsible. As an American writer on freedom of speech and assembly points out:

> The values that a community seeks from internal order are quite apparent. Indeed law and order are essential to the existence of the system of freedom of expression itself. The dynamics of disorder are apparent too. Once the degree of compliance with law declines below a certain threshold, rapid deterioration may set in. Law and

order depend upon general acceptance of the community, and that acceptance is given on the basis of fair and impartial administration of the governing rules. Violation of law, especially by the use of force, negates the whole principle upon which the structure rests. Popular acquiesence is withdrawn, institutions become corrupt and demoralized, the prestige of the Government is undermined, and the community as a whole is riven and disorganized.[2]

The exercise by protesters of the right of freedom of assembly may be seen as posing a threat to public peace and order. In some cases – but far less often than is generally supposed – it may actually pose such a threat. Demonstrations, rallies and pickets which are entirely peaceful may nonetheless disrupt traffic, shopping and other community activities and may be expensive to police. The minority of demonstrations at which violence occurs result in injuries to police, protesters and, on occasion, non-participant members of the public; they may also lead to a general apprehension of violence on the streets. Novel forms of protest, such as occupations or sit-ins of university buildings, factories or foreign embassies, may be and usually are entirely peaceful, but they challenge property rights.

But the characterization of demonstrations and other forms of public protest as a threat to normal community living obscures the basic fact that protest is a *part* of normal community life and serves a vital function in a democratic system of government. In their different and varied forms, demonstrations serve to bring issues and grievances to the attention of the public, the media and the authorities; they permit a form of face-to-face communication not offered by the media, and thus allow protesters to create and affirm solidarity with one another; as a form of political expression, representing a demand on those in power, they contribute towards the identification and, ideally, the peaceful resolution of conflict. The massing of people in the streets has been a crucial element of the struggle of working people, women and excluded minorities to wrest recognition from those in power and of the protest movements which have characterized Western societies in the last two decades.

Recent years have witnessed a number of serious, highly publicized, violent incidents occasioned by National Front meetings or marches and counter-protests. These occasions (Red Lion Square in 1974; Lewisham, in south London, and Ladywood, in Birmingham, in 1977; Digbeth, also in Birmingham, in 1978; and Leicester and Southall in 1979), together with the memory of violent clashes during anti-Vietnam protests in the late 1960s and early 1970s and similar incidents during the anti-apartheid tour protests of the early 1970s, have allowed the police and many journalists to create in the public mind an image of demonstrators as a threat to the community. Four elements may be found in this attack on demonstrations: their supposed irrelevance, the disruption to normal community life, the expense of policing them and the violence they provoke.

It is sometimes argued that the development of mass media of communication, combined with a representative electoral democracy, make protest on the streets unnecessary. For instance, in a speech in 1975 Sir Robert Mark, who was then Commissioner of the Metropolitan Police and the country's most powerful police officer, said: 'Political demonstrations seem to give satisfaction in the main to those taking part. The public as a whole are usually not interested, unless affected by inconvenience or aroused by disorder and violence.'[3] The 'satisfaction' to those taking part – the opportunity to receive a message directly from speakers, the sense of standing up and being counted, the identification with other supporters of the cause – should not be underrated. Writing off demonstrations as mere self-indulgence is one expression of a powerful strand of thought which denigrates collective action and sees civil liberties in terms of atomized individuals. The same critics deliberately underestimate the effects of public protest on the audience, whether legislature, Government or the general public. Political activity cannot be restricted to the ballot-box. Parliament may not respond directly to mass marches or rallies, but MPs undoubtedly respond to pressure from their constituents, particularly when this involves large numbers of people, while the 'creation' of an issue in the eyes of the media and the authorities generally involves a variety of highly visible activities. Rallies and marches are frequently organized by groups who might be thought to have direct access to the authorities and whose views command significant, perhaps majority, support; but they are all the more important, as a means of expressing and drawing attention to a grievance, for radical and unpopular minorities.

No large-scale protest, however peaceful, can take place without interfering to some extent with other activities. As the Metropolitan police so eloquently put it in evidence to the House of Commons Home Affairs Select Committee:

A march of 2500 persons stretches for approximately half a mile and takes about fifteen minutes to pass any given point. It plays complete havoc with traffic, not just in Oxford Street itself but also for a very wide area either side. . . . Remember that the disruption would be even greater on larger demonstrations . . . Imagine the number of aeroplanes and trains missed, business appointments spoilt and social arrangements completely ruined. Bear in mind also the bus passengers waiting for an hour or so in the confined space of one bus crawling along the road.[4]

In evidence to the same body, ACPO stated:

Today the right to demonstrate is widely *exploited* and marching is the most chosen form of demonstration adopted by protesters. Irrespective of the peaceful nature of the processions, the numbers involved bring town centres to a halt, business is seriously disrupted and public bus services thrown out of schedule. In short a general annoyance is created to the normal process of daily life. (My emphasis)[5]

Thus for ACPO even *peaceful* processions are not part of 'the normal process of daily life'. Ironically, at the same time as they try to separate 'protesters' from the 'community', the police have also been extending their definition of a demonstration. The evidence of the Commissioner of the Metropolitan Police to the Select Committee is again revealing:

Our research has been confined to those demonstrations for which police arrangements were made centrally by A8 branch, and where more than 100 officers were involved. We do not include ceremonial events, football matches and other sporting and social events. But we *do* include the Notting Hill carnival because, although it is not of course a demonstration in the true sense of the word, the disorders caused in 1976 and 1977 have many features in common with those caused by demonstrations.[6]

Since the vast majority of demonstrations are peaceful, it is quite misleading to single out one social event for inclusion simply because there have been violent incidents. But if large-scale public outdoor entertainments like Notting Hill are to be called demonstrations, there is no reason other than a judgment about the views of organisers and participants for not including royal processions, the Lord Mayor's Show, Cup Finals and so on – and thus even less reason for suggesting that 'demonstrators' are a small and unrepresentative minority.

Closely related to the argument that demonstrations disrupt 'normal' life is that of cost. The report of the Select Committee (endorsed by a majority of its members) says, for instance:

> The policing of demonstrations is expensive. . . . There is much
> public disquiet that expenditure on such a scale should be con-
> sidered necessary to deal with the activities of what many would see
> as extremist and self-indulgent groups. . . . In considering costs, one
> must also take account of the disruption of traffic and the damage to
> trade and premises that may be suffered by traders . . . the injuries to
> the police and to the public and even, on occasion, loss of life. *The
> substantial and increasing financial, political and human cost* of
> demonstrations was, and is, one of the main reasons for this
> inquiry. (My emphasis)[7]

The figures quoted by the Select Committee may seem startling:
£300,000 for the National Front march in Lewisham in April 1980,
£197,000 for a demonstration and counter-demonstration in
Leicester in April 1979 and so on. It is obvious that the police have
singled out such figures at a time of public spending cuts in the
hope of encouraging generalized hostility to peaceful demonstrations as well as to those on which violence occurs. In the Metropolitan police report for 1978,[8] for instance, a figure of £2.5 million
is offered for demonstrations, with no breakdown of how this sum
is arrived at, the extent to which it includes basic wages which
would have been paid anyway and so on. The public-order item is
the only one singled out in the report and represents less than 1 per
cent of the Metropolitan force's annual budget.

But the arguments about disruption and cost are fundamentally
unsound. First, they ignore the fact that any arrangement for
identifying, expressing and reconciling the interests and grievances of different sections of the community costs money. The
costs of holding a general election are very considerable and could
be reduced if elections were held, say, at eight-yearly rather than
five-yearly periods. But no one would seriously propose such a
'saving'. Second, those who stress the cost of policing demonstrations ignore the less easily quantified but equally real costs of
banning them. If peaceful demonstrations are routinely banned,
then protesters will sooner or later be forced to use unlawful
means, whether by holding unlawful demonstrations which are,
nontheless, designed to remain peaceful (as occurred in Queens-
land, where marches continue to be banned following disturbances
after anti-uranium mining protests) or by resorting to violent
means of expressing their views. Marches held in defiance of a ban
may require even more policing than they would have done anyway, while the greater risk is that bans on legitimate and largely

peaceful forms of protest may encourage the use of violent forms of expression.

Lord Denning made the point in his minority judgment in the case of protesters picketing a London estate agent's premises:

> the right to demonstrate and the right to protest on matters of public concern . . . [are] often the only means by which grievances can be brought to the knowledge of those in authority – at any rate with such impact as to gain a remedy. Our history is full of warnings against suppression of these rights. Most notable was the demonstration at St Peter's Fields, Manchester, in 1819 in support of universal suffrage. The magistrates sought to stop it. At least twelve were killed and hundreds injured. Afterwards the Court of Common Council of London affirmed 'the undoubted right of Englishmen to assemble together for the purpose of deliberating upon public grievances'.[9]

The passage of 150 years clearly helped here. When thousands of trade unionists assembled in North London near the Grunwick factory to defend the right of workers to join a trade union, Lord Denning's highly publicized reaction was: 'The mobs are out.' But the vital role played by public protest in achieving change is underlined by the experience in Northern Ireland, where the authorities' inability to tolerate the marches and demonstrations of the civil rights movement in the 1960s, let alone to respond to its legitimate grievances, was a crucial factor in the later resort to terrorism.

Finally, there is the argument that the growing violence of demonstrations requires new measures. In London in 1972 there were two demonstrations at which more than thirty arrests were made. In 1979 there were four such occasions – hardly a startling increase, particularly since 1979 was an election year, with highly controversial National Front meetings in Southall and Lewisham. In 1974 there was a total of 247 arrests at demonstrations in London; in 1977 a total of 1081 (over 400 of which were at Grunwick); in 1979 a total of 536 (including 345 at Southall in one day). By 1979 the number of demonstrations requiring the use of more than 100 police officers had risen to 119 from 84 in 1974.[10] On some of these occasions many police officers were injured: in Southall, 97 officers, and in Leicester in the same year, 270. Such figures are rightly a matter of serious public concern. But days lost to the police from injuries on public-order occasions (including football matches) account for only 0.5 per cent of days lost through injury in the Metropolitan police force. For the police sporting occasions are more dangerous than demonstrations.[11]

Apart from industrial pickets, which are discussed later, serious violence at demonstrations in the last six years has almost exclusively involved National Front meetings and counter-demonstrations. Instead of considering the specific factors involved on those occasions and the policing strategy adopted, both Government and the police have responded by demanding changes in the law governing all demonstrations. Although the Government admitted in its 1980 Green Paper, which laid the basis for a new Public Order Act, that 'the law is not the only factor which can maintain public order' and stressed the importance of 'the traditional police approach' towards demonstrations, its only proposals were for changes in the law.[12] Nowhere has the Government admitted that there are lessons to be learned from Southall or elsewhere about the policing of demonstrations, nor has there been any recognition that the police themselves are sometimes responsible for violence at demonstrations.

The overall picture which has been created in the last few years is that demonstrations are violent, criminal, even subversive. In his 1973 annual report as Commissioner for the Metropolitan police, for instance, Sir Robert Mark tells us that the Metropolitan force was under great strain, having to deal with '72,750 burglaries, 2680 robberies and 450 demonstrations'. Sir David McNee's first report as Commissioner[13] referred to an anti-National Front march in Haringey in April 1977 as 'a counter-demonstration organized by the Socialist Workers Party, the International Marxist Group, the Communist Party of England and others' – the others, whom he did not specify, included the Labour party, the Labour mayor and Labour and Conservative councillors. In the same report Sir David said, quite untruthfully, that the decision to hold a mass picket at Grunwick was taken 'by the strike committee, prompted by the Socialist Workers Party'. The existence of 'a minority of deter-mined militants . . . [who] judge the success of their protests by the amount of disorder they create' (in the words of Sir John Waldron, in his 1970 report as Metropolitan Police Commissioner) has become so much the leading feature of explanations of violence on demonstrations that it has apparently become impossible for journalists, politicians or even the police to describe accurately what is actually happening. In April 1979, for instance, Sir David McNee immediately attributed the violence at Southall to 'extremist outsiders', even though the timing of most serious incidents and the fact that the vast majority of those arrested came from the local Asian community flatly contradicted such an interpretation.

The construction of a general image of demonstrations as extremist, violent and outside the normal limits of acceptability may produce short-term results for the police in the form of greater powers. But it may also have unlooked for effects. General expectations of violence will condition not only the behaviour of many demonstrators but also police tactics. If growing violence at demonstrations is the result, as seems all too probable, more frequent resort to bans will be the response. And as a legitimate and traditional form of expression is ruled out of order, illegitimate and far more violent forms of expression may well take its place.

The present law

Freedom of association– that is to say, the freedom of individuals to organize themselves in groups, to attend public or private meetings, to participate in rallies or processions – should be axiomatic in a democratic society. This freedom is, of course, restricted to freedom of peaceful assembly and association. Those who set out to use violence at a demonstration should not be surprised when the criminal law is used against them, although civil libertarians will then have a different interest in ensuring the just administration of the law against those alleged to have broken it. But freedom of peaceful assembly is precisely what is exercised by the majority of demonstrators at most demonstrations which take place in Britain: just as the excesses of the police on certain occasions do not lead us to conclude that the police must not be allowed to police demonstrations, so the excesses of some demonstrators on occasion must not serve as an excuse for the introduction of unnecessary restrictions on the right to demonstrate.

I use the word 'right' only in a moral sense. English law does not often recognize rights and certainly does not do so when it comes to freedom of assembly. A brief examination of major legal provisions affecting assemblies is instructive.[14] The traditional view of English law is that what would be called 'rights' under a different legal regime are, in this country, the freedoms which are left behind after all the prohibitions have been taken into account. Street expresses it thus: [15]

> This is how English law goes about its job of defining limits on our freedoms. The citizen may do as he likes unless he clashes with some specific restriction on his freedom. The law does not say: 'You can do that'; it says 'You cannot do this', which means that you can do everything else except that which it says you cannot do.

Lord Scarman, in his report on the events in 1974 in Red Lion Square, [16] said:

> The right [to demonstrate] of course exists, subject only to limits required by the need for good order and the passage of traffic.

And the Government's Green Paper repeats the view that 'one is certainly free [to demonstrate] provided specific provisions of the law . . . are not contravened.' [17]

As a description of how the law operates, this view is now seriously misleading. Far from being a reasonably clear area of freedom in which to act, subject only to specific restrictions imposed by law, the freedom to demonstrate is at the mercy of arbitrary decisions by the police and the executive, often unchallengeable in the courts. The common law recognizes a freedom to move along the highway in a procession, but that freedom is subject not only to an ill-defined law of 'obstruction of the highway' but also to the power contained in the 1936 Public Order Act to ban processions, including those in connection with which no threat to public order is envisaged. The freedom to hold stationary demonstrations in a public place is even less well protected by common law; the police have extensive discretionary powers to disperse groups of people, to limit the numbers present and to bar access to the place chosen, against which the would-be demonstrator has no legal protection whatsoever. The freedom to demonstrate is exercised by thousands of demonstrators every year: but when the police decide that it is *not* to be exercised, the freedom to demonstrate is revealed to be an illusion, for protesters have no rights to assert against the powers of the police.

The common law protection for 'reasonable user' of the highway – to which the right to 'pass and repass' is central – has generally been held to include processions and marches. The law is not particularly clear and derives from property rights rather than conceptions of the public interest. The 'public' highway is, in reality, private land owned, usually, by the local authority and bounded by other private property. When a procession causes damage the owner could, if he chose, sue for trespass. In practice, however, civil law is not a real constraint on those organizing or taking part in processions, and, as Brownlie has stressed,[18] the law of trespass governs *private* rights and tells us noihing about public usage. The restraints which matter in practice are, first, the provisions in some local Acts which make it a criminal offence to hold a demonstration without giving prior notice; second, the power given to the police to impose conditions on a march under the 1936 Public Order Act; third, the power to ban marches under the same Act; and fourth, the range of common law and statutory offences relating to public order, of which the most commonly used are obstruction of the highway, obstruction of the police, threatening, abusive or insulting words or behaviour, affray and unlawful or riotous assembly.

In many parts of the country – including Manchester, the West Midlands, Merseyside and Cheshire – local by-laws have made it a criminal offence to organize or conduct a procession without giving prior notice to the police and/or the local council of the proposed time and route of the march. Until recently, such powers attracted little attention. In some cases they had effectively lapsed; in others, the police enforced and publicized them throughout an entire local authority area even though discrepancies between boundaries resulting from local government reorganization meant that the relevant by-laws applied only in certain districts. No record is available of any prosecution having been brought under these by-laws. In 1974 Lord Scarman, in the report of his inquiry into Red Lion Square,[19] firmly rejected a proposal by Sir Robert Mark for the creation of a similar criminal offence in London. He pointed out that on the occasion in question the police had failed to make good use of the extensive notification they had had of both the National Front and the Liberation marches.

From November 1978 onwards, following local government re-organization, a number of local councils introduced private Bills in Parliament consolidating by-laws for their new areas, which not only extended existing criminal offences to all the districts covered by the new boundaries but also, on occasion, extended the period of notice required from demonstrators. For instance, the Greater Manchester Bill, if it had been enacted in its original form, would have extended the period from twenty-four hours in one district and forty-eight hours in others to seven days throughout the area.

Opposition to these new requirements by a coalition of groups, including NCCL, Friends of the Earth, local trade unions, student unions and Labour and Liberal MPs and councillors ensured that the need for the new criminal offence was closely scrutinized in committee, and a compromise clause emerged in the West Midlands Bill providing for prior notice of seventy-two hours 'or as soon as reasonably practicable', whichever is the shorter. Although many of the prior-notice offences have not been used, and although evidence given to the committees considering the Bills made it clear that the risk of public disorder would not be reduced by the new offence, the Government has now proposed to make it a criminal offence throughout the country to hold a procession without giving prior notice. This is discussed below (see page 142).

Section 3 of the 1936 Public Order Act gives a chief police officer the power to impose conditions on a march if these are considered necessary to avoid serious public disorder. The conditions may include directions about the route of the march, as well as about banners, slogans and so on. It is not clear how extensively these powers are used. According to the Home Office, the section 'appears to have been used by the police with caution', since the police prefer to rely on agreement with the organizers. In London, however, where the majority of demonstrations take place, the police have a different power, which does *not* require the Commissioner to anticipate serious public disorder before imposing conditions. Under the 1839 Metropolitan Police Act the Commissioners for the Metropolitan and City of London police may make regulations about the route of public processions and may 'give directions to the constables for keeping order and for preventing any obstruction' in the immediate neighbourhood of 'the palaces, public offices, the High Court of Parliament, the courts of law and equity, the police courts, the theatres, and other places of public resort' and – if this were not enough – 'in any case when the streets or thoroughfares may be thronged or may be liable to be obstructed'. Sir David McNee informed the Select Committee that these powers are sometimes used 'when organizers will not voluntarily accede to police wishes'.[20]

In most cases organizers of processions reach agreement with the police with no difficulty, and the 1936 Act power to impose conditions is probably little used. But the Metropolitan police have used their more extensive 1839 Act powers to make decisions about the relative claims of protesters, pedestrians and traffic without any public debate or consultation. In evidence to the Select Committee, Deputy Assistant Commissioner Dellow, responsible for public order, gave the example of traffic congestion caused in Oxford

Street by 2500 people (see page 109 above) and disarmingly told MPs: 'We now discourage *any* processions from taking place within the Oxford Street area on the working day. Either marchers go elsewhere, or they march on Sundays.'[21] In fact, Oxford Street, which had regularly been used by processions, particularly on Saturdays, until October 1978, was unilaterally banned as a route for marches by Sir David McNee under the 1839 Act. It is possible that the House of Commons, the Greater London Council or an elected London Police Authority (if one existed) would have come to the conclusion that traffic congestion, together with the narrowing of the Oxford Street traffic lanes, demanded such a ban on processions, but they were never asked, and there is no appeal against the Commissioner's decision that processions go elsewhere.

More important in practice than the power to impose conditions under the 1936 Act is the power to ban. Within London the Commissioner may, with the Home Secretary's consent, make an order banning for up to three months 'all or any class of public processions'; outside London, the Chief Constable must apply to the district council for such an order, which, again, requires the Home Secretary's consent. A banning order may be made only if the chief officer believes that his power to impose conditions will be insufficient to prevent serious public disorder.

Although the Act states that a ban may apply to 'all or any class of processions', the Home Office and the police have now chosen to take the view that a ban cannot be used against only one demonstration or the processions of only one organization. Nonetheless, in 1961 the Act was used to ban any marches or procession organized by the Committee of 100 and, in 1976, to ban any procession connected with the death of IRA hunger-striker, James McDade. The result of the present policy is that all recent banning orders have affected processions entirely unconnected with an event from which serious public disorder is anticipated or from which no disorder at all is feared. In February 1978 a National Front march in east London during a Parliamentary by-election was to be opposed by an anti-racist march. Sir David McNee, with the Home Secretary's consent, issued an order banning *all* marches for a period of two months in the Metropolitan police area other than 'those of a religious, educational, festive or ceremonial character customarily held within the Metropolitan Police District'. At the same time a parallel order was made under the 1839 Act. The particular formula, which is now standard for banning orders, was chosen in preference to a ban on 'political processions' (the phrase previously used) to ensure that no anti-racist march by *religious* organizations – which could be described as religious, not political, processions – could be held the day after the banned National Front march.

The period of two months for this ban was chosen, according to the Metropolitan police legal adviser,[22] to provide a cooling-off period and not because of any continuing threat to public order. It is quite clear that a ban of such scope, extending for such a period, was not justified by the terms of the 1936 Act. Nonetheless, the European Human Rights Commission, to whom Christians Against Racism and Fascism applied for a review of the ban, refused even to declare the case admissible despite the protection for peaceful assembly provided by the Human Rights Convention. The Commission did, however, rule that a general ban of this kind could not qualify as 'necessary in a democratic society for the protection of public order' (the test provided by the Convention) unless it was impossible to impose a more restricted ban or to deal with the problem in some other way.[23]

In March 1981, after the National Front had announced its intention to march through south London, past the scene of an appalling fire in which thirteen black people had been killed, the Metropolitan Police Commissioner imposed a ban on marches in the whole of London for three weeks. There followed in quick succession bans in Wolverhampton for two weeks, in Leeds for three weeks, in Leicester for a month, in four districts of South Yorkshire for a week and in Strathclyde for three months – all prompted by the announcement of National Front, New National Front or similar marches. Although the south London march would have required saturation policing to prevent a violent clash between the National Front and local black youngsters, it is by no means clear that similarly serious public disorder was anticipated in the other districts in which bans were imposed. By imposing a blanket ban in response to individual National Front marches and the reaction they would provoke, chief constables and the Home Secretary have allowed the National Front to dictate the terms on which freedom of assembly may be exercised. The ban in Leeds had the effect of curtailing part of a massive trans-Pennine nuclear disarmament march which had been planned in full consultation with the police for months beforehand.

The Campaign for Nuclear Disarmament, seven of whose marches were cancelled as a result of the bans in London, applied to the Divisional Court to have the ban overturned on the grounds that, in banning peaceful processions, the Commissioner of Police had exceeded his legal authority. In upholding the Divisional Court's refusal to review the ban, the Court of Appeal said that the ban would protect Campaign for Nuclear Disarmament and other peaceful marchers from 'hooligans' and 'undesirable elements who wanted to disrupt them' – a startling extension of the hostile audience veto.[24]

Nonetheless, general banning orders have become difficult to sustain. The London police proved unwilling or unable to prevent all banned processions. In Chislehurst, for instance, a May Queen procession (clearly covered by the ban) was allowed to continue, apparently because local officers found it impossible to believe that such an innocuous event could be prohibited! In central London a march supporting the H-Block hunger-strikers was not permitted to set off in Kilburn, and a number of the leaders were arrested; nonetheless, other members of the march, who travelled by underground to central London, were then allowed to process along Whitehall.[25] The ban on almost all marches in Strathclyde, which had been imposed after the announcement of a National Front march in support of Ian Paisley, was not allowed to last its full three months. After the county council elections in May the Strathclyde Council, which had issued the banning order at the request of the Chief Constable, decided to vary its terms by exempting any march associated with nuclear power or disarmament, as well as any march on trade union or industrial issues or any march organized by a local community group. The Secretary of State (whose consent is required for a ban in Scotland) refused to accept such vaguely worded exemptions and agreed instead to a ban on processions connected with Ireland, thus restricting the ban to the situation which had originally given rise to the risk of serious violence.

The first six months of 1981 saw an unprecedented use of banning orders. The result was not only the cancellation of hundreds of entirely peaceful events but also a real fear that future events would also have to be called off. The Campaign for Nuclear Disarmament, whose Glasgow march in June 1981 was permitted only because of the change in the terms of the banning order, expressed a real reluctance to continue with plans for a massive procession in London later in the year in case the organizers' work should prove, once again, to be wasted. The Court of Appeal's refusal to review the ban and the Home Secretary's refusal to rule out the use of general bans leave peaceful processions entirely unprotected.

Once there is one procession or a combination of march and counter-march which gives rise to a fear of serious public disorder, the 1936 Act provides a power to ban *all* marches, however peaceful. The protesters have no right of appeal against the ban. And in London the 1839 Act gives the Commissioner even more extensive powers to lay down routes and impose other conditions, not in order to prevent serious public disorder but merely to avoid obstruction.

Restrictions on demonstrations

The 1936 Act to ban or impose conditions on a march does not apply to stationary demonstrations – rallies, public meetings, pickets and the like. Their status in law is extremely unclear, with the result that the police have considerable discretion in deciding under what conditions they should be allowed to take place, if at all.

In 1911 the Divisional Court decided[26] that a public meeting on the highway, provided it did not cause an obstruction or otherwise infringe the law, was lawful and was therefore protected against interference under the 1908 Public Meetings Act. In other words, the common law right to use the highway for passing and repassing was not restricted merely to walking along the street or stopping to talk to other passers-by or to conduct business but could also include a public gathering. In 1967 the same court took a similar view of the purposes to which the public highway could be put, in a case involving a member of the Committee of 100, who, with six colleagues, had tried to hold a vigil in Whitehall. The police ordered them to disperse on the grounds that they were an assembly prohibited under a Sessional Order of Parliament made by the Police Commissioner under the 1839 Act, which banned all processions and assemblies within a large part of central London on days when Parliament was sitting. Having refused to move, the appellant was arrested and subsequently convicted under the 1839 Act. On appeal, the Divisional Court held[27] that the Commissioner's ban could apply only to processions or assemblies which 'were capable of causing . . . obstruction to the free passage of members to and from the House of Parliament or disorder or annoyance in the neighbourhood or thereabouts' and that, in the absence of evidence that the vigil had caused such obstruction or was capable of doing so, the magistrate should acquit. The court explicitly concerned itself with 'the rights and liberties of subjects, and their immunity from having their *lawful activities* curbed save to the extent that Parliament has enacted' (my emphasis).

Nonetheless, the decision in that case has not prevented the Police Commissioner from continuing to obtain parliamentary sanction for Sessional Orders banning assemblies of more than fifty people within an extraordinarily wide area of central London. In March 1981, when the Young Socialists approached the police about a picket they proposed to hold outside the Home Office, near St James's, to protest against the Nationality Bill, they were told that no more than six people would be permitted, on the grounds that the police did not discriminate between non-industrial pickets and industrial pickets, for whom the Government's Code of Practice recommended a maximum of six people (see page 129). After their solicitor (NCCL's legal officer) protested, the police said that the limit would be fifty people.

To put the treatment of protesters in context, one only has to think of the complete freedom accorded to the crowds which throng the footpaths to watch the Lord Mayor's show, or to stand outside Buckingham Palace, or to see the procession of a royal wedding or state visit. The obstruction of the pavement is considerable, the delays and inconvenience to other people at least as great as that which the police condemn when caused by marches (see page 110), but no arrest is ever made for obstruction, no use ever made of the 1839 Act. If the importance of freedom of assembly is rightly recognized for those who wish to show their loyalty, and if police and public alike tolerate all the obstructions caused, equal recognition should be given to the importance of peaceful assembly for the unpopular and dissenting minority.

Although public meetings and gatherings on the highway and in other public places are lawful, there is no *right* to use any particular place for the purpose. Both Trafalgar Square and Hyde Park Corner are traditional venues for large rallies, but the courts have held that there is no right to hold meetings there. Application must be made to the Department of Environment, which refused permission to the Save Greece Now campaign in 1963, and to Colin Jordan and the Hare Krishna Temple a few years later. Since the early 1970s successive Governments have maintained a ban on the use of Trafalgar Square by any organization or rally connected with Ireland – a ban which was, however, lifted for a Peace People rally in 1978.

In 1975 the Court of Appeal took a considerably narrower view of the 'rights and liberties of subjects' than the Divisional Court had done in the cases referred to above. A weekly picket had been organized outside Prebble and Company, a north London estate agent, by a local tenants' campaign which wanted to protest against the alleged harrassment of tenants. There were no arrests for obstruction of the highway. But the company began civil proceedings for conspiracy, nuisance and defamation and obtained a High Court injunction against the pickets. Granting the injunction, Mr Justice Forbes held that the only right of the public to use the highway was for passage and repassage and 'for reasonably incidental purposes'. The protesters appealed. With Lord Denning dissenting, the Court of Appeal confirmed the injunction in a decision which, although concerned with technical matters about the appropriateness of an injunction as distinct from other remedies, accepted by implication Mr Justice Forbes's attitude towards public assemblies. But Lord Denning argued that 'picketing a person's premises (even done with a view to compel or persuade) is not unlawful unless it is associated with other conduct such as to constitute the whole conduct a nuisance at common law. Picketing is not a nuisance in itself.' He argued further that it would be wrong to restrain with an injunction the use of placards and leaflets which had not been found to be libellous: 'for aught we know, the words may be true and justifiable. And, if true, it may be very wholesome for the truth to be made known.' By granting an injunction, he said, his fellow judges nullified the protest campaign by ensuring that no picketing or leafleting could take place until a full hearing was held – possibly two years or more later. Not surprisingly, having obtained its injunction, Prebble did not proceed to a full hearing.[28]

Police powers to control and disperse gatherings on the street, even when entirely peaceful, were dramatically extended by the Divisional Court decision in *Duncan and Jones*,[29] a 1936 case which was one of the first in which NCCL represented a protester. Mrs Duncan, of the National Unemployed Workers' Movement, tried to hold a meeting outside an unemployed training centre. When a police officer told her that the meeting would have to be held 175 yards away, she refused to move and started speaking. She was arrested and subsequently convicted of obstructing an officer in the execution of his duty. Dismissing her appeal, the court held that the officer 'reasonably' feared a breach of the peace from Mrs Duncan's meeting, since a meeting in the same place a year before had been followed by disturbances inside the training centre, and that he was therefore entitled (indeed, duty-bound) to take steps to prevent a breach of the peace. The decision was strongly criticized at the time, not only for the extensive discretion which it gave the police but also for the dubious statement of facts provided to the appeal court.[30] The leading authority on public-order law, Professor Brownlie, has pointed out that the decision radically altered the definition of the obstruction of an officer in the execution of his duty, which had previously been confined to *physical* interference, and made it possible for a speaker or someone attending a meeting to be ordered to move or disperse and to be arrested even when no unlawful assembly and no breach of the peace was immediately anticipated.[31]

Even when a court subsequently acquits a defendant, an arrest for obstruction puts an end to the protest. In 1978 a small group of demonstrators stood outside Claridges Hotel to protest against the arrival on a state visit of the President of Romania. The police parked their van in front of the demonstrators so that they could not be seen. When the police refused to move the van, the demonstrators moved in front of the van and were arrested for obstructing the police in the execution of their duty. They were given an absolute discharge by the magistrates' court, which said that although the police had to do their job, in this case they were probably 'over-jumpy'!

The law relating to obstruction of the highway provides the police with their most commonly used powers against demonstrators. At common law an 'unreasonable and excessive' obstruction of the highway is a public nuisance. Furthermore, under the 1959 Highways Act it is an offence 'without lawful authority or excuse wilfully [to] obstruct the free passage along a highway'. A conviction for the common law offence of public nuisance or incitement to cause a nuisance will not be upheld unless the magistrates or jury have directed themselves to the question of whether or not the obstruction was 'unreasonable'. Although one would expect that the use of the term 'wilfully' in the statutory offence of obstruction would require evidence of intention as well as evidence of actual obstruction, in practice it is easy for the police to secure convictions even of people whose presence on the pavement or the road does not, in fact, obstruct the passage of others. In 1974 a solitary protester sitting on the pavement outside the Houses of Parliament and threatening to remain there until his demands were met was convicted for obstruction even though he had urged other people not to cause an obstruction. He was advised not to appeal, since the court had held in a 1963 case that lack of intention to obstruct the highway was no defence.[32]

A 600-year-old power of magistrates to bind over people who have been neither charged nor convicted of any criminal offence is perhaps the most arbitrary form of judicial interference with the freedom of peaceful assembly. The 1361 Justices of the Peace Act allows magistrates to bind someone over to keep the peace even if no complaint has been made. A binding-over order may be used as an alternative to prosecution when the police offer to drop charges in return; it may follow an *acquittal* on a criminal charge; it may be used even when no charge has been brought; and it may be used against *witnesses* who have appeared for either prosecution or defence. During the trials of those arrested during the anti-National Front protest in Southall, in 1979, for instance, a number of protesters or by-standers who had been called as witnesses for the defence and who had not themselves been arrested or charged, were bound over by the magistrates, who sometimes gave the impression that they believed that anyone participating in a demonstration must be a criminal. Although a binding-over order can be made only with the individual's consent, a person who does not agree will be imprisoned. In 1961 Bertrand Russell and other members of the Committee of 100 were imprisoned for refusing to be bound over, as was Pat Arrowsmith, who spent six months in prison for refusing to be bound over after a *peaceful* demonstration in 1968. In March 1980 a prosecution witness in a case against members of the Hunt Saboteurs was also imprisoned. But most victims of binding over, not surprisingly, prefer to accept the injustice of the order rather than face imprisonment. A binding-over order is recorded on the Police National Computer, along with criminal convictions;[33] any future conviction renders the defendant liable to forfeit the surety entered into for the bind-over; and, in effect, the person subject to a bind-over can attend a future demonstration only at the risk of arrest and imprisonment. It remains to be seen whether the Law Commission, which was asked in 1980 to consider the bind-over powers, will recommend their abolition in any case when the person concerned has not been convicted of an offence.

Although the common law offence of public nuisance is rarely used against demonstrators, the other common law offences of unlawful assembly, riot and affray are more frequently employed. In 1973, for instance, 112 people were found guilty of unlawful assembly, eighteen of riotous assembly and 904 of affray; in 1977 the corresponding figures were 41, 19 and 606.[34] The distinction between an unlawful and a riotous assembly is unclear. Broadly, both involve the presence of three or more people, gathered in a manner which gives 'persons of ordinary firmness' reasonable grounds to fear a breach of the peace. An affray involves fighting or other conduct which causes alarms in persons of 'reasonable firmness and courage'. The vagueness of these offences, together with the fact that, as common law offences, they carry no limit on the maximum sentence which may be imposed on conviction, makes them useful weapons for the prosecuting authorities.

From this brief review of the law it is clear that the police have a number of wide-ranging powers and very considerable discretion in dealing with processions and other demonstrations. They may decide whether or not a demonstration shall be permitted and, if so, under what conditions; whether or not a gathering should be moved on or dispersed altogether; whether or not to arrest for obstruction; which members of a demonstration to arrest and which offences to charge. We turn now to a consideration of how the discretionary powers of the police are reflected in decisions about policing policy at demonstrations.

Police practice

I have already stressed the fact that the police have no *statutory* powers to impose conditions or bans on stationary demonstrations, but that does not mean that they have no other powers. Instead of more or less clearly defined statutory powers, they have the virtually unlimited power given to them by their power to arrest for breach of the peace and by their discretion to decide whether or not a breach of the peace may be caused and, if so, how to prevent it.

The events in Southall in April 1979[35] illustrate vividly the extent of police discretion. During the general election campaign, the National Front sought and obtained a booking from Ealing Council for an election meeting in Southall Town Hall. The local community, which has a very large proportion of Asian families, planned two peaceful demonstrations in protest: a picket opposite the building, and a sit-down demonstration on the road outside. Although the organizers met with the local police on a number of occasions to discuss their plans, they were not told that the police would not allow the two demonstrations to take place. But Scotland Yard's A8 division (responsible for major public-order occasions) decided that no such protests would be permitted. On the day both protesters and other residents found that the entire central area of Southall, for a distance of up to half a mile away from the Town Hall, was cordoned off by the police.

Thus a ban on two demonstrations was imposed not by the use of a statutory banning power but by a decision which was, on the face of it, concerned only with the tactics of policing.

In fact, the decision to try to prevent any demonstration from taking place was a decision about freedom of speech and assembly. Not only were the community organizations prevented from holding their protests, but the decision also undermined the claim of the police to enforce the law impartially. Ealing Council had decided, on legal advice, that the National Front meeting in the Town Hall was protected by the Representation of the People Act 1949. The police have no power to ban an election meeting of this kind – nor do they seek such a power.[36] Faced, therefore, with a National Front meeting which had aroused the fury of the local people, the only way in which the police could impartially protect freedom of speech and assembly on both sides was by policing in such a way that the community's right to demonstrate was protected.

The police have argued that the decision to cordon off Southall, rendering the picket and the sit-down impossible and forcing the protesters to crowd around the other side of the police cordons, was necessitated by the strong possibility of a serious breach of the peace if demonstrators were allowed near the Town Hall when the National Front arrived. But the police alternative was not successful either in preventing a breach of the peace or in keeping the streets open for other users. The police cordons made it necessary to divert traffic; residents trying to get home after work could not do so. The chaos caused by the cordons rendered the stewarding arrangements completely ineffective and deprived the police of the local organizers' help in keeping the peace. There is no doubt that the anger and frustration caused by the cordons led to serious outbreaks of violence on the part of some demonstrators; equally, there is no doubt that on more than one occasion the police overreacted shockingly.[37] Ninety-seven police officers were injured; a large number of members of the public were also hurt, and one, Blair Peach, died as the result of a blow from a police officer. An unofficial committee of inquiry, established by NCCL after the Home Secretary refused to establish a public inquiry, concluded, after a detailed examination of the day's events: 'The outcome of the police operation on 23 April could hardly have been worse.'

The broad discretion given to the police in public-order matters is objectionable because it leaves individuals vulnerable to its arbitrary and discriminatory use. When the police are hostile to particular kinds of protest – as they have, on occasions, shown themselves to be hostile to anti-racist groups and distributors of left-wing literature, among others – the use of discretionary powers makes it possible for the law to be enforced in a highly partial manner. But the extent of police discretion becomes doubly dangerous when senior police officers are hostile to peaceful demonstration as such. As a result, under the guise of 'operational' decisions about policing tactics or about the competing claims of traffic and protesters, decisions are taken by the police which are of the utmost significance for freedom of speech. The police may decide to ban a long-established route for processions, or to cordon off an entire area where a demonstration is planned, or to impose, with the Home Secretary's consent, a ban on all or almost all marches. Such decisions cannot be challenged in the courts. The police, who are now explicitly hostile to freedom of assembly, are the arbiters of its exercise.

Picketing and other industrial action

The freedom to strike is an essential part of the right of workers to bargain collectively with their employers. The organization of a picket is, in turn, an essential part of the freedom to strike. But industrial pickets are also a particular form of the use of a general right, the right to assemble peacefully. For most of this century the law has given to industrial pickets a different status from that of other demonstrations. But in its most recent proposals for a new public-order law,[38] the Government has proposed extensive new restrictions on the exercise of the right to picket by simultaneously proposing new controls on demonstrations and outdoor meetings and re-defining most industrial pickets as demonstrations.

The 1906 Trade Disputes Act made it lawful to picket a workplace or home for the purposes of persuasion or peaceful communication, provided that the picket was undertaken 'in contemplation or furtherance of a trade dispute'. The formula was re-enacted in the 1974 Trade Union and Labour Relations Act (TULRA), with the omission of pickets at a person's home. Both the 1906 and the 1974 Acts were designed to safeguard trade unionists involved in a trade dispute from civil actions for damages and from the injunctions which could otherwise have been obtained by an employer. Amending legislation in 1976 specifically provided immunity for a worker involved in a trade dispute who sought to persuade other workers or suppliers to break their contracts with the employer in the dispute.

Neither the 1906 Act nor the present law provides a legal *right* to picket or to take other forms of industrial action. Nor does the immunity from *civil* actions which is offered by the formula that in certain circumstances a picket is lawful have any effect at all on a picket's liability under *criminal* law. A succession of court decisions has severely circumscribed the freedom to picket and to take other forms of industrial action. For instance, the courts have held[39] that police officers are entitled to restrict the number of pickets and to arrest for obstruction of an officer in the execution of his duty a picket who refuses to leave when ordered to do so. The Code of Practice issued by the Secretary of State for Employment under the 1980 Employment Act confirms the power of the police to limit numbers and recommends no more than six pickets at any workplace entrance. Although the Code has no direct legal effect, it can be quoted in court proceedings and is clearly designed to increase the impact of the criminal law of obstruction of the highway on industrial pickets. It is also lawful[40] for the police to form a cordon between picket and strike breakers, thus making it impossible for the picket to persuade, or even to communicate with, those entering the workplace. Finally, it is illegal for pickets to seek to stop a vehicle, thus making it impossible for them to communicate with the driver or passengers unless the police themselves decide to help.

Even before the 1980 Act dramatically extended the power of employers to sue trade unionists for damages and, most important, to obtain an injunction against those organizing or taking part in a picket, the courts themselves had narrowed the interpretation of what activities could be 'in contemplation or furtherance of a trade dispute'. The right to picket has become the rope in a tug-of-war between the Court of Appeal and the House of Lords, whose conflicting decisions have left the law in a state of appalling uncertainty.

In 1977, in a case involving the British Broadcasting Corporation and the Association of Broadcasting Staff (ABS), the Court of Appeal held that 'political' action was not protected by the 'trade dispute' formula. The ABS's action, taken to prevent an overseas broadcast of the World Cup as a protest against the regime in South

Africa, was, according to Lord Denning, nothing to do with a trade dispute but was 'coercive and interfering and nothing more'.[41] But the same court also ordered the International Federation of Seamen's Unions to call off the blacking of a Liberian ship docked in Glasgow in 1979, even though the blacking was a protest against the crew's low wages.[42] In the *Express Newspapers* case in 1979 an instruction from officials of the National Union of Journalists (NUJ) to their national newspaper members to black copy provided by the Press Association was held by the Court of Appeal to be outside the scope of immunities for industrial action.[43] Although the NUJ believed that the strike of provincial journalists was being undermined by the newspapers' use of Press Association copy and, therefore, that sympathetic action by national journalists would assist in the dispute, the court decided to substitute its own view of what was appropriate or effective action. Similarly, in January 1979 a Transport and General Workers' Union shop steward was ordered by the High Court to stop the picketing of a supplier of United Biscuits, the action being designed to put pressure on a management involved in the lorry drivers' dispute.[44] Mr Justice Ackner held that the picketing was unlawful because it was too remote from the lorry drivers' dispute; it had not helped the lorry drivers in a practical way but had given moral support only; it was not reasonably capable of, and had no reasonable prospect of, furthering the dispute. Furthermore, he considered that it was inconsistent with, and in disregard of, union instructions. A year after the decision in the *Express Newspapers* case, the House of Lords overturned the Court of Appeal, restoring the right of those involved in a dispute to decide for themselves what action would further their aims.

Nonetheless, in 1980 the Court of Appeal granted an injunction against the Iron and Steel Trades Confederation, which had called a strike of its members in private steel companies in order to put pressure on the Government to settle the union's dispute with British Steel, which had proposed to make 52,000 workers redundant. The confusion caused by the court's decision, which clearly conflicted with the Lords' decision in the *Express Newspapers* case, seriously weakened the strike, although the House of Lords, with considerable reluctance, overturned the decision a week later.

The 1980 Act radically alters the position. It remains lawful for a union in dispute with one employer to call on the workers of another firm themselves to go on strike or to take other action, provided that the purpose of this 'secondary' action is only to disrupt the supply of goods from the second firm to the employer with whom the union is in dispute. Since the Act also provides that the secondary action must be 'likely' to achieve its purpose, the courts are once again given the power to overrule a union's own judgment of the need for sympathetic industrial action. And the Act's attempt to define Dantesque circles of 'primary' and 'secondary', 'direct' and 'indirect' action is so complex that unions and their members are impossibly placed to judge the likely legal consequences of any action.

During the parliamentary debates on the Employment Bill, Government Ministers claimed that they had no intention of interfering with 'primary' industrial action (workers in a trade dispute taking action against their own employer). But the Act repealed a crucial section of TULRA, which declared that breaking a contract or calling on someone else to do so was not of itself unlawful. At the time it was predicted that the courts would step in to declare unlawful any call for industrial action which could cause the employer to fail to make deliveries specified in his commercial contracts. This is exactly what happened early in 1981, when the Court of Appeal issued an injunction against an Association of Cinematograph, Television and Allied Technicians official at Thames Television who had called on his members to black a series of ready-made programmes bought from an outside facilities company, Hadmor Productions.[45] The industrial action was directly designed to protect jobs at Thames Television by persuading the company to end its practice of buying programmes from outside companies which could have been made in-house. No 'secondary' action was involved. But Hadmor succeeded in getting its injunction. Thus the customers or suppliers of any employer involved in a trade dispute could obtain a court order preventing any call for industrial action which would interfere with the fulfilment of their contracts. Virtually all industrial action is now at the mercy of the courts.

The Employment Act was presented as a measure concerned only with *civil* liabilities. But the effects on union officials and members are not very different from those of criminal penalties. In May 1981 fifty workers who had occupied the Bestobell Insulation Plant in Glasgow in an attempt to force management to enter into negotiations over a demarcation dispute were fined £100 for contempt of court after failing to obey an injunction to end the trespass. Failure to pay the fine would, of course, have rendered them liable for imprisonment, and indeed the judge said that had the workers not apologized to the court, they would have been imprisoned anyway. In 1972, when the 1971 Industrial Relations Act was in force, five dock workers (the 'Pentonville Five') were imprisoned for six days after failing to obey a labour injunction but were released through the intervention of the Official Solicitor after threats of a general strike.

Peaceful industrial pickets will increasingly become the object of court bans. The Employment Act limits civil immunities, as far as pickets are concerned, to workers standing outside their own place of work, together with the union official representing them. A picket of workers who are not themselves in dispute, but who are seeking to prevent the direct supply of goods to the employer with whom there is a dispute, is also lawful. But more general 'secondary' picketing, or a picket by workers in dispute outside *other* premises, is no longer lawful and may be challenged through an action for damages and a claim for an injunction. At the same time the Code of Practice invites the police to arrest for obstruction everyone other than the first six pickets, regardless of whether or not the seventh and subsequent pickets are outside their own workplace. Thus, a trade unionist standing peacefully outside someone else's workplace in a gesture of solidarity with those on strike may be ordered by the courts to leave and, if he refuses to do so, may be imprisoned.

Most industrial pickets pass off entirely peacefully. An agreement is reached between pickets and local police about the numbers of people allowed at each entrance. In many cases the police are willing to halt a vehicle briefly in order to allow pickets to communicate with the driver. But as with non-industrial demonstrations, several well publicized violent occasions have been used by those generally hostile to industrial action to build up in the public mind an impression of picketing as an inevitably violent activity which undermines the rule of law. In June 1977 mass picketing outside Grunwick (where a dispute mainly involving low-paid Asian women workers had dragged on for nearly a year) led to violent clashes between police and pickets, hundreds of whom were arrested. A number of police officers were injured at Grunwick, and the strike committee itself condemned the violent activities of a small minority of those who had joined the picket line. The violence was deplorable. But it was considerably less serious than many television viewers were led to believe. As one commentator said later: 'On both sides, pickets and the police, what actually took place was less threatening than the rhetoric used to describe it.'[46] But the events at Grunwick provided an opportunity for the police and many politicians to call for new legal curbs on picketing.

Although the Government has tried to distinguish between different forms of picketing and other industrial action on the basis of how closely related the action is to the dispute, from the standpoint of freedom of assembly and freedom of communication the distinction is unjustified. Trade unionists may be standing outside their own place of work while in dispute with their own employer; they may be picketing another factory in the hope of persuading members of another union to take sympathetic action; they may be picketing a shop to persuade the public not to use services or goods from the firm in dispute; they may be joining the picket line at another workplace in order to show solidarity. In every case people are seeking to demonstrate their views through their physical presence at a particular place. In every case the main or only aim of the assembly is to let other people know what the dispute is about and to persuade people to join the strike, to cease supplying a firm which is in dispute or to cease using its products. The picket may be designed to persuade people to break their own contracts of employment or to interfere with a company's commercial contracts. The question is whether the possible damage to a firm's business should be allowed to override the rights of assembly and free speech. An employer is entitled to sue for breach of contract an employee who goes on strike or a supplier who fails to deliver the goods. In practice, such actions are almost never pursued to their end. It is the claim for an injunction that is used, pending the trial of the commercial issues involved – a trial that in practice never materializes. Thus without any hearing whatsoever on the issue of whether or not a picket has damaged a firm's economic interests and what (if any) damages would be appropriate, a firm may obtain an injunction preventing a picket from taking place at all.

The use of such injunctions is an obvious and unjustified denial of freedom of assembly and communication. But the law is not simply destructive of people's right to assemble and make their views known. Economic torts and the labour injunction are the chief legal weapons of private property against labour; they are perhaps the most naked example of the real interests of the law. The courts will readily protect an employer against a threat to his business: they will not protect an employee against the loss of his livelihood. They will not even defend the only means available to workers – collective industrial action. According to the judge in the *Bestobell* case cited above, the refusal of workers occupying a factory to obey an injunction to end the trespass threatened the rule of law itself: 'law and order, and with it civilized life, come to an end, anarchy prevails, and all are liable to suffer' if court orders are disobeyed! Trades unionists may be forgiven for thinking that factory closures and redundancies – against which an occupation may be the only effective action – are a far more real danger to civilized life.

Where a picket or demonstration goes beyond peaceful assembly and becomes intimidation or assault, then, of course, it is right for the criminal law to intervene. But the acts of violence which have been rightly condemned on the picket line and elsewhere are already criminal offences which lay the offender open to arrest and prosecution. In the aftermath of the mass pickets at Grunwick it was suggested that a mass picket, by virtue of its size alone, constituted intimidation. But a large crowd of people holding placards and shouting slogans or even insults need not give rise to any fear of violence against the strike breaker. Indeed, an assault may come from only a few people. It is also suggested, even more loosely, that the very existence of a large picket infringes the right of the non-striker to go to work. Provided that the non-striker is not prevented from entering the workplace by physical detention or threats of violence, no question of an infringement of the non-striker's rights arises: and where criminal acts take place, the criminal law already penalizes them.

In 1972, at the Saltley coke depot, a mass picket of miners succeeded in its object – the closing of the depot. At Grunwick many of the pickets hoped to prevent a coachload of strike breakers from reaching the factory, although they did not succeed. Action of this kind clearly goes beyond the purposes of peaceful demonstration or picketing and involves a serious obstruction of the highway. The question is whether, in the hope of avoiding comparatively rare incidents of this kind, new restrictions should be imposed on all pickets through civil and criminal law. I examine below (see page 141) the Government's proposals for a new Public Order Act. At this stage it must be stressed that industrial picketing serves the same essential purposes as any other form of public assembly and communication: the demonstration of solidarity, the public identification of a grievance, the opportunity to inform other people and to win their support. The risk of violence is always present when passions run high, and an industrial dispute, when the economic interests of worker and employer are most sharply in conflict, is particularly likely to inflame feelings. But the risk of violence is not a sufficient reason to *ban* people from taking part in a picket or demonstration. Mass picketing or violence on a picket line are most likely to occur when all usual forms of negotiation and arbitration have broken down, and it is a fallacy to suppose that court orders against pickets will end such conflict, with all its bitterness. The clashes on the picket line at Grunwick or on similar occasions are symptoms of an inability to resolve deep-seated economic and conflict conflicts which will inevitably manifest themselves on the streets. The attempt to keep the streets free of any such disturbances may in the long run give rise to disturbances far worse than those which are still the exception in industrial picketing.

The closed shop

Although the closed shop is not an issue directly connected with industrial action, this may be the most convenient place to consider the civil liberties issues which it raises. For some commentators the issue is simple: 'The parliamentary enforcement of the closed shop is the greatest disaster which has befallen liberty in my lifetime, a defeat for freedom comparable to those which the Stuart kings attempted to inflict – and failed.'[47] Such inflated rhetoric conceals the real and complex issues.

On the one hand, the person who is forced to join a union under a union membership agreement has his freedom of choice diminished. On the other hand, the freedom of the majority who have taken collective action in defence of their rights at the work-place may be undermined by an individual's refusal to join the union. The point is not academic. The rights and freedoms of working people at their place of employment have been protected through trade union organization, through the exercise of their freedom of association. Low wages, dangeous working conditions, long hours, inadequate holidays, works regulations which give supervisors and management excessive and arbitrary power over other employees – all these are real and extremely serious depri-vations of liberty, against which trade union organization has proved the only effective safeguard. Even today, with a high level of union organization and legislative provision on matters such as health, safety and race or sex discrimination, these problems persist. A post-entry closed shop (that is to say, an agreement requiring an employee, as a condition of employment, to belong to a recognized union) is for many trade unionists an effective way of protecting improvements in working conditions which have been won through negotiation and, possibly, industrial action. The less frequent pre-entry closed shop, which requires an applicant for a job already to hold a union card, allows the union to protect its membership from serious unemployment in a particular industry (such as the acting profession) or, in some cases, to exert control over standards of training. Of about 12 million trade unionists in this country, about a quarter are covered by union membership agreements.

The 1974 Trade Union and Labour Relations Act restored the law on the closed shop to the position which it had occupied before the 1971 Industrial Relations Act sought, entirely unsuccessfully, to outlaw such agreements. But the Act also created a new source of controversy. By retaining the protection against unfair dismissal which had been created in the 1971 Act, the 1974 Act was obliged to include a definition of a union membership agreement in order to exempt from unfair dismissal provisions those who were dismissed for refusal to join a union under a closed-shop agreement. The 1974 Act provided that those with a religious objection to joining any or a particular union or those with 'reasonable grounds' for objecting to membership of a particular union were nonetheless protected against dismissal for refusal to join a union. But this provision did not give the closed shop a new legal status. In 1976 TULRA was amended to delete the reference to the objector with 'reasonable grounds'. It is easy to see why. The original formulation gave industrial tribunals the impossible task of deciding whether or not a non-member's disagreement with his union's policies, his dislike of associations generally, his objection to paying the subscription or his willingness to work for less than the union rate was 'reasonable'. Nonetheless, the 1980 Employment Act extended unfair dismissal protection to those with a 'deeply held personal conviction' against joining any or a particular union, as well as to those employed before a union membership agreement was negotiated.

Those who object to any requirement for trade union membership would wish the closed shop outlawed entirely. The failure of the 1971 Act demonstrates the futility of such a proposal. But civil liberties principles do not require any such ban. Anyone entering into a contract of employment is required to accept a wide range of restrictions on his or her freedom in return for a wage. It is hypocritical to single out the one requirement which may be imposed by the employees and to ignore the many requirements imposed by the employer. Furthermore, objections to the closed shop in principle ignore the point made earlier, that most working people's freedoms are in practice only protected through trade union organization. The objection that compulsory union membership obliges someone to join an association whose policies may be repugnant to him ignores, first, a member's right to opt out of the 'political levy' and, second, a member's right to participate in the organization's democratic policy-making machinery.

It is true, of course, that many employers positively welcome a union membership agreement which provides an agreed mechanism for resolving disputes and reduces the risk of many small groups of workers all pursuing conflicting interests through unrelated procedures. But the common interest of management and union in reducing conflict does not of itself justify an infringement of the individual's freedom of choice. The important point is that where there is a conflict of freedoms, a choice must be made which reconciles as far as possible the competing interests. It is clearly right, for instance, that someone employed before a union membership agreement was reached should not be required to submit to such a major change in his or her terms of employment (although it should be noted that important changes in terms and conditions are frequently imposed on employees by management without their consent). The continued non-participation of an existing employee does not seriously threaten the rights of the trade unionists who, by definition, are in a sufficiently large majority to have been able to negotiate a closed shop. A case such as that of Joanna Harris, a poultry inspector dismissed by Sandwell Council in Birmingham after the negotiation of a closed-shop agreement, is rare. The majority of closed-shop agreements either explicitly or in practice exempt existing non-members, sometimes with a proviso that the equivalent of the union subscription is paid to charity. A real difficulty may arise, however, when a closed-shop agreement has been negotiated after a bitter or protracted industrial dispute during which non-members, by refusing to participate in industrial action, have deliberately set out to weaken the trade unionists' ability to improve their conditions. In such circumstances the employer may well be faced with continuing industrial conflict if he does not either move the non-members or, in the last resort, dismiss them. But in any case, when an existing employee is dismissed for refusing to comply with a subsequent union membership agreement, there should be a right to apply to an industrial tribunal for unfair dismissal. The exemption for religious objectors, whether existing or new employees, should, of course, be retained. But it is difficult to see how that exemption can be extended to non-religious, 'conscientious' objectors without leaving trade union organization vulnerable to those whose only objection is to paying the subscription (while still accepting the benefits of organization) or to those who would accept lower rates of pay or worse conditions than the union members themselves will accept.

Violence by the police

As we have noted (see page 113), the Government's discussion of public order omits any reference to the relationship between policing tactics and the exercise of freedom of peaceful protest. Nor has the Government shown any concern about police violence against demonstrators. No one doubts that on various occasions a minority of demonstrators have been responsible for serious violence against the police, nor that the law should be used against such offenders. As we have seen, the present law provides more than adequate redress against violent protesters. But there is serious doubt about whether the police themselves or the Home Secretary are prepared to act against excessive violence perpetrated by the police at demonstrations or whether present disciplinary and legal procedures are adequate.

In 1975 the then Metropolitan Police Commissioner, Sir Robert Mark, told the Police College that any police officer at a demonstration 'knows that his behaviour will be scrutinized closely, that the rules governing his conduct are more strict than those applicable to the demonstrators and the consequences for him are potentially more disadvantageous'.[48] After the events in Southall in April 1979 such a view cannot possibly be sustained. Following the serious violence on that occasion, over 300 protesters were charged with criminal offences, many involving allegations of violence against the police. But many protesters and other members of the public were also victims of violence from police officers. The Home Secretary's report[49] stated that sixty-four people other than police officers were injured; an unofficial committee of inquiry found ninety-three people who claimed to have been assaulted by the police, many of these cases being substantiated by medical evidence. The most serious injury was that suffered by a New Zealand teacher, Blair Peach, who died from what medical witnesses described as a 'deliberate' blow which would have caused extremely serious injury or death. Despite a lengthy police investigation, which, it is believed, advised the DPP of charges of riot and assault, as well as a possible murder or manslaughter charge, the DPP decided to bring no charges against any officer present at the time of the fatal blow.

The unofficial inquiry presented extensive evidence of a serious breakdown of police discipline not only in the street in which Blair Peach was hit but also during the eviction of a community centre and the dispersal of the crowd into Southall Park. Disciplinary investigations continued for two years afterwards, but in April 1981 it was reported[50] that no charges would be brought against any officer involved.

Prominent in the violence at Southall were the SPG, two of whose units were involved in the operation which led to Blair Peach's death, a third being largely responsible for the community-centre eviction, during which a number of medical attendants were injured. Established in 1965 as a mobile anti-crime squad which could carry out preventive patrols in areas particularly subject to vandalism and other crimes and could provide 'saturation policing' where required, the SPG of the Metropolitan police has come to be regarded generally as a riot squad. It is now widely used in industrial disputes and at demonstrations at which, in the words of the Police Commissioner in 1972, 'militant elements are thought likely to cause disorder'. It is also specially trained in anti-terrorist measures (SPG units have been involved in exercises carried out by the police and the Army at Heathrow Airport in the last ten years). This marked change in its function should be seen in the context of the debate in the early 1970s between the police, the Home Office and the defence authorities about the creation of a British 'third force' or paramilitary unit to stand between police and Army. The third force was never created, but the SPG has taken on many of the characteristics of a paramilitary unit. The dangers of an elite force, removed from the local command structure and from links with the community, were recognized by the Home Secretary, who directed a number of changes in 1980 after an investigation initiated by Blair Peach's death. More supervisory officers were to be appointed; command of the SPG was to come under the four Area Deputy

Assistant Commissioners; and SPG officers were to serve only four years instead of ten, as formerly. The latter change meant that more than half of the serving SPG officers would be returned to normal duties. But the changes may not make much difference. Central command by the Assistant Commissioner of 'A' Department (responsible for anti-terrorist and public-order work) will be retained 'when necessary', thus removing the SPG from local control on crucial occasions. More fundamentally, there has been no departure from the decision to create a separate, highly centralized force, specially trained in anti-terrorist and riot-control measures and used on major demonstrations. Indeed, similar units (known by names such as Public Service Units or Tactical Support Groups) are now being created in many other forces.

The Government claims[51] that it wishes to retain 'traditional' British methods of policing demonstrations. One of the reasons why Britain has largely avoided the riots between police and demonstrators which have occurred so frequently in Northern Ireland, in the USA and on the Continent, is that the police at demonstrations have remained unarmed, have largely been drawn from local forces and have relied on face-to-face persuasion and pressure to achieve their ends. The introduction of riot shields to protect police against missiles was a significant move away from this tradition and, although in some instances entirely under-standable, may in the long run make the police more and not less vulnerable if expectations of violence are fuelled.

In May 1981 the Metropolitan police launched a saturation policing scheme (code-named, with almost unbelievable ineptitude, 'Operation Swamp')[52] in the south London area of Brixton. The result was a weekend of extremely serious violence, perpetrated by hundreds of black and white residents against the police, in which, in scenes reminiscent of Belfast, petrol bombs set on fire police officers' jackets and cars were overturned and burned. The almost immediate response of the police was a demand for more effective riot-control equipment. Not only the Police Federation – which would have come under intense pressure from its own members – but also ACPO and the Chief Super-intendents Association took part in a deputation to the Home Secretary, who made it clear, however, that only defensive equipment would be considered. But as John Alderson, the Chief Constable of Devon and Cornwall, pointed out in a BBC radio interview the same weekend, the real need was to understand and tackle the causes of the complete breakdown in normal relations between the police and the Brixton community, and not to equip or train the police on the assumption that attacks of a similar seriousness were to be expected regularly in future. Despite the Home Secretary's refusal to establish a public inquiry into similar events in Bristol the previous year, Mr Whitelaw immediately announced the appointment of Lord Scarman to investigate the events under the 1964 Police Act and, more important, to examine the underlying causes of the Brixton riots. Mr Whitelaw's refusal to appoint members of the black community or other local representatives to sit with Lord Scarman meant, however, that the inquiry was unable to obtain full evidence from many of the local community organizations.

What is urgently required is a radical review of policing policies in areas like Brixton. The use of the SPG – whether at demonstrations, as in Southall, or in saturation policing of street crime, as in south London – has had a disastrous effect on relations between local communities and the local police, who have had to live with the results of the SPG's excursions into their territory. For large numbers of black youngsters the experience of unemployment, inner-city decay and inadequate education is compounded by the racism they confront, most noticeably in their dealings with the police. One does not have to believe every allegation of racist insults or police violence to appreciate the substantial evidence which exists of utterly unacceptable behaviour by many members of an almost entirely white police force.[53] Senior police officers all too often suggest that racism in the force must be expected, police officers simply being a section of the public – an argument they would never tolerate if it were advanced in relation to criminal or corrupt practice.

New restrictions on freedom of assembly

A new Public Order Bill has been under consideration by the Home Office since the then Home Secretary, Merlyn Rees, ordered a review of the law following disturbances in Birmingham and London in 1977. A further review was carried out after the events in Southall of April 1979, leading to the publication of a Green Paper[54] the following year. The matter was also considered by the Home Affairs Committee of the House of Commons, which reported in August 1980.[55] The Government's Green Paper proposals are likely to form the basis of legislation during 1982 dealing with both marches and stationary demonstrations.

The Government has proposed four main changes to the law concerning processions. The first would make it a criminal offence to organize a march without giving advance notice to the police. ACPO has lobbied for some years for a notification requirement similar to that in force in Northern Ireland (where seventy-two hours' notice is mandatory), but the argument that the police require such notice, under threat of criminal sanctions, in order to make arrangements concerning the route, police manpower and leave and so on simply does not bear examination. As Lord Scarman pointed out in his report on the Red Lion Square disorders,[56] the majority of processions, including the vast majority of large processions, are notified to the police in advance by organizers who wish to ensure that there is no difficulty about their arrangements. Since no large procession can be organized without publicity, the police always know of any major event even without formal notification. Prior notice is not related to the prevention of violence. As Lord Scarman concluded, the Metropolitan police had known for weeks about the proposed National Front meeting and Liberation march in central London in June 1974 but had not profited by that knowledge to make arrangements which would have kept the two groups apart. In Southall in April 1979 the community organizations notified the police of their plans at numerous meetings but received no indication in return of what the police operation would be. Police evidence to the Select Committee confirmed[57] that there was no occasion when serious public disorder had taken place without the police knowing in advance of the organizers' plans.

The proposed criminal offence and prior-notice requirement creates a real threat to the spontaneous procession. Even if the notification provision contained an exception for marches organized at short notice, the specified period will be thought by many organizers to be an irreducible minimum. This is particularly true of those most likely to organize small processions with little warning – for instance, workers at one workplace wanting to march to another factory in support of a strike, or mothers wanting to march to a town hall after an accident at a pedestrian crossing. The minimum notice requirement, if observed on such occasions, would completely destroy the immediacy of the protest. Furthermore, if the notification requirement were not observed, the organizers of a procession would be liable to prosecution – even though the procession itself had been entirely peaceful.

It may be suggested that the new criminal offence would not be used against peaceful protesters. In November 1979, however, a 13-year-old Cheshire schoolgirl, Penny Lloyd, organized a protest march to a local building firm in order to hand in a petition complaining about the lack of promised play facilities. On her return home she was confronted by a police officer who threatened her with a court injunction ('just as we did to the Shotton steel workers') for failing to give three days' notice of her march, as required by the by-laws then in force.[58]

That the Government recognizes the potential of the new criminal offence created by a notification requirement is suggested by its proposal for a new power of arrest.[59] It is possible that it would be an arrestable offence not only to organize a demonstration without giving notice, or to organize a demonstration which fails to keep to the notified route, but also to participate in an unnotified procession. Such offences, coupled with a power of arrest, would provide the police with a dangerously broad and entirely unjustified discretion to prevent peaceful marches.

But the real significance of the notice requirement is to be found in its association with proposals for imposing conditions or bans on processions. The Government has argued[60] that the 1936 Act power to impose conditions is little used; instead, the Chief Constable (or senior officer present on the march) should be able to re-route the march if there is any risk of 'disorder' and not only, as at present, if 'serious' disorder is feared. The Select Committee went even further,[61] proposing that there should be an additional power to impose conditions if there were 'a reasonable apprehension of serious disruption to the normal life of the community'.

As I have argued above, the view that demonstrations disrupt the community's 'normal' life is simply wrong. If the Select Committee's proposal were accepted, the police would have an extraordinary power to re-route processions away from any large shopping area, town centre or park. The decision about what constituted 'normal' community life, or when and whether a particular route would seriously disrupt it, would be left entirely to the police officers in charge. Such a power could relegate all processions to deserted back streets – even when a procession was entirely peaceful.

The Government's proposed test of 'disorder' is open to similar objections. It might be argued that any large procession causes disorder – more people on the streets, more litter, more noise –

even when no actual violence occurs. Any procession on a controversial issue might be thought to carry a risk of disorder if there were any suspicion that opponents might stand by the side of the road to heckle or try to attack the marchers. (Indeed, the Court of Appeal justified its decision in the Campaign for Nuclear Disarmament marches case partly on the ground that the police ban protected the Campaign against the interference of imaginary hooligans.)[62] And since the power to impose conditions extends beyond the route of the march to banners, placards, flags and other items carried by protesters, a new power to impose conditions on the grounds of 'disorder' would give the police complete freedom to censor any messages which could conceivably cause offence.

Similarly, the Government has proposed that the risk of any disorder should become the criterion for imposing a ban on marches. Indeed, it is even suggested that 'the effect of the event on the policing of an area as a whole' could justify a ban – inviting the police to decide, first, that a particular march requires large numbers of officers and then that the resources are simply not available. The Select Committee quite rightly rejected the proposal for any lesser criterion than 'serious public disorder', stressing that 'if bans were to be made on the apprehension of *any* violence, many marches, responsibly organized and intent only on a peaceful demonstration of view, could, in effect, be vetoed by the threat of violence from opponents.'[63]

A minority of the Select Committee rejected completely the need for any bans on processions: 'Bans are wrong in principle and unnecessary in practice.' They argued: 'the Coronation or the Lord Mayor's Procession attract larger numbers and cause greater congestion than most political processions but few would want to ban them.'[64] Furthermore, a ban could lead 'to an equal expenditure of money and police resources to contain public reaction'. Repeal of the power to ban, requiring the police to make greater use of their re-routing powers to control serious disorder, would undoubtedly strengthen freedom of protest. In a large metropolitan area containing traditional routes for processions through the city centre, proper use of the re-routing powers should be adequate to deal with marches which might otherwise result in serious violence. But in a smaller town, particularly when a racist march is proposed in opposition to the local ethnic minority community, a ban may be the only way of avoiding violent confrontation.

On the question of stationary demonstrations, the Government has broken completely new ground. Noting that the present power to impose conditions or a ban applies only to processions, the Government has proposed[65] to extend that power, along with the new criminal offence of demonstrating without notice, to any stationary demonstration held outdoors. Organizers of pickets (whether connected with industrial disputes or not), rallies, public meetings, 'vigils' and other forms of stationary protest would have to give prior notice to the police, would be subject to conditions concerning the location of their protest, the placards and banners displayed, the numbers present and so on, and could be banned altogether. Such sweeping controls have never previously been considered necessary, even during the 1930s.

It is indeed true that it is not only processions or marches that may lead to serious public disorder. In most of the clashes between the National Front and the anti-racist movement or between the police and the latter a stationary meeting has been involved, in some cases a meeting held indoors by the National Front or a protest outdoors organized by its opponents. The assumption behind the new proposals is that they would pre-empt violence of the kind seen in Southall, Birmingham or Red Lion Square.

But the new controls would do nothing to eliminate disorder at demonstrations. Prior notice would not have eliminated any of the violent clashes which have taken place in recent years: the police knew of the events well in advance anyway. The 're-routing' of a proposed demonstration was tried in Southall in April 1979 – with disastrous results, as we have noted.

The real target is industrial picketing. The 1980 Employment Act has already restricted such pickets to workers in dispute with an employer, standing outside their own workplace and accompanied only by their union official. The Code of Practice issued under the Act has restricted the number of picketing workers to a maximum of six. All others – whether workers in dispute, or trades unionists showing their support – would constitute a 'demonstration in support of a picket' and thus liable to the new restrictions. But a power to redirect or ban a mass picket would not necessarily avert clashes between pickets and police. When large numbers of people wish to demonstrate about any cause about which they feel extremely strongly, they may decide to do so in defiance of a ban. The more frequently such bans are imposed, the more likely they are to be disobeyed; and the disorder which would result from police attempts to enforce a ban may well be far more serious than the conflict which originally gave rise to the ban.

A ban on racist demonstrations?

It has been strongly argued in recent years that marches and meetings of the National Front and similar organizations – the trigger-points for much of the violence on the streets – should be banned. The Trades Union Congress and the Labour Party have argued that the police should have a power to ban a march which would cause incitement to racial hatred. The Legal Action Group has proposed [66] that bans on marches should be confined to those held by racist organizations. Such proposals are immediately attractive for all those concerned to eradicate racist prejudice and violence. They must, nonetheless, be rejected.

It is a crucial principle of democratic political organization that no Government should be allowed to curtail the rights of its opponents to enjoy freedom of association and of expression. The views of the National Front are repugnant to many, probably most, people in this country. But the views of many other groups are also deeply offensive to some sections of the community and, in particular, to those in authority. A Government with the power to ban is inevitably tempted to deny to people holding views which the Government itself finds threatening or obnoxious the opportunity to associate with others or to express themselves.

It is sometimes argued that the expression of racist views does not fall within the limits of democratic or political activity. The Legal Action Group has suggested that 'demonstrations aimed at . . stirring up racial hatred or prejudice are clearly distinguishable and in a separate category from demonstrations which are genuine expressions of concern about matters of public importance.' [67] But the real threat of racism to the safety and wellbeing of Britain's ethnic minorities comes precisely from the fact that many people, including many political leaders, genuinely believe that the existence of those minorities somehow threatens the rest of the population and that 'immigrants' should be persuaded or forced to leave this country. Proposals for repatriation are no less objectionable when they come from Conservative MPs or Enoch Powell than when they are advanced by an avowedly racist and neo-Fascist organization.

Bans do not, of course, prevent politicians or anyone else from holding racist views; nor can they prevent racist violence. It is worth recalling that bans, as instruments of public policy, have been used for decades in Northern Ireland, the Irish Republican

Army (IRA) and four other organizations currently being proscribed under the Emergency Provisions Act. But the organizations continue to exist. Their leaders are well-known. Support for their views has not been diminished by the bans. And the violence has not ceased. A ban on racist organizations or their activities might be said to be a statement of official opposition to racism even if the ban has no other effect, just as it was argued that the ban on the IRA in Britain, under the Prevention of Terrorism Act, was needed to placate public opinion even though it might make the police's job rather more difficult. Such posturing by Governments is the worst possible reason for making membership or participation in an organization illegal. If there were any evidence that bans could reduce racist prejudice or violence, a real conflict between the right of freedom of assembly and the rights of racial minorities would arise. But there is no such evidence. There is, as I argue elsewhere (see chapter 8), a desperate need for Government to lead public opinion against racism and to eradicate the racism of its own policies: until that is done, official condemnation of racist organizations is the merest hypocrisy.

The only legitimate ground for interfering with freedom of assembly is the threat of serious public disorder which cannot be averted in any other way. If bans are not to become the automatic response to any major demonstration on a controversial issue, far more attention must be paid to policing methods. National Front election meetings have sometimes, as in Southall, been the focus of extremely serious violence; they have also, on other occasions, passed off with little or no disorder when the police, instead of cordoning off or banning protest demonstrations, have ensured that members of the public have been able to attend what are meant, according to the Representation of the People Act, to be public meetings.

But banning orders must always remain a last resort, to be used exceptionally and in the narrowest possible terms. The 1936 Act does not distinguish between the *sources* of violence and thus leaves open the serious possibility that one group, by disrupting its opponent's march or meeting, will force a ban to be imposed. The right of individuals to express their views is destroyed if a hostile audience can impose a veto. If the reception of the audience were to be the criterion for permitting or denying a speaker the right to speak, Martin Luther King would never have been able to organize civil rights marches in the southern states of the USA. It is for this reason that the Supreme Court of the USA, in deciding freedom of speech issues, has never upheld a ban on a meeting on the grounds that the audience would be provoked to violence. Unfortunately, the British courts have been all too willing to allow the threat of public disorder, however remote, to be the overriding criterion for deciding whether or not a speaker should be allowed to speak. And the test of serious public disorder, under the 1936 Act, does allow the threat of violence from counter-demonstrators to become the grounds of a ban.

Any departure from the 'serious public disorder' test would, however, result in a far more grave threat to the right of protest. If, for instance, the Act were to be amended to allow a ban on marches or meetings which might incite to racial hatred, or prejudice 'good race relations', or promote hostility to racial, ethnic, religious or other groups, there is no doubt at all that the powers would be used extremely widely by those who wish to outlaw 'totalitarians of the right and the left'. The *Berufsverbot* of West Germany, under which thousands of teachers and civil servants have been purged, provides a telling illustration of the risk of trying to protect a community against 'extremists'.

Protecting peaceful protest

The right to assemble peacefully on the streets and in other public places is too important to be left to the diminishing gaps between ill-defined and arbitrary police powers. It may be suggested that since most marches and demonstrations pass off peacefully, un-hindered by the police or anyone else, the present legal position is satisfactory. But the vulnerability of protest is revealed on those occasions when the police, through operational tactics, violence, administrative or legal bans, arrests or the arbitrary selection of defendants and charges, make it impossible for a peaceful demon-stration to take place. The unwillingness of the courts generally to overrule police discretion (indeed, the complicity of the courts in extending that discretion), the failure of the European Human Rights Commission to consider the matter, the inability of the police authorities to call the police to account for their handling of public disorder – all reveal the frailty of institutions designed to protect fundamental freedoms against excessive police powers.

The legal problem of freedom of assembly is twofold: it involves the absence of any positive right to assemble, and the existence of discretionary police powers that are increasingly widely defined and open to serious abuse. The solution, likewise, is twofold: to reverse the traditions of English law and carve out for peaceful assemblies a protected status, and to curtail the discretionary powers of the police.

The creation of a statutory right to peaceful demonstration would not be easy. Such a right was, in a sense, created for industrial disputes by the 1906 Trade Disputes Act, but it was a right which, as we have seen, was easily whittled away by convictions for obstruction of the police or the highway which enlarged the powers of the police to reduce the numbers of pickets or to send them elsewhere. Nor did the 1906 Act provide a remedy for those whose 'right' to hold a peaceful picket was infringed.

It may be more profitable to turn the common law concept of the 'reasonable user' of the highway to our purpose and to provide, by statute, a definition of 'reasonable user' which includes both processions and stationary gatherings, whether small groups distributing literature or large outdoor meetings or rallies. The problem of balancing the rights of protesters against those of shoppers, pedestrians, drivers and other users of the highway is already generally dealt with when it comes to processions. There is general public acceptance of the inevitable disruption caused by any large-scale procession, whether associated with the Lord Mayor's Show or a march against nuclear weapons. There should, however, be a right of appeal to the High Court against the imposition of conditions or a ban under the 1936 Act, while the additional powers of the Metropolitan police under the 1839 Act should be abolished or severely curtailed, in particular by making their exercise subject to the scrutiny of an elected Police Authority.

Where stationary demonstrations are concerned, the balance is more difficult to draw. The new definition of 'reasonable user' should protect, for instance, Mrs Duncan's attempt to hold a meeting outside an unemployed training centre (see page 123) or, in the autumn of 1980, the attempt by a number of MPs and others to hold a picket outside an unemployment office in south London. In order to ensure that small, peaceful and essentially undisruptive events are not banned by police arrests, the offence of obstruction of the highway or pavement should be redefined to include only the situation in which there is a real, and more than trivial, obstruction of other passers-by.

Next there is a pressing need to restrict the powers which are conferred on the police by their duty to disperse an assembly, regardless of whether or not the assembly is unlawful, for they reasonably fear a breach of the peace. Although the requirement that their fear be 'reasonable' appears to offer a balance between the demands of public order and the claims of free speech, in practice the courts have been unwilling to overrule the judgment of the police officer on the spot, however remote the possibility of any disorder. Instead of relying on a notion of 'reasonableness' which has proved unsatisfactory, we should look to the notion of 'clear and present danger' adopted by the Supreme Court of the USA in a series of free-speech cases. Thus the power to disperse an assembly or to arrest for breach of the peace should be available only where there is evidence of a 'clear and present danger' of serious disturbance. Finally, the offence of obstructing the police in the execution of their duty should be restricted, as it is in Scotland, to cases in which the officer is physically obstructed and should not include mere disobedience of an order.

The law has failed to protect freedom of assembly and protest. Far from requiring new and sweeping powers to restrict, ban or disperse processions and other demonstrations, the police already have objectionably wide powers to employ against peaceful protest. The protection of free speech and assembly requires not only a restriction of police discretion but also the legal recognition of the right of people peacefully to meet or march in the streets and other public places.

III

Test Cases for Civil Liberties

6

Civil Liberties and Northern Ireland

The violence of the last twelve years in Northern Ireland was born of the denial of civil rights to the Roman Catholic minority. The conflict itself has given birth to new violations of human rights, which have, in turn, been the impetus for further fighting. Guarantees of human rights will not themselves produce a resolution of the conflict: but no solution will be found without them.

The minimum requirements for the constitution of a community divided on religious or ethnic lines have been described (in the context of Cyprus) thus:

> a sound constitutional policy with regard to bicommunal societies . . . should, at the very least, be directed towards, first, the successful institutionalization of the co-operation of the various ethnic groups in the running of governmental affairs and the sharing of power; secondly, a fair allocation of the structures and functions of the state, and the achievement thereby of a satisfactory power balance between the various ethnic groups excluding both political dominance over and oppression of the smaller group as well as the frustration and alienation of the larger and major group; and thirdly, the provision of revision procedures and adequate readjustment machinery for the amicable resolution of inevitable disputes and the renegotiation of the political and constitutional arrangements in the event of their proving unworkable or unsatisfactory.[1]

Intercommunal conflict in Northern Ireland is made peculiarly complex by the fact that there are not one but two minorities: a Roman Catholic community, in the minority in Northern Ireland, bordering on an independent republic in which, until recently, the Roman Catholic Church was an established part of the constitution; and a Protestant community, forming the majority in Northern Ireland but fearing minority status in a reunited Ireland. But the

153

settlement of 1920, permitting the creation of 'a Protestant Parliament for a Protestant people', failed to meet the basic requirements of a political and legal system which could reconcile, or at least minimize conflict between, the two communities.

Until its disbandment in 1972, the Stormont Parliament was permanently dominated by the Ulster Unionist majority. In local government, where the Catholic community had a majority in some areas (such as Derry), Unionist domination was guaranteed by the manipulation of electoral boundaries and a deliberate policy of council-house allocation which maintained the Unionist vote in marginal wards and concentrated the Catholic community in wards which the Unionists could never hope to win.[2] Discrimination against the minority is well documented: in some Unionist authorities Catholic applicants were unlikely to be considered for local government appointments, particularly senior posts; employment opportunities were often segregated, much of the new economic development taking place in predominantly Protestant areas (an example being the location of the New University of Ulster at Coleraine, rather than Derry); and, although the Catholic community obtained a larger share overall of public housing, the Cameron Commission (established after the violence of August 1969) found that houses allocated to the minority were generally needed to rehouse families from the slums, while Protestant allocations more frequently went to new families.[3] Segregated schooling helped to maintain the sense of two embattled communities.

From the outset the Unionist majority protected themselves against the possibility of Republican agitation by the Special Powers Acts – 'temporary' legislation introduced first in 1922 and re-enacted on a permanent basis in 1933 – which gave the security forces the power to arrest without warrant, to detain without trial, to enter and search homes without warrant, to impose a curfew and to prohibit meetings, assemblies and processions. The Royal Ulster Constabulary (RUC), it was estimated in 1969, was 90 per cent Protestant, while the part-time Special Constabulary was entirely recruited from the Protestant community, a large proportion of its members coming from the Orange Order.[4] Over thirty years before the present troubles began, a Commission of Inquiry established by the NCCL concluded:

First, that through the operation of the Special Powers Acts contempt has been begotten for the representative institutions of government.

Secondly, that through the use of Special Powers individual liberty is no longer protected by law, but is at the arbitrary disposition of the Executive. This abrogation of the rule of law has been so practised as to bring the freedom of the subject into contempt.

Thirdly, that the Northern Irish Government has used Special Powers towards securing the domination of one particular political faction and, at the same time, towards curtailing the lawful activities of its opponents. The driving of legitimate movements underground into illegality, the intimidating or branding as law breakers of their adherents, however innocent of crime, has tended to encourage violence and bigotry on the part of the Government's supporters as well as to beget in its opponents an intolerance of the 'law and order' thus maintained. The Government's policy is thus driving its opponents into the ways of extremists.[5]

It is indeed remarkable that the system lasted as long as it did.

What finally brought down the Unionist Government was the failure of the civil rights movement – that is to say, the failure of the Unionists and the failure of the Westminster Government, which retained ultimate responsibility for the province under the 1920 Government of Ireland Act, to meet the legitimate demands for an end to religious discrimination, gerrymandering and special powers. In campaigning for an end to discrimination, the civil rights movement was asking only for the fulfilment of the assurance given in the 1920 Act that prohibited Stormont from legislating against religious equality and prohibited religious discrimination in the exercise of the Governor's executive powers. The assurances, when tested, proved wanting. In 1964 the newly formed Campaign for Social Justice in Northern Ireland tried to obtain the intervention of the then British Prime Minister, Sir Alec Douglas Hume, who had rashly informed a press conference in Belfast that religious discrimination could be dealt with 'by law'.[6] In 1966 the Campaign tried to obtain legal aid for a test case against housing discrimination, but the refusal of the legal aid committee to finance the case led the Campaign to conclude that legal redress was unachievable.[7] It was not until 1968 that civil rights issues were brought before the courts, in a case on behalf of someone charged with membership of the (by then illegal) Republican Clubs. The case was finally lost in the House of Lords in June 1969, a few months before the breakdown of civil government in Derry and Belfast persuaded the Westminster Government to send in the Army.[8] Thus, in striking contrast to the black civil rights movement of the USA, the minority in Northern Ireland found themselves unable to pursue grievances through the courts.

The courts cannot be entirely blamed for their failure to provide a means of redress, although the legalistic refusal of the House of Lords, in the Republican Clubs case, to review ministerial decisions in the absence of proof of 'bad faith', ended any real hope of improving the position of the minority through the legal machinery. The response of the politicians and the police was far more culpable. By 1968 the civil rights movement had begun to organize peaceful rallies and marches to demonstrate its grievances. Until then the Campaign for Social Justice had been able to write that 'with some notable exceptions, relations between the police and the minority were normal.' However, not only did the police prove incapable of protecting the civil rights marchers against the attacks of Protestant extremists, but the police themselves met the marchers with violence. In October 1968 a march in Derry was banned, allegedly because it would clash with an Apprentice Boys (i.e. Orange) march, which, the Cameron Commission found, had been invented for the occasion. The civil rights march took place and was violently attacked by the police. In January 1969 members of the 'B' Specials were involved, unofficially, in an ambush of a march organized by People's Democracy between Belfast and Derry. In August the RUC failed to prevent a number of houses in Catholic areas of Belfast from being burned out; that same month the British Army was sent into Northern Ireland to take over from the police and to protect the minority from further Protestant attacks.

By November 1968 the then Prime Minister of Northern Ireland, Captain O'Neill, had been persuaded, under pressure from Westminster, to accept a package of reforms, including the establishment of an Ombudsman, the reform of the system of housing allocations, the reform of local government and the amendment of the Special Powers Act. In January 1969 a Commission was appointed under Lord Cameron to investigate the causes of the disturbances. But the deepening conflict between different wings of the Unionist Party made it clear that no rapid implementation of the reform programme could be expected from Stormont. The double frustrations of the unwillingness or inability of the courts to handle civil rights litigation and the failure of the reforms to meet the expectations of the minority have been traced by Tom Hadden and Paddy Hillyard.[9] Although the Specials were disbanded in October 1968, the reconstituted RUC and the new Police Authority were unable to regain the minority community's confidence. The two offices of Ombudsman (one for central, the other for local government) were set up in late 1969, but, restricted as they were to procedural rather than substantive issues concerning individual cases, they were unable to tackle the general patterns of discrimination which were the real, and justified, grievance of the minority. Full-scale reform of local government did not take place until 1973, the only action in the years immediately following the violence of 1968 and 1969 being the replacement of the grotesquely gerrymandered Derry Council with a non-elected Derry Commission. Thus although the Commission's work was generally praised, the minority continued to be denied control in the city in which they formed a local majority. Similarly, the housing functions of local government were removed to a non-elected Northern Ireland Housing Executive, which did not start work until 1972.

By then the operations of the British Army provided a new and far more dangerous source of grievance. In 1969 the soldiers were, on the whole, welcomed by the minority community; the IRA did not (except in the imagination of some Unionist politicians and the RUC Special Branch) exist. But the warnings apparently offered by senior officers that the Army was untrained for a peace-keeping role were ignored. Relationships between the soldiers and the minority deteriorated; the Army stepped up its 'policing' role, conducting extensive searches for arms in Catholic, rather than Protestant, areas. In July 1970 a routine arms search led to a curfew in the Lower Falls area of Derry and to serious fighting between soldiers and the community. As the Army became not the protector of the minority but the inheritor of the Unionists' Special Powers Acts, so the IRA was able to move on from manning the barricades in Catholic ghettos of Belfast to more violent offensives. In 1970 the first person died at the hands of the Army, in February 1971 the first soldier at the hands of the IRA.

In August 1971 internment was introduced. No decision could have been more destructive of remaining hopes of a peaceful resolution of the conflict. The internees were drawn exclusively from the Catholic community (although Protestants were added later). The ramshackle intelligence of the RUC ensured that a large number of the internees could not possibly have been suspected of any criminal offence. In any case, regardless of the characteristics of the victims, detention without trial signalled the abandonment of any pretence at upholding the rule of law. Not only were suspects arrested without warrant and locked up without any term being set to their imprisonment, but twelve of them were brutally ill-treated. The use of the 'five techniques' – forcing the men to wear hoods over their heads except when alone or being interrogated, continuously subjecting them to electronic noise, spread-eagling them against a wall for periods of up to forty-three hours, depriving them of sleep and beating – were eventually condemned by the European Human Rights Commission (which held that the techniques amounted to 'torture', in breach of the Human Rights Convention) and the Human Rights Court (which regarded them as ill-treatment rather than torture but nonetheless in violation of the Convention) in an inter-state case brought by the Dublin Government. The interrogation methods were abandoned, well before the European case was concluded. But the fury of the minority community (and, of course, that of many among the majority) was hardly appeased by the report of the Compton Commission, which investigated and substantiated the complaints of the internees. Two of its members, both Privy Counsellors, *upheld* the use of 'in-depth interrogation', although the third, a former Lord Chancellor, Lord Gardiner, condemned them as 'illegal, not morally justifiable and alien to the traditions of what I still believe to be the greatest democracy in the world'.[10] No action was ever taken against the officers or the MI5 interrogators responsible for the torture of the detainees, and the British Government has never been prepared to acknowledge the level at which knowledge of and responsibility for the operation rested.

It was over three years before the authorities publicly admitted that internment had been a mistake. Internment was, as has often been said, the Provisional IRA's most effective recruiting sergeant. The escalation of violence was immediate, forty members of the security forces being killed in the four months after August 1971. In 1975 the then Secretary of State, Merlyn Rees, announced that no further use of the internment power would be made, and by the end of the year the last internee had been released. But the process of 'normalization', of dealing with those suspected of terrorist offences through the criminal courts, has produced its own sequel of human rights violations. The Emergency Provisions Act, which replaced the Special Powers Act in 1973, abolished jury trial for 'scheduled' offences (i.e., those thought likely to relate to terrorism), reversed the burden of proof in bail applications, abolished the prohibition on hearsay evidence and rendered admissible as evidence 'confession' statements which, although involuntary, had not actually been obtained by torture, inhuman or degrading treatment, threats or inducements. The difficulty of obaining bail for those charged with a scheduled offence, together with lengthy pre-trial delays, led a number of community groups to condemn remands in custody as internment under another name in the period immediately following the phasing out of internment itself. Pre-trial delays have now been considerably reduced, and 27 per cent of bail applications made by those tried during 1977 and 1978 were granted. But the requirement that bail applications be made to the High Court continues to deter some would-be applicants.[11]

The allegation of sectarian bias among Northern Ireland juries – the reason given for their abolition – was never substantiated. Although both independent research and figures published by the Attorney-General showed a higher acquittal rate on serious charges among Protestants than among Catholics,[12] it must be remembered that the property qualification required for jury service in Northern Ireland inevitably discriminated in favour of Protestant electors. More important, as NCCL stressed in its evidence to Lord Gardiner's inquiry into the operation of the Emergency Provisions Act, the two communities in Northern Ireland had effectively been policed under totally different systems since 1970. The Protestant community had not rejected the largely Protestant RUC, which was therefore able to persist with more or less normal policing methods, relying on information from within the community itself, and was able to bring suspects before the courts. But the RUC was unable to enter many of the Catholic areas, which were therefore policed by the Army, suspects ending up only too often in internment rather than before the courts.[13] The absence of juries is a major factor in the lack of confidence, particularly within the minority community, in the special courts; and in 1980 a public opinion survey carried out for the Standing Advisory Commission on Human Rights revealed a majority within both communities in favour of the restoration of jury trial. Depressingly, however, there is no movement in support of juries among community organizations or even among defence lawyers, who seem to prefer well-known judges, however case-hardened, to the unpredictable verdicts of the jury.[14]

The Emergency Provisions Act also authorized the detention of suspects for up to seventy-two hours and provided – in contrast to the common law rule that confession statements should be admitted as evidence only if 'voluntary' – that confession statements would be *excluded* only if the defence could prove that they were obtained by prohibited means. Thus when the courts replaced the internment camps there was an immediate inducement for the police to use extended interrogation, detention, isolation, inducements, threats and, in some cases, violence in the hope of obtaining 'evidence' which would persuade the suspect to plead guilty or would be accepted by the courts.

In practice, the courts themselves have resisted the standards of the Emergency Provisions Act, continuing to exclude some statements even when there is evidence of a lesser degree of violence than that tolerated by the Act.[15] But the risk of exclusion in a few cases did not prevent the police from developing interrogation practices which involved serious violence against some suspects. In 1977 two special RUC interrogation centres were opened at Castlereagh in Belfast and at Gough Army Barracks in Armagh, both designed so that neither cells nor interview rooms had windows. Police doctors themselves became increasingly concerned about police behaviour, but representations from the Association of Forensic Medical Officers and from police surgeons at Gough were ignored by the authorities. One particularly courageous police doctor, who spoke out publicly about violence against suspects, was even subjected to a vicious smear campaign by senior officials.[16] In November 1977 an Amnesty International mission investigated a number of complaints of ill-treatment, concluding that many of them were well founded.[17] In 1978 the Government, unable any longer to dismiss evidence of violence as 'self-inflicted', established the Bennett Committee on Police Interrogation Practices, which reported in March 1979 that in some cases 'injuries whatever their precise cause had not been self-inflicted and had been sustained in police custody.'[18] The Bennett Committee recommended that closed-circuit television be installed in all interview rooms and monitored by uniformed officers (the report made it clear that the uniformed branch had not been the subject of complaints); that limits be placed on the duration of interviews and the number of interrogating officers; that suspects be given an absolute right of access to a solicitor after forty-eight hours; and that a code of conduct for interviews be introduced. The Government, a year later, accepted the recommendations, although the recommendation of access to a solicitor has been nullified by the insistence that a police officer may be present at the interview. An analysis of the court records of those arrested and charged since then is not yet available,[19] but the number of complaints has dropped, and it appears that the new Chief Constable of the RUC, who took office during 1980, has succeeded in rooting out the worst violence.

The procedure for handling complaints against police officers, however, remains entirely unsatisfactory. As in Britain, the independent Police Complaints Board is little involved in serious complaints, all of which are referred to the DPP for a decision on criminal charges. Very few prosecutions are brought: in 1978 only 3 per cent of complaints referred to the DPP led to a charge. But the remainder of the complaints cannot be reopened by the Board unless some separate disciplinary offence apart from the possible criminal offence is involved. The need for a visibly effective and independent police complaints system is even more urgent in Northern Ireland than in Britain, and it is therefore essential that the Board be given the power to consider afresh the possibility of disciplinary charges in any case in which the DPP has decided not to prosecute.

The existence of special no-jury courts, with special rules of evidence designed to obtain convictions which might not be obtainable otherwise, has lent support to the demands of the Provisional IRA for 'special category' status for those convicted of scheduled offences. 'Special category' status was introduced in July 1972, when the authorities agreed that those convicted of terrorist offences should be allowed to enjoy the same conditions as those who had been interned and who were organized in POW-like camps, under the direction of their own political leaders. When internment was phased out in 1975 it was decided to end 'special category' status as well. But those who had been convicted before February 1976 were permitted to retain their privileges, which were also extended to those convicted subsequently of offences committed before February. The authorities knew that demands for 'special category' status would arise as soon as those convicted of later offences entered the prisons but were determined to enforce its abolition. In 1977 prisoners began to protest by refusing to wear prison clothes or to do prison work; the authorities responded by charging offences against prison discipline, for which the penalty was loss of remission of sentence, and by refusing to allow prisoners to wear their own clothes. By 1980 over 300 prisoners were 'on the blanket'.[20] During 1978 the protest escalated, as prisoners refused to take exercise or to use toilet facilities, and the 'dirty protest', with prisoners occupying cells smeared with their own excreta, became notorious throughout the world. In 1980 a number of IRA prisoners began a hunger-strike in support of their demands and were apparently successful in reaching a compromise with the authorities shortly before Christmas. Early in 1981, however, the 'settlement' collapsed and the hunger-strike was resumed. By July 1981 eight hunger-strikers had died.

Earlier in the year the first by-election for the parliamentary seat of Fermanagh and Tyrone had produced an overwhelming majority for one of the hunger-strikers, Bobby Sands. Although his victory was widely interpreted as a show of support for the Provisional IRA and the hunger-strikers, it is probably more accurately seen as a reflection of the overwhelmingly anti-British feelings of the Catholic population there. As the Social Democratic and Labour party failed to stand and the only other candidate was a Unionist, the Catholic vote united behind Sands. The new MP was unable to take his seat and died soon after his election. In order to prevent a repetition of the election result, the Westminster Government introduced legislation to amend the Representation of the People Act, banning serving prisoners from standing for Parliament. It was characteristic of successive Governments' attitude towards Northern Ireland that, having urged the two communities to abandon the bullet for the ballot-box, the Government then changed the rules of the ballot when the outcome was too much to stomach. The new Act failed to have the desired effect, Bobby Sands's former election agent being nominated as a Republican candidate in the second by-election in August 1981.

Bobby Sands' death was followed by those of two other hunger-strikers, and in the rioting which exploded again in Belfast and Derry a number of civilians, as well as soldiers and police officers, were killed. In what has become a standard response to evidence of law breaking by the security forces, the Government refused to establish a public inquiry into the deaths of two young men in Derry who were run over and killed by Army land rovers on Easter Sunday, in circumstances which suggested a shocking degree of negligence and possibly a deliberate intention to kill. Instead the RUC were left to investigate and issued a statement to the effect that the matter was being treated as a 'road accident'.[21] In August it was announced that the two drivers would be charged with dangerous driving; no mention was made of the senior officer or officers who apparently ordered them to drive at high speed into a stationary crowd. But demands grew for an end to the use by the Army of plastic bullets, which, between January and July 1981, killed at least five people.[22]

The Government was right to resist the demands for a return to 'special category' status. Both Republican and Loyalist organizations have been responsible for an appalling catalogue of murders, kidnappings, bombings and robberies. Some victims have died simply because they were of the wrong religion or lived in the wrong area, others because they were soldiers, police or prison officers or were, for some other reason, regarded as 'legitimate' targets. The loss of lives, the bereavements and the terror created among entire communities is the direct price of political violence. But the price has also been paid in the form of the operations of the security services, the imposition of emergency powers and the deaths of innocent people shot by soldiers.[23] There are circumstances in which the extent of repression and the impossibility of effecting change through peaceful political means justify insurrectionary violence as the only way of achieving or restoring human rights for the oppressed. But those circumstances did not exist in Northern Ireland. With the exception of those who have been convicted only of membership of an illegal organization and who are therefore 'political prisoners' (in the sense of having been imprisoned for their beliefs and associations), the prisoners who are calling for 'special category' status have been convicted of serious offences, violent or otherwise. The process of their conviction is indeed open to rigorous criticism: but the solution to the problem is to restore the normal process of criminal justice, not to entrench the special courts by giving special status to those convicted in them. (It should also be noted that the prisoners have no claim under international law[24] to 'special category' status.)

There is, however, a very strong case for compromise on the prisoners' 'five demands'. Particularly as women prisoners throughout the United Kingdom are already allowed to wear their own clothes, there is no reason why men should not be given the same right. Compulsory prison work, at derisory wages, is an unjustified infringement of the rights of those whose freedom has already been ended. Adequate provisions for education, for association with other prisoners and for contact with the outside world through visits and letters should form part of any humane penal system. The European Human Rights Commission, which in 1980 rejected the prisoners' complaints of inhuman and degrading treatment, nonetheless strongly criticized 'the inflexible approach of the state authorities, which has been concerned more to punish offenders against prison discipline than to explore ways of resolving such a serious deadlock'.[25] Presumably in the hope of strengthening its position against those who wanted no compromise with the prisoners, the Northern Ireland Office gave a surprising amount of publicity to the Commission's criticisms; and, as Provisional Sinn Fein itself said, the settlement which was reached before Christmas 1980 apparently resolved virtually all the differences between the prisoners and the authorities. It is not yet clear why that settlement broke down: but those who refused to implement the agreement, or to introduce an appropriate programme of reforms for *all* prisoners, bear a heavy responsibility for the deaths which have followed both inside and outside the Maze Prison.

A Bill of Rights?

Given the history of discrimination against the minority and the use of emergency powers against members of both communities, it is not surprising that support for a Bill of Rights, at least during the last decade, has been widespread in Northern Ireland. In 1972 both the Ulster Unionist Party and the Alliance Party made proposals for a Bill of Rights, which were also referred to in the Government's Discussion Paper *The Future of Northern Ireland*, published that year. In 1975 the Northern Ireland Civil Rights Association (NICRA) and the Ulster Citizens' Civil Liberties Centre (UCCLC) each published a detailed model for a Bill of Rights. The NICRA proposal[26] dealt in particular detail with emergency powers – for instance, by restricting the powers of the security forces to collect information, to search private premises and to seize property, by outlawing internment and by providing safeguards for suspects, including the right to see a lawyer in detention. The UCCLC model,[27] although outlawing some features of emergency powers, acknowledged the need for some departure from basic standards in times of serious violence.

The Government responded by inviting the Standing Advisory Commission on Human Rights to consider whether or not a Bill of Rights should be introduced and, if so, in what form. In an excellent report[28] published in 1977, the Commission recommended the introduction of a Bill of Rights for the whole of the United Kingdom, while accepting that if such a proposal were to prove unacceptable, legislation should be introduced for Northern Ireland alone. The Bill of Rights, which would incorporate the standards of the European Human Rights Convention, would take precedence over all other legislation unless Parliament specifically stated in a later enactment that its provisions were to override those of the Bill of Rights. The merits of this and other proposals for a new Bill of Rights are discussed in detail in chapter 10. At this stage it should be stated that a Bill of Rights could never be a substitute for political change. No Bill of Rights, for instance, could put an end to emergency powers as long as the Westminster Government remains committed to the use of such powers. A Bill of Rights, providing a pledge of minimum and equal rights for both communities in Northern Ireland, will have to be part of any new political structure, but it cannot solve the problem of what political structure or what kind of government that should be. No Bill of Rights, whether for the United Kingdom as a whole or for Northern Ireland alone, has yet been enacted, and the focus of debate has shifted, rightly, from that issue to the broader question of a new political initiative.

The Prevention of Terrorism Act

Neither terrorism nor emergency powers have been confined to Northern Ireland. In November 1974 twenty-one people died after two bombs exploded in Birmingham pubs. The fury of the public, which had taken rather limited notice of the years of violence on the other side of the Irish Sea, led to demands for a restoration of capital punishment and a ban on the IRA. On 28 November the then Home Secretary, Roy Jenkins, responded to the demand that the Government 'do something' by introducing the Prevention of Terrorism Bill, which was rushed through all its parliamentary stages in little over twenty-four hours.

The 1974 Act (now replaced by the 1976 Act) banned the IRA and gave the Home Secretary the power to add other groups to the schedule of proscribed organizations. The Irish National Liberation Army is the only other group to have been banned, after claiming responsibility for the murder of Airey Neave, Conservative spokesman on Northern Ireland, shortly before the May 1979 election. The Act created new offences of membership of, or support for, a proscribed organization, which were extended by the 1976 Act to support for 'terrorism' itself (even though 'terrorism', as such, is not a criminal offence). Proscription was largely a cosmetic exercise, designed to placate public opinion. The police, apparently, had argued that bans made it more difficult to keep an eye on those who might become involved in terrorist crime, and only thirty-six people have been charged with offences under this part of the Act, twenty-seven having been convicted. But the bans offend against the principle that people should be punished for their actions and not for their beliefs or their associations with others. They serve no overriding public purpose, and, the offensiveness of certain views, however repugnant they may be to the majority of people, is not a sufficiently compelling reason for making it a crime to hold or express those views.

Second, the Act gave the police a new power to detain those 'reasonably' suspected of being involved in the commission, preparation or instigation of acts of terrorism. 'Terrorism' is defined throughout the Act as the use of violence for political ends – a definition wide enough to include, for instance, the demonstrator who assaults a police officer, or a trade unionist, on a mass picket where violence occurs. Nor is the test of 'reasonable suspicion' any safeguard against random arrest. Someone arrested under the Act may be detained, on police authority, for up to forty-eight hours and, with the Home Secretary's consent, for a further five days. Thus the Act nullifies the provision that a suspect should be brought before a court as soon as practicable after being charged. But the period between arrest and charge had never been controlled, and it was not uncommon, even before the introduction of the Act, for suspects in serious cases to be held for days on end before being charged or released. In that sense, the Act legitimized previous malpractice; but it also abolished the residual safeguard of *habeas corpus*, since the Home Secretary's consent (which has never been refused) is sufficient to make detention lawful. Nor is the detention power restricted to cases in which a person is suspected of involvement in terrorism *relating to Northern Ireland*. The Home Secretary has stated[29] that an extension of the detention period would be authorized only 'where a connection with terrorism related to Northern Irish affairs is established or suspected'. But there is nothing to prevent the arrest and detention for up to two days of those who have no connection at all with Northern Ireland, and nothing to prevent the Home Secretary from changing his policy and permitting the detention of such people for up to seven days.

In Northern Ireland these detention powers were added to those which the security forces already had under the Emergency Provisions Act. It seems that the RUC had little use for the new law. Between September 1977 and the end of August 1978, for instance, 2814 people were held under the earlier powers, compared with only 156 under the Prevention of Terrorism Act. It would appear[30] that in Northern Ireland the more extensive detention powers are used in cases in which the police have a particular wish for lengthy interrogation. Nearly half of those held under the Prevention of Terrorism laws in Northern Ireland were then charged with a criminal offence, and of those charged, over 90 per cent were held for over forty-eight hours.

In Britain, however, the detention powers have been used for the widescale harassment of people connected, often very remotely, with Irish affairs and for low-level information gathering; only a tiny proportion of detainees have been brought before the courts. Between November 1974 and the end of June 1981 5191 people were arrested and detained. Most were released after forty-eight hours, 694 (or 13.4 per cent) being held for an extended period. Only 352 (or 6.8 per cent) were charged with a criminal offence, seventy-six of those being charged only with an offence under the Act itself (typically, support for 'terrorism' or for a proscribed organization).[31] Those charged with serious offences (including murder and firearms offences) could, of course, have been arrested under normal police powers without resort to the Act.

The most deplorable feature of the Act is the exclusion power given to the Home Secretary and the Secretary of State for Northern Ireland. Under the 1974 Act a United Kingdom citizen born in Northern Ireland could be banned from living in England, Scotland or Wales by being restricted to the province; a citizen of another country could be excluded from the United Kingdom altogether. Protests from Ulster Unionist MPs at the one-way nature of the traffic in alleged terrorists led to the introduction, in 1976, of a power to exclude from Northern Ireland to Great Britain, a power which has never been used. The power to exclude is available against a person who, the Secretary of State believes, has been, or might be, involved in the commission, preparation or instigation of acts of terrorism, and people in connection with whom exclusion would be 'expedient in order to prevent acts of terrorism'. A person born in Britain, who has lived there all his life, may not be excluded to Northern Ireland, nor may someone who has lived in Britain for the last twenty years.

Like internment, exclusion denies the principles of the rule of law. The excludee is not charged with a criminal offence. He has no right to know the evidence against him. He has no right to a trial, nor to an appeal against the decision. He may make 'representations' to a Government-appointed 'adviser', who may be in the same state of ignorance as the excludee about the police case. The decision is taken in secret by the police, Home Office officials and the Minister. Between November 1974 and June 1981 310 applications for exclusion orders were made, of which 272 were accepted. Twenty-four exclusion orders have been revoked, some following a review of longer-standing exclusions instituted after Lord Shackleton's inquiry into the operation of the Act.[32] The majority of excludees (213) have been sent to Northern Ireland.

If the excludees are indeed men of violence who are involved in terrorist crime, then their exclusion to Northern Ireland is an extraordinary policy for a Government of the United Kingdom to adopt. The removal of allegedly dangerous suspects to that part of the United Kingdom which has suffered most from terrorism is in direct contradiction to the purpose of exclusion contained in the Act – the *prevention* of acts of terrorism. In fact, there is no evidence at all that most excludees have been involved in terrorist activity. Of all those returned to Northern Ireland, only one has subsequently been arrested and charged with an offence. The real targets of exclusion seem to have been those politically active in the Republican cause, including most of the leading members of Clann n'ha Eireann. Many of the excludees have been forced to separate themselves from their families, who are unwilling or unable to make a new life in Northern Ireland. Exclusion has in fact created a system of internal exile by executive order, a system which the Government itself condemns when applied in the Soviet Union but which the majority of British MPs and most of the British press condone in this country.

The use of exclusion orders, and the powers of extended detention have been challenged in a series of cases to the European Human Rights Commission.

The future

I have tried to give only the briefest account of the civil rights movement and the subsequent attempt to defend civil liberties against terrorism and against the emergency state built up by successive Governments at Westminster. A full history of the last two decades remains to be written. Some of the reforms sought by the civil rights movement have been achieved – but through direct rule, not through the transformation of elected institutions in the province. The worst excesses of the first half of the 1970s (internment, massive house-to-house searches, the 'screening' of large sections of the population) have ended, but the decade's conflict has created a settled determination within the minority community not to be governed by Westminster or Stormont and a willingness to support, or at least to protect, the Republican paramilitary groups. The Government has exhorted the community to return to democratic politics but was appalled by the result of the Fermanagh and South Tyrone by-election, which demonstrated the willingness of the Catholic community to turn out and vote for the hunger-striker who was the only anti-Unionist and anti-British candidate. The support commanded by the hunger-strikers has been illustrated, too, by the willingness and ability of mourners in Derry and Belfast to protect masked and armed Provisional IRA men who have fired salutes over the coffins of dead hunger-strikers.

Within the Protestant community the old Unionist monolith has been irrevocably broken. With the Unionist parties divided, Ian Paisley has emerged as the key political leader. The Ulster Defence Association (UDA), notorious for its involvement in earlier sectarian warfare, has established a political wing, the Ulster Political Research Centre, committed not to the Union but to independence for Northern Ireland. Its proposals have received little support, and the discovery of arms in UDA offices in May 1981 suggests that terrorist activity may once again take over from political initiatives.

The alternatives for British policy in Northern Ireland were set out by Professor Richard Rose some five years ago:[33] continued direct rule from Westminster, an independent Northern Ireland, reunification with Southern Ireland, the destruction of Northern Ireland (for instance, through repartition), and self-government within the United Kingdom. With the addition of some form of self-governing Northern Ireland, associated in a loose federation with Britain and the Republic, these remain the options available today. It must be clear by now that Britain cannot continue its attempt to impose civil government in Northern Ireland. In 1980 it was perhaps possible to envisage a gradual, if uneasy, process of normalization, with a continuing reduction in troop levels and activity, further amendments to the Emergency Provisions Act, improved structures of accountability for the police, possibly some increase in local government powers. But the Army rightly warned that victory over the Provisional IRA was impossible and that its highly disciplined cell structure made the detection of offenders extremely difficult. The Mountbatten murders amply illustrated the Provisional IRA's lethal abilities, while an analysis of Republicans convicted of scheduled offences has shown that the Provisional IRA can continue to recruit young, often unemployed, working-class men and women to its cause. The polarization in Northern Ireland caused by the hunger strikes and the rallying to Ian Paisley on the one hand and to the Provisional IRA on the other, together with the threat to the stability of the Irish Government posed by the hunger-strikers' campaign, suggests strongly that no normalization is likely. The continuation of direct rule will mean a permanent commitment of troops, a permanent structure of emergency powers, permanent subsidies on a large scale, all punctuated by serious rioting and deaths. That is the answer to those who argue that there is no alternative to direct rule as long as Northern Ireland remains part of the United Kingdom and no alternative to the Union as long as a majority of the population in Northern Ireland support it. The price of the Union is direct rule, and the price of direct rule, in terms of people's lives, is too high.

But withdrawal is not, by itself, an acceptable option. The Republic cannot impose civil government in Northern Ireland any more than can Westminster. The withdrawal of British troops would trigger off massive fighting between Protestant and Republican paramilitaries, the former considerably more numerous and better armed. The outcome could well be the establishment of an independent Protestant Northern Ireland with somewhat different boundaries and the prospect of continuing border fighting, if not worse, within Ireland.

The priority now must be the creation of a constitutional forum in which political discussion and negotiation about options for the future could take place. The political problems associated with any such initiative are immense: to persuade the paramilitary organizations to take part in talks rather than to step up the conflict, and to involve the Dublin Government without setting off the civil war (or even the unilateral declaration of independence) which an immediate announcement of withdrawal would provoke. For this reason the British Government cannot rule out the possibility of some form of self-government in Northern Ireland. But any new constitutional arrangement must provide what the 1920 Government of Ireland Act tragically failed to achieve: tough guarantees of basic rights for the minority as well as for the majority community, together with accessible and representative institutions to enforce them. That challenge will be just as crucial in a united Ireland as under any other constitutional settlement.

7

The Other Half

⌊The rights and freedoms of 'the freeborn Englishman' have generally been the prerogative of men⌋ Despite the attempts of early feminists to assert the rights of women,[1] it is only in the last fifty years that women in this country have begun to achieve their claim to full citizenship.⌊Even now the rights of women are not always regarded as a civil liberties issue⌋ (Two recently published civil liberties casebooks omit the subject altogether.)[2]⌊And yet it is absurd to speak of the achievement of human rights if half of humanity is to be omitted⌋ Women's acquisition of citizenship is a landmark in the struggle for civil liberties: and by 'citizenship' I mean not only the literal right to acquire and transmit citizenship on equal terms but also the acquisition of full legal capacity, of full participation in the rights and duties of citizenship. The economic, legal, financial and social status of women is a key measure of the extent to which a society takes human rights seriously.

I shall concentrate in this chapter on women's *legal* status. The inequalities of women are not merely reflected in discriminatory legal provisions: as Sachs and Wilson[3] have cogently demonstrated, the structures of legal thinking and of the legal profession are deeply flawed by sexism.⌊The struggle for legislative reform to remove disabilities imposed on women has been counter-pointed by judicial decisions which reinforce male prejudice⌋ In their discussion of the series of cases in which, from 1873 onwards, women tried to establish their claim to be included in the judicial definition of 'persons', Sachs and Wilson comment:

> What was self-evident truth to feminists . . . was manifest absurdity to most of the judges. Far from viewing the women as victims of oppressive and capricious behaviour, they treated them with varying degrees of courtesy as misguided attention seekers, much as members of the women's liberation movement would be treated by most men today.[4]

Indeed, in July 1981 a claim by two feminists under the Sex Discrimination Act against a wine bar which persisted in refusing to serve women at the bar was rejected by a county court judge (not one of the bar's many judicial customers) on the grounds that no 'reasonable' woman would object to such treatment and that women's rights activists were clearly not 'reasonable' people.[5]

It was not until 1926 that women acquired the vote on equal terms with men. But the vote did not bring with it other significant changes in women's legal position. Despite the Sex Disqualification (Removal) Act of 1919, women remained effectively barred from access to, and promotion in, many jobs, while continuing to be paid less than men even for those jobs that they shared. The retention of the property qualification for jury service meant that few women could serve. Transmission of citizenship to a child continued to pass only through the male. The father remained legal guardian of his legitimate children, while the mother's domicile was determined by that of her husband. It was another forty years, during which a new women's movement gained momentum, before further substantial legislative reform was won.

In 1970 the Matrimonial Proceedings and Property Act recognized that a woman who had been at home, caring for husband and children, should become entitled to a share of the family home and property even when, as was generally the case, these were owned by the man. In 1973 the married woman became equal guardian of her children and was entitled to acquire her own domicile, independent of that of her husband. In 1976 the Domestic Violence Act enabled a woman to obtain an injunction against a violent husband without commencing divorce proceedings, while the Sexual Offences (Amendment) Act 1976 provided anonymity for victims of rape and placed some restrictions on cross-examination of a woman about previous sexual experience. But legal changes have done little to transform the prejudices of those who administer them. Despite the 1970 Act, divorce judges have often returned to the earlier formula of giving the wife only one-third of the joint family income and property, while magistrates are generally reluctant to use their new powers against violent husbands or cohabitees without proof of repeated injury to the woman. And the 1967 Abortion Act, although removing from women and their doctors the threat of prosecution for an abortion performed with two doctors' consent on specified grounds, failed to ensure that abortion counselling and provision was available

through the National Health Service throughout the country.[6]
∟ Among the most basic constitutional provisions of any country's laws are the definitions of a citizen and of a taxpayer. In both cases British women remain second-class.⸝

It is generally accepted that a British man has the right to marry, to bring his wife to live with him in his own country and to extend his citizenship to her and to their children. As we will see in chapter 8, these rights are in practice persistently denied to black British men. But there is no acceptance, even in principle, that women should exercise such rights. Until 1969 a woman born or settled in this country had been able to bring a foreign-born fiancé or husband to join her here, although there was no statutory recognition of her right to do so. In that year, as part of the Labour Government's panic-stricken attempt to curb migration of black and Asian men, the then Home Secretary, James Callaghan, introduced new Immigration Rules which barred fiancés and husbands from Commonwealth countries. The 1971 Immigration Act extended the ban to Commonwealth and foreign fiancés and husbands other than those in exceptional compassionate circumstances, a proviso of which very few were able to take advantage. In 1974 the new Labour Government was persuaded to drop the ban and to restore to women settled in this country the right to be joined by a fiancé or husband, although an entry visa continued to be required for husbands (but not for foreign wives). But in 1976, bowing to racist scares of 'marriages of convenience', the Home Secretary introduced a new rule which gave immigration officers the power to refuse entry clearance to a man suspected of using marriage in order to avoid immigration control. A foreign husband was only to be admitted, if at all, for twelve months, after which settlement could be refused if suspicion of a marriage of convenience had arisen.

The Conservative election manifesto of May 1979 promised a withdrawal of this 'concession' to foreign husbands. After a sustained campaign, supported not only by women's groups, black organizations, the churches and the Labour movement but also by some Conservative MPs and Conservative women, the Government retreated, finally imposing a ban on the fiancés or husbands of women who were not themselves born in this country and neither of whose parents were born here. Even then the Home Secretary retained a discretion which, he assured backbench Conservative MPs, would benefit those (white) women whose foreign-born parents had been in Crown service. The result is that thousands of women, mainly of Asian origin, have been deprived of their right to be joined here by their fiancés or husbands, while others, although born in this country themselves, continue to be separated from their partners by the use of the discretionary power to reject alleged marriages of convenience.

In early 1981 a number of cases of women affected by the new rules were submitted to the European Human Rights Commission by NCCL and the Joint Council for the Welfare of Immigrants on the grounds that the women had been deprived of their right to marry and to found a family, that the rule was racially discriminatory and that, because it could not be justified by reference to the needs of immigration policy, it was inhuman and degrading. There is little doubt that the Commission and (if the Government insists on referring the case for further consideration) the Human Rights Court will find in favour of the women applicants,[7] but the years of separation and hardship suffered by the couples involved concerned will be added to the record of this country's shameful treatment of minority women.

The discriminatory provisions of immigration law are compounded by citizenship law. Under the 1948 British Nationality Act a foreign woman who married a United Kingdom male citizen acquired a right to take his citizenship, even after divorce. But a foreign husband had no similar right, being required to apply for naturalization after five years' residence. As long as the man could obtain entry to this country and settle here, the acquisition of citizenship was not, in most cases, a problem, although the absolute power of the Home Secretary to refuse naturalization left some foreign husbands unable to obtain employment and permanently at risk of deportation. The new barriers to settlement by a foreign husband make the problems of acquiring citizenship even more important. The obvious solution – to extend to British women the right of British men to transmit citizenship to a spouse – was rejected by both the 1974 Labour Government and the 1979 Conservative Government on the usual ground that such a measure would encourage marriages of convenience. (It should be noted that no Government has been able to provide evidence that more than a handful of such marriages ever take place;[8] that if the right to citizenship were to result in fake marriages, there would be some evidence of a number of foreign women acquiring British citizenship through such means; and that the willingness to allow a foreign wife to acquire citizenship while denying the same citizenship to a foreign husband assumes that the foreign man is more important or more dangerous a threat.)

The 1981 British Nationality Act has removed the right of a foreign wife to acquire citizenship on marriage. Instead, any foreign spouse may apply for naturalization after three years' residence. Although the Government has repeatedly claimed that the new provision is not sex-discriminatory, it is, in fact a classic example of indirect discrimination, which, in employment and other fields, is outlawed under the Sex Discrimination Act. In other words, the apparently equal provision of the Nationality Act has quite different effects on the two sexes. Because the Immigration Rules make it impossible for some foreign husbands to achieve residence, their 'right' to apply for naturalization under the Nationality Act is meaningless. Furthermore, the retention of the Home Secretary's discretion to refuse naturalization without providing reasons (and an applicant has no right of appeal against his decision) will permit civil servants and Ministers to refuse citizenship, even to those who qualify on residence grounds, because of race or sex prejudice.

Like citizenship and immigration law, the laws on social security and income tax continue to reflect and to perpetuate the notion of breadwinner husband and dependent wife. Until 1977 a married woman in employment could opt out of insurance cover for sickness, unemployment, maternity and retirement and could rely instead on her husband's contributions. The removal of this option and the institution of equality of contributions was followed some years later by equality of benefits: the lower rate of sickness and unemployment benefit for married women was abolished, and from 1972 a married woman who received benefit became entitled to additions for her dependent children on the same terms as her husband. But an addition for a dependent husband is paid only if the husband is 'incapable of self-support', despite the fact that a married man claiming benefit can obtain an addition for his 'dependent' wife even if she is earning herself (although if her earnings are above a prescribed limit, the addition is correspondingly reduced). Even these changes were forced on the British Government by the EEC Directive on equality of treatment in social security schemes, which will not come fully into force until 1984. The Directive will not, however, affect the continued application of the cohabitation rule, which prevents a woman living with a man 'as husband and wife' from claiming supplementary benefits in her own right.

The 1975 Social Security Pensions Act took a considerable step forward in equalizing retirement benefits for men and women. Its most radical provision is the 'home responsibilities' protection, under which pension rights earned by a man or woman while in employment are fully preserved during periods spent at home caring for children or other dependent relatives: twenty years' paid employment will be sufficient for a full pension once the scheme comes fully into effect in 1998. But the scheme cannot be completely non-discriminatory. It preserves unequal retirement ages, under which women may – and are often obliged to – receive a retirement pension at 60 but men are required to wait until the age of 65. By retaining the possibility of deferring retirement and earning an additional pension, the scheme allows a woman who manages to keep her job until 65 to earn a pension one-third *higher* than that of a man retiring at the same age with the same level of previous earnings. At a time of declining job opportunities, few women will benefit. But the linking of a substantial part of the pension to previous earnings (even with the proviso that only the twenty highest years' earnings will be counted) means that women's pensions will continue, on average, to be substantially lower than men's. Furthermore, occupational pension schemes, which are a major factor in the income of many retired men, continue to discriminate against women. Although equal access at the same age and on the same terms is required by the Equal Pay Act, schemes are not required to provide for women's dependants on the same terms as they provide for men's, while the fact that pension rights need only be preserved after five years' membership of the scheme excludes younger women in particular from receiving a pension eventually. Proposals for a new Sex Discrimination Bill that would extend the provisions of the 1975 Sex Discrimination Act to occupational pension schemes were shelved by the last Labour Government and have not been revived.

Income tax laws illustrate perhaps the crudest bias towards the married man. For tax purposes, the married man owns his wife's income, is responsible for paying the tax on it and, until recently, was entitled to receive any rebates due. In return for marriage, the man obtains a personal allowance which is substantially higher than that received by his wife or by a single person. The married woman, in contrast, may only receive the benefit of her tax allowance – claimed for her by her husband – if she is in employment. The higher tax allowance for the married man makes nonsense of equal pay laws, since a married woman earning the same as a married man takes home (at 1981/2 tax rates) £4.40 a week less after deduction of tax. Furthermore, the man's 'ownership' of his wife's income entitles him to receive all the tax relief due on a mortgage held in his wife's name – even when she makes all the mortgage repayments! Separate taxation of a wife's earnings (valuable only to the very well-off) and separate assessment of a couple's income (little publicized and claimed by few) do not remove the fundamental inequities of the system.

⌐A Green Paper on the taxation of married couples published in December 1980[9] reveals considerable reluctance on the part of the government to make any radical changes. Among the options described, the most favoured appears to be a system of 'transferable' allowances, under which a wife or husband without any income or with insufficient income to make full use of the personal tax allowance would be able to transfer part or all of the allowance to the wealthier spouse. Such a system would not only be extremely expensive (the Green Paper estimates a cost of £3 billion in a full year), but it would also benefit a spouse at home regardless of whether or not she or he had dependants to care for without providing him or her with any additional income (since the extra benefit of the tax allowance would go to the partner in employment). It would also make nonsense of the principle of treating each taxpayer as an independent individual, regardless of sex or marital status, which should be the fundamental principle of tax reforms in this area.⌐

Inequalities in the workplace

The underlying effects of sex inequalities – loss of self-esteem, fear of violence, the stunting of emotional development in both sexes – are impossible to measure, but the effect of inequalities in employment are all too visible: low pay, poverty, the waste of skills, a divided workforce. In 1970, when the Equal Pay Act was passed, women's average earnings, excluding the effect of overtime pay, were 63.1 per cent of men's. By 1977 the gap had narrowed to 73.5 per cent. But that progress has not been maintained; the most recent figures, those for 1979, show that women were earning on average only 73 per cent of men's earnings.[10]

The 1970 Act has now exhausted its usefulness. During the five years which were permitted to employers to reorganize their wage structures before the Act became enforceable through industrial tribunals and the Central Arbitration Committee (CAC), many of the sex-segregated pay scales were redrafted – sometimes to provide a genuinely integrated scheme but more often to preserve women's jobs at the bottom of a superficially non-discriminatory structure. For instance, in 1977 the CAC considered the case of a motor construction firm which paid the majority of its women employees the unskilled male rate, although they were semi-skilled workers. The male employees in the female-dominated bottom grade all received a higher personal wage than the women. The CAC ordered that the women be moved up a grade, pending a full job-evaluation scheme. Between 1975 and 1979 many such pay structures were successfully referred to the CAC, which used its power to rewrite pay structures, with separate men's and women's grades, to order employers to rise the lowest women's grade at least to the lowest male-dominated grade. But in 1979 the Court of Appeal overturned a CAC ruling of this kind,[11] ordering the CAC to operate only within a strict construction of its powers and to amend only explicitly segregated pay structures – of which, of course, very few remain.

Other than via an application to the CAC, the Act is enforceable through an individual complaint to an industrial tribunal, which may order an employer to pay a woman complainant the same wage as a man employed by the same firm who is doing the same or broadly similar work or work which has been rated as equivalent in a job-evaluation scheme. While some women have succeeded in such applications, the usefulness of the Act is severely restricted by the requirement that a woman compares her pay with the pay actually received by a man doing comparable work. Although job-evaluation schemes may be used to compare jobs which are entirely dissimilar in content, the woman who believes that she is unequally paid cannot insist on a job-evaluation scheme: she can rely on an existing scheme only if it has rated her job as equivalent to a higher-paid job held by a man. Although an industrial tribunal may overrule a job-evaluation scheme which is proven to be discriminatory (for instance, because it awards men higher points for the same skill), such a scheme is rarely proven to be unlawful. Nonetheless, these schemes often leave the majority of women employees at the bottom end of the pay scales. Thus in order to succeed in an equal pay claim, a woman must normally find a man doing the same or similar work as she herself is. And this is a test which most women simply cannot pass. In 1979 2 million women, over one-fifth of those in employment, were working in jobs wholly or mainly done by women.

Nearly half the female workforce is employed in part-time jobs. Its members suffer particularly from the inadequacies of legal protection. In one of the first cases brought under the equal pay and sex discrimination legislation, an agricultural worker, Mrs Meekes, complained of indirect discrimination on the grounds that her hourly pay rate as a part-time worker was less than that of the full-time workers. Because all the full-time workers were women, she could not establish a case under the Equal Pay Act, and since the Sex Discrimination Act does not deal with pay rates, she could not succeed in her complaint of indirect discrimination.[12] A similar complaint was brought by Mrs Jenkins, whose hourly rate was also less than that of male full-time workers doing the same job. The Court of Appeal held initially that the very fact that Mrs Jenkins was a part-timer was a 'material difference' which negated her claim to equal pay: the employer was entitled to pay her less, since employing part-timers made it more difficult to use the machinery to maximum efficiency [13] The case was, however, referred to the EEC Court of Justice in Luxembourg for a ruling on the provisions of the Treaty of Rome concerning equal pay. In June 1981 the Court of Justice held [14] that part-timers were not necessarily entitled to equal pay, provided that the employer could establish that economic criteria, and not sex, were the basis for the differential. The decision leaves the way open for employers to plead, as Mrs Jenkins's employers did, that they would not dream of discriminating against women; that part-timers were simply a less efficient means of organizing the workforce; and that it was pure coincidence that most or all of the part-timers were women. The Court of Appeal had not ruled, at the time of writing, on how the Court of Justice decision would affect Mrs Jenkins's application.

The deficiencies of the equal-pay legislation are now clear. Because many women work in women-only jobs, no comparison with similar work done by men is available. Although a job-evaluation scheme may provide a means of overcoming this problem, a woman claiming equal pay cannot insist that her employer and union undertake a job-evaluation exercise: and, in any case, such a scheme certainly would not guarantee an upgrading of women's wages. Part-time workers – who are almost all women and who account for nearly half the female workforce – may be paid a lower hourly rate, and in most cases the law provides no redress. The power of the CAC to intervene in wage structures which are discriminatory in practice, if not in name, has been severely curtailed. And the only other route open to women in low-paid, segregated work (to claim the 'going rate' for the job in a particular area or industry through an application to the CAC) was abolished by the 1980 Employment Act.

Despite the submission of detailed proposals for amending the legislation by the Equal Opportunities Commission (EOC) and the Trades Union Congress, the only prospect for amendments by the present Government comes from the EEC. Article 119 of the Treaty of Rome, which requires equal pay for work of equal value, is binding on all member states. Direct access to the Court of Justice is therefore available, even where domestic legislation provides no effective remedy. In 1981 the EOC supported a complaint by women employed at Lloyds Bank, which operated a discriminatory system of arrangements for younger workers' contributions to the bank's occupational pension scheme. The Court of Justice's finding in favour of the women [15] was the first case in which employers were faced with a very considerable bill in order to remedy their discrimination.

Even more important, the Commission of the EEC, after investigating member states' compliance with Article 119 and with the Directive on equal pay, issued a 'reasoned opinion' to the United Kingdom Government to the effect that the 1970 Act, by failing to provide for equal pay for work of equal value except under the extremely limited provisions for job-evaluation schemes, is in breach of the Treaty of Rome. Although the 'reasoned opinion' is itself confidential, it is known that the Government has rejected the Commission's view, thus challenging the Commission itself to commence proceedings in the Court of Justice against the United Kingdom.

The fundamental problem revealed by the failure of the Equal Pay Act is that of job segregation. As we have already noted, most women work in women-dominated employment. This concentration of women in a few areas of the job market – primarily unskilled and semi-skilled manufacturing jobs in the distribution and catering trades and the clerical and technical services – has intensified since the early years of this century. In 1911 the proportion of women and men in clerical and secretarial work reflected their proportions in the labour force as a whole: by 1970 those jobs were largely the women's preserve. The 1975 Sex Discrimination Act was designed to tackle the problems of low expectations, inadequate training and intense job segregation which lay behind the continuing problems of women's lower pay.

The task of equipping girls with the skills and confidence to move into new and better-paid areas of work begins in the schools. Sex discrimination is no longer as crude as it was in 1961, when local education authorities provided 69p for science facilities for each grammar-school boy but only 57p for each girl. The Act outlawed both direct and indirect discrimination by local education authorities, boards of governors and teachers, although single-sex schools were permitted to remain in existence. A 1975 Department of Education survey revealed widespread segregation in time-tabling, and, despite complaints to the EOC, the Act has not abolished the practice of timetabling 'boys' subjects' and 'girls' subjects' simultaneously. Allowing one girl to opt to move into a woodwork or technical drawing class or allowing one boy to move into a girls' needlework or cookery class neither encourages equality of opportunity nor enables both girls and boys to acquire the range of skills which they will need as parents and as workers. (Unfortunately, the first case which would have challenged simultaneous timetabling was abandoned after delays in obtaining finance meant that the girl concerned had left school before the case would have been heard.)

Sex stereotyping of subjects is reflected in General Certificate of Education 'Ordinary' Level results. In 1975, for instance, boys obtained 61 per cent of maths passes (grades A to C), 58 per cent of physics passes and 98 per cent of technical drawing passes; girls obtained 58 per cent of French passes and 98 per cent of those in cookery. Since technical drawing, for instance, is often a prerequisite for an apprenticeship leading to skilled employment, the vast majority of girls are effectively excluded from a wide range of higher-paid jobs even before they leave school. Programmes for unemployed school-leavers could have compensated for some of these deficiencies. They have not done so. In 1977, when half the unemployed 16–17-year-olds were girls, only one-fifth of the job-creation placements went to girls, although girls did get 46 per cent of the community industry placements. Of the 25,000 people who qualified from skill centres in 1978, less than 1000 were women. Nor has the retraining of older women done much to affect the traditional segregation of the workforce. Of the 41,000 women who completed training in 1977 under the Training Opportunities Scheme, 76 per cent trained for traditionally female occupations in courses such as typing and office skills.

The 1975 Act has so far had little effect on the under-representation of women on day-release, in industrial appren-ticeships and in other forms of training for non-traditional work. The Act only requires employers and training organizations not to discriminate, directly or indirectly, against someone applying for a job, for training or for promotion. But a woman cannot successfully complain of unlawful discrimination if she is not qualified for a particular job or if she does not have the prerequisite school results for a particular training programme. Nor can the use of individual complaints to enforce the Act tackle the problem that low expectations, fear of discrimination and an entirely justified fear of the treatment that a lone woman will receive from a male workforce prevent the majority of women from considering training for a job in, say, engineering, the construction industry or vehicle maintenance.

Potentially the most far-reaching of the Act's provisions is its ban on unjustifiable, indirect discrimination. In the case of Belinda Price, a 35-year-old mother who was refused employment at the Civil Service Executive Officer grade, it was held that the age limit of 28 applied equally to men and to women, who were particularly likely to be out of employment in their twenties and thirties while caring for small children.[16] Since the age limit could not be justified as necessary for workforce planning or for training and promotion, the Civil Service was required to redraw the age limit, which was raised to 45 in 1980. The provisions on indirect discrimination would, therefore, make it possible to challenge other requirements – such as mobility conditions, lengthy residential training or a condition that a foreman must have worked on night shifts – which disqualify many women from certain jobs. Unfortunately, too little use has been made of this section of the Act, either as the basis for legal action or in trade union negotiations.

In recognition of the fact that more is needed to balance the effects of centuries of inequality, the Act also permits positive discrimination by employers, training organizations and trade unions; special courses can be run for women in fields in which they have previously been under-represented or, as has been arranged by a few trade unions, seats may be reserved for women on a national executive committee. But there is no compulsion to provide for positive action, and the relevant provisions of the Act have barely been used. By contrast, in the United States of America, affirmative-action programmes require institutions and companies receiving federal funds to analyse their hiring and personnel policies and the composition of their workforce and to draw up programmes to increase the representation of women and minority-group workers in jobs in which they have been under-represented. By establishing goals and timetables (but not quotas) institutions are encouraged to implement special requirements, to undertake training programmes, to redesign jobs in order to provide opportunities for people lacking recognized qualifications and to make efforts to provide in-service training for people locked into dead-end jobs. The problems encountered in implementing equal opportunities laws in the United States should not be underestimated: women's earnings, as a proportion of men's, have actually declined in the last two decades. Nonetheless, affirmative-action programmes have assisted many women in overcoming the barrier of segregation, particularly in middle-management grades and in some non-traditional craft jobs.

As positive-action programmes are developed in this country, they may be expected to generate a controversy similar to that which arose in the USA over cases like *Bakke,* when it was argued, on the one hand, that discrimination on grounds of race was never permissible and, on the other hand, that without positive 'race-conscious'- policies previous discrimination would never be overcome. (I have touched on this debate elsewhere: see page 214.) But it is clear that positive-action programmes are here to stay. Both the Trades Union Congress and the NCCL have held major conferences designed to develop detailed proposals on recruitment, promotion and training policies based on a comprehensive analysis of the position of women employees in a particular firm and a programme of targets designed to reduce job segregation and pay inequalities. Financed by the EOC, the NCCL has initiated pilot positive-action projects. In Thames Television, for instance, an NCCL consultant on positive action was seconded to the company to undertake a detailed survey of the workforce and to hold a series of lengthy discussions with women workers. Her report, which recommended in particular the appointment of a women's employment officer and special measures to train women for technical posts, was largely accepted by the managing directors, while a special women's committee was established to monitor the programme's implementation. A pilot project in a major clearing bank has been undertaken by Professor Nancy Seear of the London School of Economics, in which considerable stress is placed on the need to keep women in touch with their former employers and with developments in the banking world while they are out of work, caring for small children.

The problems raised by special measures for women were also at issue in the proposed repeal of protective legislation which restricts the total number of hours worked and prohibits night work by manual women workers in factories. When the Sex Discrimination Bill was introduced, there was considerable pressure from the

Confederation of British Industries for repeal, and in 1979 the EOC recommended that most of the restrictions be abolished. The EOC argued that by denying women the opportunity to increase their earnings with shift premiums and overtime pay and by banning them from jobs which required night work, the protective legislation led to discrimination; that the legislation could not be extended to men without complete disruption to industry; that the laws restricted women's freedom to arrange their work at home and in the factory to suit themselves; and that its continued existence was incompatible with the principle of sex equality.

But the arguments in favour of repeal are less convincing than they may appear at first sight. Men and women are not equal in the home or in the job market. Most employed women continue to do a second job at home, carrying the prime responsibility for looking after children and the home. The repeal of protective legislation would leave many women faced with a choice between working antisocial hours or losing their jobs. The EOC itself admits that some women would be dismissed for refusing to accept new working arrangements, and those women would be unprotected by the laws against unfair dismissal. The protective laws do need amendment, but this should be designed to extend their benefits to men wherever possible (for instance, in the provision of meal breaks and rest periods) and to provide both men and women workers with more control over the hours they work.

The EOC has said that abolition of the protective laws should be accompanied by new provisions for employed parents, such as increased maternity and paternity leave, and a major expansion of child-care facilities, proposals which are quite unlikely to be implemented in the present economic climate. As long ago as 1965 it was estimated[17] that 1 million mothers required day-care places for their under-5s and that over 1 million needed out-of-school places for their over-5s. In 1974 64 per cent of mothers wanted some form of day care for their under-5s,[18] while a survey of three inner-city areas in London found that 90 per cent of mothers wanted day care for their 3- and 4-year-olds. But local authority targets for day-care places remain 8 per 1000 under-5s; priority waiting lists included 12,601 children in 1976. In 1973 only 29 per cent of children under 5 received some form of child care, including those places with childminders, and the proportion is unlikely to be any higher now. Without a massive expansion of resources to meet the needs of both children and their parents, and without a change of attitude on the part of employers, fathers and the community generally enabling and encouraging fathers to share the task of looking after children, anti-discrimination laws are unlikely to make more than a dent in the problem of women in employment.

The assumption that women's chief task in life is to bear and bring up children – the assumption from which legal, economic and social inequalities spring – now has nothing to do with reality. As Richard Titmuss pointed out nearly thirty years ago,[19] the average working-class woman at the turn of this century could expect to spend some fifteen years pregnant or nursing her youngest child. By the time the youngest left school, her life expectancy was only 15 years. By 1955 (some years before the introduction of the oral contraceptive, to which so many changes in the position of women are wrongly attributed) the average time spent pregnant or nursing a child had been reduced to about four years, while the woman who had completed bringing up her family still had another 30 years ahead of her. The realization of equal rights means not only that the care of children should no longer be used as an excuse to maintain women's legal and financial dependency and to relegate them to the least skilled, lowest-paid sectors of the job market, but also that the care of children should be shared by men.

But the reality still in Britain is that poverty and powerlessness are women-dominated conditions. By 1986 half the workforce will be women, most of them married. Women's earnings already support, wholly or partly, one in six non-pensioner households, while the number of families living below the poverty level would be trebled if it were not for women's earnings. Yet low pay is almost entirely women's pay. In 1978, for instance, nearly half of the employed women were earning less than £50 a week, compared with only 10 per cent of men – at a time when average full-time earnings were £86.90. The majority of poor pensioners, who form one of the largest groups of those living in poverty, are women, as are the majority of single parents dependent on welfare benefits. Unemployment among women is growing at nearly twice the rate of that among men, while the services most threatened by public-sector spending cuts – education, social services and health care – are those in which a high proportion of women are employed and on which women particularly rely for assistance with the care of children and other dependent relatives. Despite legal reforms in the status of women – reforms which, as we have seen, have not yet encompassed such basic questions as citizenship and taxation – women are derisorily under-represented in Parliament, on official bodies, in the professions and in other higher-paid jobs and in the leadership of the trade union movement. Women will not be able to achieve equal rights and status through changes in the law and at the workplace as long as they are left with the main responsibility of caring for children and other dependants and maintaining the home. Better maternity-leave provisions and the massive expansion of child-care facilities, although urgently needed, will alleviate but not solve the problem. Equality between the sexes demands a radical alteration in the organization of work in the home and outside it, so that men as well as women take a full part in caring for the family, and women as well as men are enabled to gain access to the full range of employment opportunities and to play a full part in trade union and political activities.

8

Free and Equal?

The persecution of racial and religious minorities was the evil which, more than any other, international human rights standards were designed to combat. The opening provision of the Universal Declaration of Human Rights, 'All human beings are born free and equal in dignity and rights', echoes the far older wording of the Bill of Rights of the United States of America. But the enslavement of black Americans, permitted by the courts and Congress until 1865, is a telling reminder that apparently universal categories may be of narrow application. The United Kingdom subscribes not only to the Universal Declaration and the European Human Rights Convention but also to the International Covenant for the Elimination of Discrimination. British society's image of itself relies heavily on notions of tolerance and fair play, while the theory of the rule of law encompasses the central principle that all are equal before the law. Thus the treatment of racial minorities – in law, in administrative policy and in social practice – is a crucial test of the community's commitment to, and understanding of, its own legal norms as well as of international human rights standards. I shall argue in this chapter that those standards are utterly compromised by the almost casual acceptance of racism which is now an institutionalized part of British law and society.

Migration to and from this country is as old as the country's history. British culture, which, according to the Prime Minister, is in danger of being 'swamped' by 'immigrants', is a product of centuries of population movement: successive generations of conquerors and settlers from Scandinavia and the Continent; the colonial empire and trading relationships dating at least as far back as Tudor England; the deliberate policy of settling Protestants in Ireland; the influx of persecuted religious minorities, such as the Huguenots; the arrival of Jewish refugees during this century; the movement of Irish families seeking work; the emigration to and return from Commonwealth countries; and so on.

The debate about the 'problem of race relations' is not new. The first formal controls on immigration into this country were introduced in 1905 to keep out 'the most undesirable class of aliens in the Continent', 'the backward march of physical degeneration,' 'the people dumped down on this country because no other country will take them' – as the Honourable Members of the House of Commons and the Lords described the European Jews who were then settling in Britain.[1] Prime Minister Balfour claimed for this country 'a right to keep out everybody who does not add to the strength of the community – the industrial, social and intellectual strength of the community'. As Anne Dummett has pointed out, 'this last phrase rings ironically in the ears of anyone now even vaguely aware of the industrial, social and intellectual strength added to this country by the Jewish immigration of those years.'[2] If the rhetoric of parliamentarians in 1905 is perhaps more akin to the propaganda of the National Front now than to the language of parliamentary debates, then the terms of the 1914 debate on German immigration ('If we could get rid of those 200,000 aliens, probably we might relieve very considerably the housing difficulty in this country')[3] are all too familiar.

Debates about immigration in this country have always been debates about minorities. For the last twenty years the issue of immigration has never been far from the centre of public controversy. But the particular nature of the immigration debate must be understood. It has not, in fact, been a debate about immigration at all – about its extent or the policies which should govern its control. Increasingly rigorous immigration controls on black people and their families have been counterpointed by the removal of controls from a growing number of white people and their families. 'Immigration' has become a code word for 'black immigration' and 'immigrant' a substitute for 'black'. The propaganda of the neo-Fascist groups in Britain has concentrated almost entirely on the issue of immigration; their demand for the 'repatriation' of the black minorities – in other words, for the mass expulsion of people born or settled here – has now been taken up by some Conservative MPs.[4]

But the most pernicious contribution to the debate has come from this country's political leaders, for whom the conventional wisdom is that strict immigration controls are necessary to improve race relations. The 'tolerance' of the British people must not be over-stretched by the arrival of too many black or Asian migrants, they claim, but those black people who are here must be 'treated fairly'. Thus the development of immigration laws from 1962 onwards has been paralleled by the introduction of anti-discrimination laws and the creation first of the Race Relations Board and Community Relations Commission and later of the Commission for Racial Equality.

The official assumption that immigration controls help good race relations has been disastrous. First, the implied or explicit hostility of successive Governments, vociferously backed by the media, to migration from the West Indies and the Indian subcontinent (euphemistically named the 'new Commonwealth') has legitimized and encouraged racial prejudice within the rest of the community. Instead of campaigning against racism and stressing the evils to which racism gives rise and against which this country fought less than forty years ago, successive Ministers have encouraged white voters to believe that they are right to regard immigration as a problem, have praised their 'tolerance' while appealing to and inflaming their intolerance. Not surprisingly, efforts to reduce racial discrimination have had little chance of success.

The black minorities have suffered, directly and indirectly, from this official hypocrisy. West Indian mothers and Asian fathers who have settled in this country have found themselves forcibly separated from their families. Asian workers, many of them born in this country, find themselves faced with passport checks when they apply for jobs or the victims of passport raids aimed at illegal entrants. Increasingly, black citizens seeking official services, such as the use of the National Health Service, are required to prove their immigration status first.[5] The present Government's proposal to charge foreigners for the use of the National Health Service will only accelerate the tendency to treat black British citizens as if they were indeed foreigners. Michael Dummett has most eloquently summarized the impact of official policies on the minorities:

> Black people . . . see themelves constantly the target of attacks from
> the leaders of society, scarcely ever the object of appreciation,
> respect or sympathy. Naturally they feel alienated from the society
> in which they find themselves: told continually by the extremists
> that neither they nor their children can ever be accepted as English
> or British, treated by the rest as manifestly undesirable and
> unwelcome, they can hardly see that society as anything but hostile
> to them. In particular, the effect on those who directly experience

the harsh workings of the immigration controls which are supposed to ensure harmonious community relations should not be overlooked. It may appear to a white person that, in supporting a policy which means interminable delay and often unjust refusal for a family seeking to join the husband and father, he is doing his best for racial harmony: it will not strike a man who is prevented for years, and in many cases for ever, from being reunited with his family in this light; nor will it so strike those many whom he will tell of his agony.[6]

The development of immigration controls

The 1948 British Nationality Act created a single class of 'British subjects' or 'Commonwealth citizens' (the terms were interchangeable), all of whom had the right to come to the United Kingdom. Citizens of the United Kingdom and Colonies were only one of the categories included in British subject status, and the civic rights of United Kingdom citizens, including their right to live in this country, to vote, to stand for public office and to work in the public sector, depended not on their citizenship of the United Kingdom but on their being British subjects living in this country. Immigration control, which operated only against aliens, was still governed by laws introduced in 1905, 1914 and 1919.[7]

The policy of free entry from other Commonwealth countries to the 'mother country' was of considerable assistance during the decade after the war, when the economy was expanding and Britain's public services needed new labour. Both London Transport and the National Health Service (Enoch Powell, MP, being the Minister for Health from 1960 to 1963) were among the employers with recruiting stations in the West Indies. According to a 'rough count' kept before 1962 of Commonwealth migrants from the Caribbean, Asia, East and West Africa and the Mediterranean, the *net* intake was around 42,000 in 1955 and 1956 but had dropped to about 21,000 in 1959. By 1961, by which time it was clear that immigration controls were to be imposed, the figure had risen to over 136,000.[8] In 1962 the first Commonwealth Immigrants Act required Commonwealth citizens, other than citizens of the United Kingdom who had been born in this country or had been issued with UK passports by UK Government representatives abroad, to seek entry permission as visitors, students, work-permit holders or people of independent means. It was clear from the outset that although the Act was, on the face of it, non-racist, the people most affected would be not Australians, Canadians or New Zealanders but 'new Commonwealth' citizens. In 1963 and 1964 the three white Commonwealth countries, all with fairly small populations, supplied Britain with between 130,000 and 150,000 visitors, while fewer than half that number were admitted from the more populous black Commonwealth countries.[9]

In 1965 the new Labour Government published a White Paper[10] heralding the double-edged policy which has governed official thinking on race relations ever since. Its two sections were entitled 'Control of Immigration' and 'Integration', and, in a phrase which has remained an unexamined assumption of public debate, the White Paper spoke of 'our small and overcrowded country', proposing to remove the right of 16- and 17-year-old children of Commonwealth families settled in this country to join their parents. The Government also proposed a new power of 'repatriation', which would allow the Home Secretary to deport a Commonwealth citizen who breached his entry conditions by remaining longer than specified. Medical tests, including X-rays, were to be introduced in immigrants' home countries (needless to say, Australians, Canadians and New Zealanders who came to this country to study or visit were rarely required to submit to such tests).

The White Paper paved the way for the shameful betrayal of principle involved in the 1968 Commonwealth Immigrants Act. The 1962 Act, although it had affected those UK citizens from the Colonies who were not born in this country, had not altered the status of UK citizens who had been guaranteed the right to retain their citizenship after the former Colony in which they lived had become independent. Many of those who had exercised their right to retain citizenship were people of Asian origin living in the newly independent territories of East Africa. The 1968 Act was a panic measure prompted by the imminent expulsion of this community of UK citizens of Asian origin from Kenya, victims of Kenya's Africanization policies. The Act was a double insult. On the one hand, it *extended* the number of United Kingdom citizens born abroad who were to be freed from immigration control by exempting any UK citizen with a parent or grandparent born or naturalized in the United Kingdom. On the other hand, the Act deprived citizens of this country, carrying passports issued by representatives of the Westminster Government and able to claim no other country's citizenship, of their legal entitlement to enter the

United Kingdom. In place of the right of entry, a quota of 1500 vouchers a year was created. The scandal of the 'shuttlecocking' of United Kingdom citizens between Heathrow Airport and the countries which had expelled them, highlighted by a series of complaints to the European Human Rights Commission,[11] persuaded the Government to introduce in 1969 a system of appeals against refusal of entry clearance. As Uganda began to expel British Asians and other non-Ugandan citizens, the quota was increased to 5000. But many of the United Kingdom passport holders who were unable to obtain a quota voucher (in 1970, for instance, the High Commission in Kampala had a waiting list of 2000) went, temporarily as they thought, to India. Although the Indian Government had insisted, and British Governments have accepted, that entry clearance will eventually be given to the 25,000 or so East African refugees in India, successive Governments have in fact refused to allow the annual quota for India to be increased beyond 500, even though for some years now the quota for the African countries has not been fully used.

The Conservative Government's 1971 Immigration Act, which remains in force today, adopted the 1968 Act's test of birth in this country as the basis for the concept of 'patriality'. United Kingdom citizens born, registered or naturalized in this country, or one of whose parents or grandparents had been born, registered or naturalized here, were 'patrial', with a right of entry and abode. All the rest, including not only the East African Asians but also many citizens from the Colonies, were 'non-patrial'. But the patriality test was extended to all Commonwealth citizens, with the result that some millions of people (almost all white), one of whose parents had been born in this country, were *freed* from the immigration control to which they had been subject since 1962. The racist intentions of the new scheme were made even clearer when an amendment to the Bill was accepted which gave any Commonwealth citizen with one grandparent born here the right to enter this country to seek work. The Act came into force in January 1973. The following year, when the United Kingdom joined the EEC, freedom of entry into this country was extended to over 200 million citizens of other Common Market countries, who are now permitted to come to the UK for up to six months to seek work and are free to settle if they obtain employment.

Thus the United Kingdom has not one but two immigration policies. For millions of white Commonwealth citizens and all Common Market citizens, there are no immigration controls at all:

entry to this 'small, overcrowded island' is entirely free. But for non-patrial United Kingdom citizens, for families or dependants trying to join a New Commonwealth migrant settled here, for the fiancés or husbands of women settled here but born abroad and for anyone outside the EEC or the favoured families of the white Commonwealth, immigration controls present an often insuperable bar.

The operation of the 1971 Act has been significantly modified by changes in the Immigration Rules made under its authority by successive Home Secretaries.[12] Their course can be traced elsewhere.[13] What must be stressed here is the injustice caused by the present system of immigration control. Two themes emerge: the interruption, even the destruction, of the family life of many migrants, almost all of them black; and the quite extraordinary increase in executive power which immigration law had permitted.

An individual's right to marry and to found a family is explicitly protected by the European Human Rights Convention. Most people would agree that a British person should be able to marry the person of his choice and live here with his family. But the present system of immigration control violates the right to family life not only of many people who have settled in this country but also of many who are themselves citizens of this country. That the contradiction is uneasily perceived is suggested by the outcry prompted by individual cases of hardship – such as the Home Secretary's refusal to permit Mrs Anwar Ditta, a United Kingdom citizen *born* in this country, to be joined by her three children who had been born in Pakistan[14] – even though many of the journalists and members of the public who protest at such cases themselves condone or positively support 'tough immigration controls' in general.

The 1971 Act provides a statutory right for the wife and for the children up to the age of 16 of a Commonwealth citizen settled in this country to join him here, provided that the man settled here before January 1973. Other families may also be permitted to enter, but their position depends on the Immigration Rules, which are subject to frequent change on ministerial initiative. The husband or fiancé of a *woman* settled in this country has no statutory right of entry; the position is entirely governed by the Rules, which have been radically altered in recent years. Thus the legal recognition of the rights of settled migrants' families is tenuous. The position in practice is even worse.

An American or non-patrial Australian woman seeking to come

to. this country as the fiancée or wife of a British-born man is, in theory, in exactly the same position as the Indian wife of an Indian citizen or the Pakistani wife of a UK citizen of Pakistani origin who has been settled here since before 1973. The gulf between them is illustrated by trying to imagine public reaction to the proposal that Australian or American wives be required to wait up to two years for an interview with an entry certificate officer, submit to a further delay before a decision is made – with the strong possibility that an entry certificate will be refused – and then be offered a right of appeal, months or even years later, to an immigration adjudicator in London. But a system or bureaucratic delay so effective that it negates the statutory 'right' of a wife and children to join a husband and father here is exactly what successive Governments have created in the Indian subcontinent.

In 1975 the Court of Appeal considered the position of patrial wives (that is to say, women who were themselves citizens of the United Kingdom or another Commonwealth country and were married to a patrial UK or Commonwealth citizen). In a decision which was for a brief period a landmark of enlightenment, Lord Scarman condemned the queues – 'Justice delayed is justice denied' – and enjoined those operating the Immigration Rules to have regard to the European Human Rights Convention.[15] Following the decision, a system of priority queues was created for wives with children under the age of 10. For such families the delay before being granted a first interview was, in the first quarter of 1980, three months. But in the same period families with older children faced delays of up to ten months in New Delhi, twenty-one months in Islamabad and up two years in Dacca, with similar delays operating against husbands and fiancés.[16]

The delays which Lord Scarman condemned might seem a little more tolerable if there were a certain prospect of admission at the end. What makes the position even more disturbing is the rate at which entry certificates are refused to wives and children – and the extraordinary variation in the refusal rate. There has been no change in the statutory position of wives and of children aged under 16 of Commonwealth citizens settled here before 1973 since then, and no reason to believe that the proportion of women and children falsely claiming to be related to a man here should vary from year to year. Nonetheless, the refusal rates in the Indian subcontinent have varied dramatically, reaching a low point in 1975 after a visit by the then Minister of State at the Home Office, Alex Lyon, MP. Mr Lyon reported that the main message delivered to the immigration officers was that they were to implement the civil standard of proof (as required by the law) that they be satisfied on a balance of probabilities as to the actual identity of the applicant. Instead, the officials had been treating applicants as though they were conducting a criminal trial and demanding proof of identity beyond reasonable doubt.

Refusal rates at Heathrow Airport have also showed a steady upward trend over the last three years. The Joint Council for the Welfare of Immigrants has calculated[17] that refusals in the ten months following the change of Government in May 1979 increased by 30 per cent, although no changes in the Rules were brought into effect until March 1980. The Home Secretary refused to accept the implication that immigration officers' application of the Rules varied with a change of Government. But a similar shift in refusal rates – inexplicable by any change in the Rules or any new policy directive – occurred in 1976, after the dismissal of Mr Lyon from the Home Office.[18]

Members of a family applying in the Indian subcontinent for permission to join their relatives here face lengthy and intrusive questioning about family relationships. Minor discrepancies in replies, possibly compounded by problems of interpretation, may lead to a refusal. Even more offensive is the use of medical examinations as an instrument of immigration control. In 1979, following international uproar over the revelation that a woman entering this country as a fiancée had been subjected to a 'virginity test' at Heathrow Airport, the Home Secretary terminated the use of vaginal examinations by port or High Commission medical officers. X-rays of adults and pregnant women were stopped at the same time. But X-rays of children, designed to establish their age, continue – and were, indeed, upheld in the report by Sir Henry Yellowlees, who was appointed in January 1979 to consider the use of medical techniques in immigration control. Ignoring the medical evidence about the dangers of even small doses of radiation, and ignoring the discrepancies of up to two years between 'bone age' as suggested by X-rays and chronological age – discrepancies which make the X-rays worthless for a decision about whether or not a child is under or over the age of 16 – the Yellowlees Report concluded: 'it is ethical to carry out an X-ray examination of bone age on a child. . . . I conclude that the use of X-rays of the bony skeleton provides a useful, fairly accurate and acceptably safe way of estimating the age of children.[19]

Before 1980 it was possible for older children of a family to join their relatives here. The new Immigration Rules, which came into effect in March of that year, only permit, in rare cases, the admission of a dependent, unmarried daughter. The older relatives of the sponsor settled here are also harshly affected. Many families, whatever their ethnic origin, would welcome the possibility of having elderly parents living with them and, if necessary, extending financial help as well. But the Rules will only allow the admission of a widowed mother, or a widowed father aged over 65, if the parent is wholly or mainly dependent on the child or grandchild here and if there are no close relatives in the country of origin. A father aged below 65, or parents who are both alive, will be admitted only if they have a standard of living 'substantially' below the average of their own country – a condition which cannot possibly be fulfilled by anyone receiving financial help from relatives in Britain. In one case a widowed father of 67 applied to join his son, who was willing and able to house and support him. The father, who was due to retire in a few months' time, would receive no pension and would therefore be destitute. He was refused admission on the ground that he was not dependent on his son at the time of application.[20]

An elderly person able to support him- or herself through independent means (which, under the new Rules, means an income of at least £10,000 a year) is likely to be admitted. An elderly person who was born in this country, or a Commonwealth citizen with a parent or grandparent born here, will be able to return to this country on retirement, regardless of his income or how long he has lived abroad. But an elderly relative from the 'new Commonwealth' whose family in this country can prove that it is able and willing to house and support him or her will almost never be admitted.[21] And once refused permission to enter for settlement, the parent or grandparent will almost certainly be denied entry as a visitor. Thus, although the rules concerning elderly relatives are not explicitly racist, they seriously disrupt the lives of the Asian, but not the white, community in this country.

Immigration as it is generally thought of – that is to say, Asian and West Indian immigration – is by now almost entirely a matter of wives, children and some other relatives joining someone settled in this country. The categories of jobs for which no work permits are required has been drastically restricted and the number of permits given considerably reduced in the last few years. Single men from Bangladesh, India or Pakistan who could have qualified to come here for employment in the 1960s can no longer do so, and they have not been able to since 1973. The wives and children who remain in the queues are, for the most part, the dependants of men who have been settled in this country for a decade or more. They are the 'problem' to which a Conservative MP, Ivor Stanbrook, referred during the second reading of the British Nationality Bill in January 1981, when he said:

> there is one aspect of the immigration problem that impinges on nationality. The British public is being kept completely ignorant of it. I refer to the thousands – perhaps hundreds of thousands – of dependants of immigrants settled here, who are still on the Indian subcontinent, but who have the right to come here to settle and, in turn, to acquire British citizenship. The Government have a manifesto commitment to set up a register of such people, and ultimately, to impose a quota on admissions. They have not yet done so. We should at least know the size of the problem if such a register were to exist.[22]

But if the official rhetoric about treating alike *all* residents, black and white, were to mean anything, it would mean that the Asian wives and children of Asian men settled here, many of whom have become British citizens, would be regarded in practice as having exactly the same right to come here as the foreign wife of any other British citizen.

But the forced separation of Asian and West Indian families is only part of the price of Britain's racist immigration laws. Parliament and the public have also condoned an extension of executive powers which would not be tolerated for a moment if it were tax inspectors, not immigration officers, exercising the power and white taxpayers rather than Asian workers who were the victims. Labour and Conservative Home Secretaries have actively sought and obtained an extension of their powers and of those of their officials, and the highest court of the country has endorsed their claims.

The 1971 Immigration Act gave the Home Secretary the power to remove an illegal entrant, who had no right of appeal until he was returned to the country from which he came. The power was specifically intended for use against those who arrived at the ports without entry clearance and who were refused admission: by a legal fiction, they were held never to have entered the country and did not qualify for the appeal rights of those who were faced with deportation after settlement. But a succession of court decisions since 1976 has extended the definition of 'illegal entrant' to include those who obtained permission to enter and settle allegedly on the basis of false documentation, or by allegedly deceiving the immigration officer in some other way, or by failing to disclose some material fact – even if the deception was practised by soneone else or if the person concerned had no idea that a particular fact was 'material'.

Mrs Claveria came to this country from the Philippines as a resident domestic worker at Charing Cross Hospital in London. She applied for permission for her husband to join her but, in March 1978, he was refused. Furthermore, she was informed that she was herself an illegal entrant and would be removed, since she had not disclosed to the immigration authorities in the Philippines that she had children when she applied to come here. Mrs Claveria had never been asked by the immigration officer whether she had a family and had no idea that she would have been refused if that fact had been known; all arrangements had been made by an agency supplying the demand for unskilled hospital workers in Britain by arranging jobs for women who could not support their families in the Philippines. Nonetheless, Mrs Claveria and about 250 other women in a similar position were all threatened with removal as illegal entrants, and in November 1979 the Divisional Court held that Mrs Claveria was indeed an illegal entrant. A major public campaign on behalf of the women persuaded the Home Secretary to allow many of them to remain here. (By September 1980, of ninety-three cases in which decisions had been taken, fifty women were allowed to stay, the remaining forty-three being removed.)

In July 1980 the House of Lords dismissed an appeal by Mohammed Zamir, a Pakistani citizen who had applied in December 1972 for permission to join his parents, who had been settled in Britain for the previous ten years. Zamir was aged 15 at the time of the application, but his entry certificate, which was initially refused, was not granted until November 1975. A few months later he married and shortly afterwards arrived alone in this country. When his wife, two years later, applied for permission to join him, the entry clearance officer in Islamabad notified the Home Office that Mr Zamir had been married before his arrival in the United Kingdom. Mr Zamir was arrested on suspicion of being an illegal entrant. He applied for a writ of *habeas corpus*, which was refused. The Home Office argued throughout that Mr Zamir's marriage terminated his status as a dependent son and that, therefore, he was not entitled to the entry certificate which had been granted him in that capacity. Neither the Home Office nor the courts seem to have paid any attention to the three years' delay in allowing Zamir to join his family. In what the Lord Chief Justice described as 'a modest step forward in the law on this topic', the High Court decided that there is a duty on the part of a would-be immigrant to disclose any changes of circumstance 'if he knew, or ought to have known, that those changes were material to the immigration history'. Confirming the decision, the House of Lords held that the courts will not examine the facts which lead to the Home Office's decision that someone is an illegal entrant, but will merely decide whether the Home Office has reasonable grounds to think that the entry has been illegal.[23]

The result is now that the police, acting on the authority of the immigration service, may arrest without warrant someone suspected of being an illegal entrant. The suspect will be detained – without charge and with no right to bail – for an indefinite period. If he applies for *habeas corpus*, he must prove to the court that there were *no* grounds on which the immigration officer could have acted or that no reasonable person could have come to the decision reached by the immigration officer. The Home Secretary's order for the detention of an allegedly illegal entrant is otherwise a complete answer to an application for a writ of *habeas corpus*.[24] If the Home Office later decides that it was wrong in its suspicions, the entrant will be released without compensation. But if the Home Office sticks by its original decision, the suspect will be removed by administrative order, unable to appeal to the immigration appeals adjudicator or tribunal except from the country to which he is returned.[25]

Even Merlyn Rees, who, as Labour Home Secretary from 1976 to 1979, administered this system, has begun to have doubts about it. Two months after the 1979 election he told the House of Commons:

I found – and I started to have the matter looked at – that someone can be locked up for a long period, purely by administrative order. I ask the Home Office to keep looking at that, because it should not happen in this country unless we are sure that it is necessary [*sic*] and that the procedures are right. I was beginning to question that.[26]

In 1979 585 people were removed as illegal entrants. By 1980 the numbers had almost doubled, with 319 Commonwealth citizens and 589 foreign nationals removed (a total of 908). During that year 669 people were held in custody on suspicion of being illegal entrants. And in forty cases dealt with during 1980 the Home Office admitted to a mistake, classifying them as 'Illegal status not established'.[27] In their pursuit of suspects, the immigration service and the police have begun to raid workplaces employing black workers. In May 1980 ten establishments connected with Bestway Cash and Carry were raided. Of thirty-seven people arrested and detained, twenty-eight were here entirely lawfully: indeed, nine of them were patrial United Kingdom citizens. One man, detained for seven hours, had been settled here for twenty-three years but was held in detention even after his documents had been examined. The Joint Council for the Welfare of Immigrants has reported[28] that shortly after this and similar raids the employees of a north-east London factory with a substantially black workforce were required to bring in immediately their 'work permits, passports, naturalization certificates or birth certificates' for checking and copying.

It is impossible to stress too heavily the insecurity which passport raids and the detention and removal of *settled* immigrants have created in the ethnic minority communities. It is now possible for someone who came here as a child, who was given permission to settle here and who has known no other home to be picked out by the Home Office years later, on the suspicion that he is not, in fact, the child of the man who claimed to be his father and that his passport was therefore obtained through deception. He can be detained without warrant or charge and removed in the exercise of 'administrative duty' – and the courts offer him no protection whatsoever. It is no longer true that refusal of bail to a defendant on a criminal charge is the one occasion on which the law permits detention without trial; nor is it true that repatriation is a demand only of the extreme right. Under the name of administrative removal, the Home Office and the courts have already created and sanctioned a system of repatriation.

Nor can the acquisition of United Kingdom citizenship protect the settled migrant. The 1948 British Nationality Act provided that someone alleged to have obtained citizenship by fraud, false representation or concealment of a material fact may be deprived of his citizenship only after a hearing by a specially constituted committee of inquiry. But this entirely proper provision was bypassed by the Court of Appeal, which held in 1978, in the case of Sultan Mahmood,[29] that citizenship allegedly obtained by dubious means is void from the outset. It is up to the individual to prove that his acquisition of citizenship was valid. No special committee of inquiry is required, since no deprivation of citizenship is intended: the citizenship will simply be declared never to have been acquired. Thus the courts have given the Home Office a new power to strip a

British citizen of his citizenship by administrative *diktat* and to repatriate him from the country which has become his home.

The categories established by the 1948 Act – citizenship of the United Kingdom and Colonies, and Commonwealth citizenship, embracing citizens of all independent Commonwealth countries, including the United Kingdom – have been thrown into thorough confusion by two decades of immigration law. Under the 1971 Act thousands of United Kingdom citizens became non-patrial, although millions of other Commonwealth citizens were patrial. It has been common ground between the political parties for some years that a new citizenship law is needed. In 1976 the then Labour Government proposed in a Green Paper[30] to create two citizenships in place of the present United Kingdom citizenship: a British citizenship, carrying a right of abode in this country, and a British overseas citizenship for citizens in the Colonies and other non-patrial citizens. Although strongly criticized at the time by the Labour Party itself and now disowned by Labour's parliamentary leadership, the Green Paper proposals were closely followed in the Conservative Government's new Nationality Act of 1981. That Act has created *three* new citizenships: British citizenship, citizenship of the British Dependent Territories and British overseas citizenship.

But only the first of the new citizenships carries with it the right to live and work in a named territory. The rights of citizens from the Colonies to live in a particular Colony depends not on their citizenship but on each Colony's immigration laws. And holders of British overseas citizenship have, quite simply, no rights at all. Even British citizenship carries with it only the right to live in the United Kingdom. The grant of a passport remains at the discretion of the Foreign Secretary, proposals from Justice and NCCL for a right of appeal against refusal or withdrawal of a passport having been refused. The right to vote, to stand for office and to work in the public sector will continue to depend on the status of Commonwealth citizen, with citizens of other Commonwealth countries settled here having these rights in common with British Citizens. The Government has, however, suggested, that voting and similar rights may at a future date be withdrawn from settled Commonwealth citizens, whose right to register automatically as full British citizens will also be withdrawn five years after the commencement of the new Nationality Act.

Far from concerning itself with the major constitutional issues involved in nationality, the new Act is in reality an immigration law. It takes patriality as the crucial criterion for acquiring British citizenship and makes the right of abode the only explicit consequence of such citizenship. The Government had also hoped to restrict the rights of people who had acquired United Kingdom or (later) British citizenship by registration or naturalization by denying them the right to pass on their citizenship to a child abroad – a proposal which it was forced to withdraw even before the Bill went into its committee stages. But the Government has, despite considerable pressure from the Churches and community organizations, stood by its plan to abandon the long-standing principle that a child born in this country is a citizen by birth (the *jus soli* principle). Under the new scheme a child born in the United Kingdom will become a British citizen only if one parent is either a British citizen or is legally settled here at the time of birth or subsequently. As a result, someone born here who later applies for a passport will be required to supply proof of his parents' immigration and citizenship status – proof which it may be difficult or impossible to supply if the passport application is not made until many years after the birth. Futhermore, where a parent is deprived of settled status by being removed as an illegal entrant, the child will retrospectively be deprived of citizenship as well. By ending the right of settled Commonwealth citizens to register automatically as British citizens, the Act will substantially increase the numbers required to apply for naturalization, a process which is already extremely slow and expensive and which leaves the decision entirely in the hands of the Home Secretary.

But there are alternatives, at once simpler and fairer, to our present immigration controls and the new citizenship law. Accepting the need to disentangle the confusion of citizenship and immigration laws, the most satisfactory scheme would be to create a separate citizenship for each of the present Colonies, each such citizenship carrying with it the right to live, work, vote and exercise the other rights and duties of citizenship in that territory.[31] British citizenship would carry with it the right to live, work and vote in the United Kingdom and would be acquired at the outset not only by those who become United Kingdom citizens by birth, adoption, naturalization or registration in this country, but also by the non-patrial United Kingdom citizens outside the colonies, including the East African Asians, who have no other citizenship.

Before any such changes are made, however, full consultations with the Commonweatlh should take place, particularly with a view to establishing a proper status for those non-patrial United

Kingdom citizens in Malaysia and Sri Lanka who do not yet hold those countries' citizenships. Once the new scheme was established, British citizenship would be acquired automatically by any child born in this country and by any child born abroad to a British citizen, unless the parent was also a citizen by descent, in which case the child would acquire British citizenship only if one parent was working in government or similar service or if the child would otherwise be stateless. The husband or wife of a British citizen would also be entitled to register as a citizen.[32] Naturalization would be available after five years' residence in this country, provided that the applicant had no serious criminal conviction, and a right of appeal to a Citizenship Appeals Tribunal against refusal of citizenship or of a passport would be provided.

Such a citizenship scheme would form the basis of a complete overhaul of immigration controls, with the aim of establishing a system which encouraged and assisted family reunion, enabled this country to obtain from abroad badly needed skills, acknowledged our international commitment to refugees and provided effective rights of appeal against administrative decisions. The present power to remove a settled migrant or to deprive a citizen of citizenship without a proper hearing of the accusations against him would be abolished.

I make no apology for dwelling at length on this country's immigration and citizenship laws. It is impossible to understand the position of the ethnic minorities in Britain without appreciating the effects of these laws. Not only have the security and the family life of the black communities been eroded, but the commitment of successive Governments to restricting ethnic minority migration and to removing as many black and Asian immigrants as possible has resulted in an intolerable extension of ministerial and administrative power. Parliament has been unwilling or unable to curb these powers. And the courts – in sweeping aside *habeas corpus* and refusing to scrutinize administrative decisions when they affect racial minorities – have actively connived at a system of arbitrary and racially biased executive power.

It is in this context that one must consider the other forms of racism from which the black British communities suffer and the attempts made by Government to deal with racist violence, racial disadvantage and discrimination.

In February 1981 the Home Secretary announced a new investigation of racist organizations in Britain and the possibility of establishing special police units to deal with racist violence. The

Joint Committee Against Racialism (JCAR), a body sponsored by the Labour, Liberal and Conservative Parties, had collected reports of at least 1000 specifically racist attacks on ethnic minority families in the previous eighteen months.[33] It would appear that the Asian community has been the main target of racist violence, although Jewish synagogues and cemeteries are being desecrated on a growing scale. The National Front, the British Movement and similar neo-Fascist bodies explicitly encourage such attacks, although it is not clear to what extent the violence which has terrorized Asian families in areas like the East End of London has been deliberately planned and co-ordinated. Many of the victims have criticized the police for failing to come to the rescue rapidly enough or to investigate the crime rigorously; the police themselves claim that many of the attacks are not specifically racist but part of a general problem of urban violence. But the explicitly racist content of the kind of attacks documented by JCAR cannot be denied, while the consequence of apparent police indifference or hostility has been the resort in some areas to self-defence groups. A massive reinforcement of beat policing, together with strong, repeated, public commitments from the police, the Police Authorities and the Home Secretary to defend racial and religious minorities, are urgently needed. But it is also essential that racism within the police force is effectively tackled, that stop-and-search powers cease to be used as a form of harassment against young blacks and that more effective structures of police accountability are established (see page 65). Nor can we expect more effective and responsive policing to cope with the problems generated by rapidly rising rates of youth unemployment and, in particular, the ability of organizations like the National Front to recruit white pupils and school-leavers. Racist violence is part of the price which this country is paying for gross economic mismanagement. The return to economic policies designed to achieve full employment must underpin any serious commitment to protecting ethnic minorities.

The law against incitement to racial hatred

Revulsion against racist and anti-Semitic propaganda in the early 1960s led to the introduction in 1965 of a Race Relations Act, which not only established the Race Relations Board, with powers to conciliate in a limited range of cases of discrimination, but also

made it a criminal offence[34] to distribute material or to use
which were threatening, abusive or insulting with an inter
incite to racial hatred. Of the fourteen people prosecuted
citement to racial hatred between 1965 and 1970, nine were white,
five were black. The most prominent of the white defendants was
Colin Jordan, who was sentenced in 1967 to eighteen months'
imprisonment, and of the black defendants, Michael Abdul Malik
(Michael X), sentenced in the same year to twelve months'
imprisonment. In 1968 the acquittal of members of the Racial
Preservation Society, whose more carefully expressed racism did
not, in the judge's view, reveal an intention to stir up racial hatred,
made the authorities reluctant to risk prosecutions which might
legitimize the propaganda they were trying to suppress. Proposals
were made to strengthen the incitement law by, among others,
Lord Scarman, in his report on the Red Lion Square disorders in
1974,[35] and in 1976 the new Race Relations Act included an amendment to the 1936 Public Order Act which defined the incitement
offence by reference to the *likelihood* of stirring up racial hatred.
Although it was hoped that the removal of the requirement to
prove intent would make prosecutions easier to bring, in fact only
25 prosecutions were authorized by the Attorney-General between
1976 and 1981.

It is now once again suggested in many quarters that the incitement to racial hatred laws be further amended, possibly by making
the advocacy of repatriation a criminal offence and by providing a
new power to ban a march which might inflame racial hatred.

The introduction and development of the incitement laws raise
serious civil liberties issues. Freedom of speech is not an academic
question or a white liberal myth: the right to express one's views in
speech or in writing is fundamental to the process of securing
political change. The only context in which interference with what
someone chooses to say or to write is justified is if there is a serious
likelihood of violence or other serious criminal acts following
directly from what is said or written. Those who supported the
initial introduction of the law against incitement to racial hatred
argued that the law would reduce the propaganda that leads to the
hatred which results in violence. But the law is also now defended
on the grounds that it protects black minorities from abuse and
from having their freedom to live a safe and equal life infringed.

Racial discrimination and racist violence destroy the rights of
minorities to live equally in dignity and security. In our desire to
eradicate racism, therefore, it is not surprising that the case for the

methods adopted, or their likely efectiveness, is not always carefully analysed. The case made for the incitement law is by no means
clear-cut. When NCCL launched its campaign for an incitement to
racial hatred law in 1959, it argued that the Notting Hill riots were
deliberately incited by printed material.[36] After so many years, it is
impossible to judge the truth of that claim, although NCCL itself also
blamed the riots partly on the Government's failure to deal with
discrimination. In some cases it is possible to establish a clear
connection. For instance, in March 1981 bricks were thrown
through the window of Peter Hain's house in south London after
his name and address, and those of other leading members of the
Anti-Nazi League, had been published in a National Front news
sheet, with an exhortation that they be harassed. But in a case in
which the incitement to violence is clear, the incitement to racial
hatred law is an unnecessary addition to the criminal law. The
assumption behind the incitement law is that racist violence will be
reduced if the most objectionable expressions of racism are
curtailed. But the experience of the last two decades suggests
otherwise. Surely no one now would support Donald Soper's
view, expressed in 1963, that the incitement law 'is the genuine
medicine that can begin to cure racial discrimination, and without it
any other medicament will be ineffective'.[37] It is hard to believe that
a 'strengthened' incitement law would be any more effective. A ban
on the advocacy of repatriation would be absurd when repatriation
is practised in reality by the Government. The repeal of the 1971
Immigration Act and the 1981 Nationality Act, and their replacement by just and non-racist laws, would do far more to restore the
security of the black minorities than the occasional prosecution of a
neo-Fascist leader.

The use of the incitement laws against black militants in the 1960s
should also serve as a warning of the use to which a 'strengthened',
and therefore probably vaguer, incitement law could be put in
future. Similarly, the current resort to blanket bans on marches (see
page 119) should warn against the acceptance of proposals of new
banning powers. No one doubts the deep offensiveness of National
Front and similar slogans to the black and Jewish communities
(and, of course, to millions of other people as well). But offensiveness cannot by itself be an acceptable criterion for prosecuting a
speaker or banning a march. Nor can a march of itself be described
as intimidation. Where criminal acts are involved – threats of
violence by the marchers, for instance – the criminal law already
applies. But the suggestion made by some sections of the anti-racist

movement that a march can *of itself* constitute a threat to the rights of others offers dangerous grounds for new restrictions on the right to protest.

Racism and racist violence are political problems with complex causes. Those who still believe that the criminal law can play any significant part in reducing racial prejudice or violence should consider the experience in Northern Ireland, where laws against republicanism and against incitement to religious hatred did nothing to prevent the present troubles or to reduce their seriousness. The unsuitability of the criminal law as an instrument for reducing the indirect causes of violence, and the danger of using the law to suppress the expression of views, even when those views are deeply objectionable and threatening to many people, should lead to the conclusion that no further strengthening of the incitement laws is necessary or desirable. The real need is for the ethnic minority communities to feel that Governments are on their side against a racist minority: and that can be achieved only by a transformation of Government policies as part of a political offensive against racism.

Discrimination

The black British communities mostly live in inner-city areas, where the accumulated disadvantages of poor housing, inadequate public services, high crime levels and over burdened schools are suffered by black and white alike. The urban black family suffers from the double disadvantage of race and class.

Comprehensive information about the employment position of black workers (comparable with details available about women workers) is not available. But the 1971 Census revealed a heavy over-representation of West Indian, Pakistani and Indian workers in unskilled and semi-skilled employment. Although Indian men were represented in the same proportion as in the population generally in non-manual work, West Indians and Pakistanis were considerably less likely to be employed in non-manual jobs. A survey by Political and Economic Planning (PEP) in 1974 showed that although black semi-skilled and unskilled manual workers earned on average exactly the same as white workers, black skilled manual workers earned on average nearly £4 a week less and black non-manual workers £12 a week less than white workers in the same jobs.[38] Both the PEP study and the Tavistock Institute's more recent investigaton of employment in government Departments[39] made it clear that the under-representation of minority workers in clerical and professional work could not be explained by a lower level of educational qualifications or by difficulty in obtaining recognition for foreign qualifications. According to the PEP study, even when allowance was made for a possible difference in educational standards in Britain and the Indian subcontinent, black men were in less senior jobs than white men with directly comparable qualifications. The Tavistock Institute's study similarly showed that when a comparison was made directly between white and minority-group applicants with the same qualifications, minority-group applicants were less likely to be called for interview, less likely to be appointed if interviewed and less likely to have reasons noted for their rejection.

Racial discrimination is clearly reflected in unemployment levels. Even in 1971, when unemployment among the Asian community was at about the same level as that in the country as a whole, the level of unemployment among West Indian men and women was over twice the average. Between February 1979 and February 1980 registered unemployment among black workers rose four times as fast as unemployment generally.[40] Young West Indians are the worst affected. A study in the London borough of Lewisham of 1977 school-leavers[41] found that the West Indians were three times as likely to be unemployed as their white contemporaries, and that those who had found a job had taken longer to find work, had made more applications and had been to more interviews before getting employment, and were less satisfied with the jobs they had obtained.

West Indian parents who came to this country not only to obtain employment for themselves but also to improve their children's prospects are now widely convinced that the British education system has failed their children. Despite the evidence from some schools, where children of West Indian origin do at least as well as their white counterparts,[42] the general picture is depressing. Surveys undertaken in the Inner London Education Authority area revealed persistent under-achievement among minority-group children, even among those who had been entirely educated in this country.[43] Those surveys were undertaken in 1966 and 1968, although follow-up studies of reading levels in 1971 and 1975 confirmed the under-achievement of West Indian children. A 1970 survey[44] of pupils in a London borough again placed West Indian pupils in the lowest band of achievement, although children born in this country of West Indian origin did significantly better than those who had migrated here. A study published in the London borough of Redbridge in 1978 [45] found that at one comprehensive school 46 per cent of West Indian pupils were receiving remedial help, compared with only about a quarter of pupils generally. West Indian pupils were also less likely to achieve 'O'-Levels and none had achieved 'A'-Level passes in 1977.

A 1971 study in two London primary schools suggested that social class rather than race was the crucial factor in under-achievement. [46] The first report on the Rampton Committee, which investigated the education of black children, strongly suggested that a combination of teachers' own prejudices and expectations, the living conditions of poorer urban families and the language problems of West Indian children were the likeliest causes of their poor educational results. That racism alone, or the problems of migrant families generally, cannot account for educational disadvantage is underlined by the experience of children of Asian origin, whose performance at school is generally at least as good as that of white children. [47] But Asian pupils often come from professional or business families, and the needs of those who had arrived from abroad for special teaching in English were recognized by education authorities. A child from an Asian family, particularly if he or she has been born here, may well encounter the same treatment and expectations as a white middle-class pupil. Certainly, it is the West Indian pupils who are dramatically over-represented in schools for the educationally subnormal: in 1970 they were between three and four times more likely than other pupils to be in such schools, and it is believed that the proportion may have increased since then. [48]

The inequalities of the black communities in employment are only partly explained by educational disadvantage. Where qualifications are equal – as they are particularly likely to be for Asian applicants – racial discrimination is clearly the overriding factor. But for West Indian jobseekers, and particularly the young, for whom unemployment is most severe, racial discrimination has combined with the failure of the educational system to meet the needs of both first-generation and second-generation black children. The low expectations from which West Indian pupils and their teachers often suffer are reinforced by the experience of black school-leavers who fail to find satisfactory jobs, or indeed any job at all.

The 1971 Census also disclosed the appalling housing problems of the black communities. Department of Environment analysis of the Census data[49] revealed that 70 per cent of ethnic minority communities were concentrated in 10 per cent of Census districts, which contained nearly three times the average number of households sharing or without hot water, twice as many sharing or without a bath, nearly three times as many living at a density of over 1.5 people to a room, twice as many lacking exclusive use of all basic amenities, half as many living in council housing and twice as many in private furnished accommodation. The National Child Development Study (using 1974 survey material) found that first-generation Asian children and their families, and West Indian families including those with children born here, suffered particularly from poor housing conditions.[50] Census information on the housing pattern in Greater London in 1971 showed that 44 per cent of non-white tenants lived in inter-war, unmodernized housing, compared with only 15 per cent of white tenants. Even taking into account the concentration of black housing-list applicants in the lower-priority categories and the preference of many black families for inner-London accommodation, minority-group families remained worse off than white families.

The 1965 Race Relations Act was the first attempt to outlaw discrimination by legislative action. But its scope was extremely restricted, the Race Relations Board being limited to attempting to conciliate. The 1968 Act extended anti-discrimination provisions to housing, employment and a wider range of goods and services. Private clubs, however, where racial bars were widespread, remained exempt. The 1968 Act enabled the Board to refer complaints of discrimination in cases of dismissal to industrial tribunals, but of the discrimination complaints handled by tribunals before 1976, not one ended in success for the complainant. The 1976 Act – modelled on the 1975 Sex Discrimination Act, which, in its turn, had been greatly influenced by the failures of the 1965 and 1968 Acts – outlaws both direct and indirect discrimination in recruitment, promotion and other aspects of employment; education and training; housing; the provision of goods, services and facilities; and advertising. The Act also replaced the Board and its fellow, the Community Relations Commission, with a new Commission for Racial Equality (CRE), with powers parallel to those of the Equal Opportunities Commission.

The 1976 Act envisaged a dual attack on racial discrimination. Individual cases would be pursued (with CRE backing, if necessary) through industrial tribunals and the county courts, while the CRE would devote its energies primarily to the 'strategic' job of identifying key areas of discrimination and, through its powers to investigate and to issue non-discrimination notices, would tackle general patterns of discrimination which could not be altered through individual complaints. The CRE has, in fact, found it necessary to assist a large number of individual complainants, sometimes with notable success. In 1978 the CRE represented a number of Asian men who had formerly been employed by British Steel but who, on reapplying, had been rejected on the grounds that they did not meet the new language requirements. Although the employers refused to admit liability, the case was settled with large amounts of compensation for the complainants and an indication that the imposition of language requirements could fall foul of the ban of unjustified indirect discrimination.

But the overall success rate of individual complaints is appallingly low. In 1978 of 298 cases taken to industrial tribunals, only twenty (about 7 per cent) succeeded after a hearing. The following year the number of successes remained at the same level, less than 6 per cent of a total of 366 cases. The individual who seeks to prove race discrimination in a tribunal or court faces problems similar to the victim of sex discrimination: he or she must prove not only that less favourable treatment occurred but also that race discrimination was the cause; evidence may be extremely difficult to come by; and those hearing the case may share the employer's prejudices or regard a complaint of racist behaviour as unimportant.

Even if individual complaints were successfully brought in far larger numbers, policies and patterns of discrimination would probably remain untouched. The CRE has been rather more successful than the EOC in launching formal investigations, either in response to complaints about a particular agency or as part of a general attempt to tackle the disadvantaged employment position of black minorities. A formal investigation into the National Bus Company, which began in May 1978 and has not yet reported, was the result of the CRE's conclusion that it needed to identify the major sectors of employment in which black workers were concentrated – passenger transport being one key area. But many of the investigations, particularly those which have been completed and resulted in non-discrimination notices, have so far had little effect outside the firm concerned.

The CRE has been widely criticized for its failure to combat discrimination and racist prejudice more energetically or to take issue outspokenly on behalf of black minorities. It has suffered from severe internal disagreements, some inherited from its predecessors, and does not seem to have developed either a coherent strategy or an effective internal structure. But not even a more aggressive Commission would necessarily have been able to overcome Government indifference.

As the largest employer in the country, national government has a major responsibility for tackling race discrimination. The Tavistock Institute report of November 1978 on discrimination inside the Civil Service should finally have convinced government sceptics that they too had a problem. The Institute's study of clerical recruitment[51] in the headquarters of the Department of Health and Social Security (one of a number of surveys) showed that although 45 per cent of the job applications received by the department came from black job seekers, only 2.5 per cent of those appointed were black. At every stage of the recruitment procedure, right through to the evaluation of those who were appointed, black applicants were less likely to succeed. The Institute's findings could have been the basis for a massive equal opportunities programme in the Civil Service. But the request of the Civil and Public Services Association (one of the main non-industrial unions involved) for continuous monitoring of the position of ethnic minorities in the Civil Service has been rejected, and the joint working party established to consider the report had not reached its conclusions by May 1981.

Monitoring the treatment of black job seekers and employees – which is all that the Tavistock Institute did – is the prerequisite for an equal opportunities policy designed to deal with the problems of discrimination, job segregation and under-achievement revealed by the analysis. Monitoring is also essential to establish the effect of an equal opportunities policy, although it çan never be a substitute for full implementation of such a policy. But even the collection of information based on people's race or colour has proved an extremely controversial exercise. Many union branches and some black organizations have seen the collection of racial data as itself discriminatory or have feared that the inclusion of details about racial origin on, say, a job-application form would simply encourage discrimination. Objections were also raised to the proposal to include a question on racial origin in the 1981 Census (a proposal abandoned by the Conservative Government). Fears about the misuse of racial information are often well founded and any policy on ethnic records must take account of them – for instance, by providing that the racial origin of job applicants is recorded anonymously and not made available to the interviewer, and by including with the job-application form a full explanation of the equal opportunities policy on which the racial-origin question is based. But any serious attempt to formulate an equal opportunities programme must include an agreement to obtain regular information about ethnic minorities, whether in a particular workforce or among those on the council housing waiting list.

National and local government could also have taken a lead in tackling racial discrimination through its contracts with suppliers of equipment and services. Since 1969 a standard clause has been included in all national government contracts requiring compliance with anti-discrimination law and asking contractors to ensure that their employees and subcontractors are also observing the law. But in twelve years, despite the recommendations of a series of parliamentary and other bodies, nothing whatsoever has been done to ensure compliance with this clause. It is not adequate to require the contractor to provide information about his policies to the Department of Employment, as was suggested in the White Paper which preceded the 1976 Act: what is needed is a specialist team of investigators, armed with the power to demand and obtain detailed information about the recruitment, employment and promotion of ethnic minority workers in a contractor's firm, coupled with the use by the CRE of its power to issue non-discrimination notices where appropriate.

But just as the segregation of women in lower-paid, less skilled jobs has not proved amenable to laws against discrimination, so racial discrimination requires positive policies to promote equal opportunities. Like the Sex Discrimination Act (see page 182), the 1976 Act permits training bodies and employers to organize training for black workers or applicants who are under-represented in a particular field and to encourage them to apply for those jobs. (Discrimination in favour of black applicants simply because of their race remains unlawful at the point of recruitment or promotion.) Under these provisions, a south London project has established a basic training course in community work for West Indians who lacked the academic qualifications for established courses. But even less advantage has been taken of the permission given to positive discrimination in training of black workers than of the similar provisions for women (see page 183). There is a pressing need for Government, employers, trades unions and the training bodies to use the positive discrimination provisions to their full, so that special opportunities for training and recruitment, designed to compensate for the disadvantaged position of the black minorities, are placed at the centre of detailed equal opportunities programmes.

In the United States affirmative action is backed by legal sanctions. The Office of Federal Contract Compliance monitors the observance by government contractors of non-discrimination clauses, under which contractors are required to provide a detailed breakdown of the ethnic origin of their workforce at every level and to establish programmes and targets for reducing racial imbalance. Where an action is brought to the courts against an employer who has discriminated, the court may and often does make a detailed order designed to eradicate previous discriminatory practices and to compensate for their effects; again, goals for recruitment and promotion are normally included. Whereas in Britain a complaint of discrimination can be brought only by an individual acting on his or her own behalf, the courts in the USA can deal with a 'class action', which may affect hundreds of thousands of actual and future employees. The affirmative-action guidelines drawn up by the Equal Employment Opportunities Commission (a statutory body with responsiblity for ensuring compliance with laws against both race and sex discrimination) stress the need for 'specific, measurable, attainable hiring and promotion goals, with target dates, in each area of underutilization'.

The development of affirmative action has triggered a national debate in the USA about the validity of programmes which may involve 'reverse discrimination' against white males in favour of women and ethnic minorities. In the *Bakke* case,[52] the Supreme Court overruled a scheme for admissions to medical school which, by reserving a certain proportion of places for minority candidates, led to the rejection of a white candidate who would otherwise have qualified. But the court also held that the programme which took race into account would be lawful and has since upheld an affirmative-action programme in the Kaiser Corporation, which reserves 50 per cent of places in certain in-plant training programmes for black employees. The court stressed that the programme did not require the dismissal of white employees and their replacement by black workers; that it did not bar the promotion of white employees, who could still qualify for half the places on the training programme; that the programme was temporary; and that it was designed to manifest the obvious imbalance in Kaiser's almost entirely white craft workforce.

The arguments used by the Supreme Court in *Kaiser*[53] are directly applicable to the case for positive action in this country. Where minority group workers do not have the qualifications which would gain them entrance to apprenticeships or other training schemes or to skilled or professional employment, a 'neutral' non-discrimination policy which merely requires employers to treat candidates with equal qualifications equally is manifestly inadequate. The provisions for positive action in the 1976 Act would, in fact, allow an employer or training body to reserve *all* the places on a particular training scheme for minority-group workers if the scheme were designed to equip them for jobs which were exclusively or mainly done by white workers. But the 1976 Act prohibits any discrimination at the point of selection for recruitment or promotion, thus ruling out any system of quotas. But an equal opportunities programme which committed employer and union to trying to achieve, say, representation of black workers in skilled and managerial positions in numbers equivalent to their proportion in the workforce as a whole over a period of years, and which included positive-action training programmes, special measures to encourage black workers to apply for jobs where they were now under-represented and a training programme to tackle explicit or unconscious prejudices among white supervisors and management – such a programme would be entirely lawful under the present law. In the absence of legal measures which would require such programmes, it is up to the trade unions, the CRE and the Government itself to commit themselves to this development.

Race relations and civil disorder

The urban riots of July 1981 shocked the nation. But it is too early to say whether they shocked people and the Government into recognizing the depths of despair to which working-class, young black and white people in the cities had been driven, of whether the shock of seeing televised, on English streets, the burning cars and missile throwing which had come to symbolize the H-Block protest of Belfast and Derry would prompt only an increase in aggressive policing and sentencing powers. The immediate response of Government Ministers was extremely discouraging.

But there are lessons enough for Ministers wishing to learn how to avoid the recurrence of violent civil conflict. Economic deprivation, discrimination, racial prejudice and racially motivated violence, harsh and apparently biased policing, inadequate means for dealing with grievances and a lack of effective political power – all these are paralleled by the situation that obtained in Northern Ireland in the late 1960s. It is surely not too much to expect that the lessons have by now been learned: that normal policing relation-ships cannot survive where a police force drawn almost entirely from the majority community is felt systematically to be harassing and abusing the minority; that where peaceful political means of meeting the minority community's aspirations and dealing with their grievances do not work, the grievances will find violent expression; and, perhaps most important of all, that increasing the use of the state's coercive powers to deal with street violence produces further injustices and further grievances, which only make the violence worse and delay even more the possibility of a political resolution. It is argued – as it was in relation to terrorist activity in Northern Ireland – that some freedoms must be sacri-ficed in order to protect the freedom of people to walk about the streets in safety or to conduct their businesses without fear of looting and arson. But that is not the choice that has to be made. Internment in Northern Ireland did not produce safety for most of the community at the cost of locking up some innocent people: the injustice of internment directly increased the danger both to the security forces and to the community they should have protected.

Similar lessons may be found in the rioting in North American cities in the summer of 1967: but in striking contrast, they were immediately acknowledged by the Government of the day and underlined in the Report of the Commission established by Presi-dent Johnson to investigate the disorders. The Kerner Commis-sion, which reported in March 1968,[54] spelled out the basic issue:

> White racism is essentially responsible for the explosive mixture which has been accumulating in our cities since the end of World War II. At the base of this mixture are three of the most bitter fruits of white racial attitudes: pervasive discrimination and segregation . . . black migration and white exodus [with] the massive and growing concentration of impoverished Negroes in our major cities . . . black ghettos [where] segregation and poverty have intersected to destroy opportunity and hope and to enforce failure.[55]

The Commission wrote of a 'reservoir of grievances' that finally spilled over into violence in response to some apparently minor, even trivial, triggering incident. After extensive interviews with thousands of people in different cities, the Commission concluded that the riots were directed largely against the police, who 'have come to symbolize white power, white racism, and white repression': they were not inter-communal riots. Nor was there any evidence that they were the result of an organized conspiracy or attempt to overthrow the Government.

In response to serious disorders in Brixton, in south London, in April 1981, Lord Scarman was requested by the Government to undertake an inquiry into the immediate and underlying causes of the violence and to make appropriate recommendations. Despite considerable pressure on the Government from community organizations, no representatives of the black community or other independent figures were appointed to sit with Lord Scarman; nor was he given anything approaching the highly skilled, multi-racial staff which had assisted the Kerner Commission in its task. As rioting broke out in Liverpool, in Manchester, in Coventry and in other parts of London, Lord Scarman's terms of reference were rapidly widened. But whereas the Kerner Commission had been established by a President who had told the nation: 'The only genuine, long-range solution for what has happened lies in an attack – mounted at every level – upon the conditions that breed despair and violence', Lord Scarman was effectively faced with trying to convince a Government which preferred to look on the breakdown of parental indiscipline and the intervention of left-wing agitators as the causes of the problem. Despite acknowledgments from some Cabinet Ministers that unemployment must have been a factor in the breakdown of order, there was no sign of significant change in economic or employment policies.

The first task in dealing with civil conflict on this scale is simply to ensure that police measures do not make matters worse. The police have an obligation to protect people and property: but they cannot discharge that duty if the measures they take bring on to the streets more people prepared to attack the police themselves. The immediate response of the police and the Home Secretary, however, was to look to more effective riot equipment to deal with the problem. CS gas was used in Liverpool at the beginning of July, and the Home Secretary sanctioned its use, suggesting that water cannon and rubber bullets might even become necessary. But CS gas was abandoned as a crowd-control weapon in Northern Ireland in the early 1970s because its devastating effects on rioters and bystanders alike, even if providing a temporary respite, guaranteed more trouble later. Rubber bullets were found to be lethal at close range; the injuries and, in some cases, deaths which

both they and their later replacement, plastic bullets, have caused
have added to the bitterness of the Catholic community's hostility
towards the security forces. Thus any immediate measures taken to
contain the rioting must not exacerbate the hostility to the police
that is one of the factors in the present fighting. More efficient
protective clothing; rigorous control by senior officers of the use of
force so that, as far as possible, innocent people are not injured;
close liaison with local councillors and other community representatives; and the support of what the Kerner Commission called
'counter-rioters' to encourage community self-policing: all are
crucial to an immediate strategy for dealing with the disorders. A
more effective and visibly independent method for dealing with
grievances against the police and new means of ensuring their
accountability to elected representatives will be essential if normal
policing relationships are to be rebuilt.

In addition to new riot equipment, the Government has proposed new criminal sanctions. Parents are to be made responsible
for fines imposed on their children, a provision which has, in fact,
existed since 1977, with very little effect. Indeed, it is a striking
measure of the Government's ignorance of the condition of the
cities that it should regard fines as an effective sanction in areas of
massive unemployment. More seriously, a new Riot Act is likely to
be introduced, not because it will assist the police in affecting
arrests in the midst of disorder, but because according to the Home
Secretary, it may help to process suspects more quickly through
the courts. In other words, it will be possible to obtain convictions
without the inconvenient necessity of establishing any criminal
activity or intent: mere presence on the streets after the Riot Act has
been read will be sufficient for conviction. The Home Secretary's
emphasis on the need for speed suggests that jury trial is not to be
available for the new offence – and, presumably, police officers'
identification evidence is to be sufficient proof of guilt. This combination of a curfew and a new 'sus' law could hardly be better
designed to step up warfare against the police and to ensure that
the full sympathy of their community will be behind the rioters.

The police are part of the problem. But they are also victims of
economic, social and political conflicts whose results they are
supposed to contain. Reforming police practice and tackling the
problem of racism within the police force will not prevent the police
from being seen as a symbol of a racist and divided society as long
as those basic conflicts exist. The Kerner Commission responded to
President Johnson's call by outlining a major programme of

employment (2 million new jobs in three years), education, housing (6 million new or improved housing units in five years) and welfare, in addition to a new structure of neighbourhood 'city halls' and improved policing methods and accountability. The Scarman inquiry will need to recommend a similar programme of economic and social reconstruction. But the reversal of at least two decades of official racism will also be required, an acknowledgement at last that racial equality in the cities cannot be built on racial inequality in the ports of entry. And, finally, the political parties must tackle seriously the appalling under-representation of the black minorities in local politics and their absence from the House of Commons.

When injustice is so serious that civil disorder results, then civil liberties are most in danger. Equal protection and equal rights are insulted by the deprivation, the discrimination and the violence from which black families suffer. Street violence is a further threat to the freedom of entire communities to lead safe and peaceful lives. And the repressive measures with which the Government is likely to respond to the violence will create new injustices and will pose new threats to community peace. As we know from what has happened in Northern Ireland, this triple threat can destroy the most basic standards in human rights. In the words of the Kerner Commission, violence and destruction must be ended – in the streets of the cities and in the lives of people.

9

The Homosexual Minority

The bedrock of civil liberties is the setting of limits on the power of the state to interfere with the private lives of citizens. But the retention of laws against male homosexuality, together with structures of punishment and discrimination which affect homosexual men and women alike, reveals how inadequate is our conception of the proper limits of state action – even when it affects that most basic issue, the individual's choice of private sexual activity.

During the celebrated debate two and a half decades ago which surrounded the report of the Wolfenden Committee on laws concerning homosexuality and prostitution, Lord Devlin offered as a justification for the continuation of criminal penalties against homosexuality the view that such laws, by cementing the moral bricks of society, protected the continuation of society itself.[1] Recognizing that laws against private behaviour required strong justification, he argued that a majority of the community would need to feel 'intolerance, indignation and disgust' in order that the activities of a minority could be curtailed by the criminal law. His thesis has been convincingly demolished by Professor H. L. A. Hart[2] and, more recently, by Professor Ronald Dworkin,[3] and I need only summarize the most obvious faults of the argument. First, the assumption that a majority feel 'intolerance, indignation and disgust' may not be accurate; second, the notion of a society whose moral code must be protected excludes from its membership those minorities, membership of which may be substantial, whose moral code differs from that of the majority; third, there is no evidence that the blunt weapon of the criminal law can impose a uniform moral code; and, fourth, there is no evidence that the disappearance of a uniform moral code leads to the disintegration of society. 'Intolerance, indignation and disgust', even if such emotions are deeply rooted in a majority of the community, cannot

220

overcome the rights of other people to privacy, dignity and the right to pursue happiness and the fulfilment of their individual potential. The grounding of the criminal law on the assumed or actual prejudices of a majority is entirely incompatible with respect for the rights of a minority.

The Wolfenden Committee, established by the Home Secretary in 1954, reported in 1957.[4] The Committee argued that the functions of the criminal law were to preserve public order and decency and to protect the weak, *not* to impose morality on a dissenting minority. They recommended in particular, that consenting homosexual acts performed in private by adult men (that is, men aged 21 or over) should be decriminalized. Although their recommendations concerning prostitution were the basis for legislation in 1959, it was not until 1967 that the Sexual Offences Bill, introduced by Lord Arran in the House of Lords and by Leo Abse, MP, in the Commons, was enacted. The 1967 Act was defective in many respects; it did not apply to Scotland and Northern Ireland, where *all* male homosexual acts remain illegal; it did not apply to the armed forces and the merchant navy; the extremely narrow definition of 'public place' meant that homosexual activity behind the locked door of a public lavatory, or in a public park at night when no one else was present, or in a private home where more than two people were present all remained within the scope of the criminal law. The Act did not legalize homosexuality; it merely removed criminal penalties from a fairly narrow range of homosexual activities, leaving the way open, for instance, for a series of prosecutions for conspiracy to corrupt public morals of publishers who accepted advertisements from those seeking to take part in legal sexual activity (see page 97).

The 1967 Act has not secured for homosexual men and women a rightful and equal place in society. It was not intended to. The comparison with the Wolfenden Committee's proposals on prostitution is revealing. The Committee wanted to get prostitutes off the streets, to preserve 'morality' through the use of the criminal law against women openly soliciting for custom, while securing the satisfaction of their male clients to whom the criminal law did not apply. Similarly, the sponsors of the 1967 Act hoped that by allowing homosexual couples to do what they liked in private, they would keep homosexuality off the streets and out of the public eye. Lord Arran said of the Act: 'I ask those who have, as it were, been in bondage and for whom the prison doors are now open to show their thanks by comporting themselves quietly and with dignity.'[5]

But there is nothing dignified about the present state of the law. Far from concentrating on cases of violence, coercion or pressure on the very young or those who are otherwise vulnerable to unwelcome attentions (as, by and large, the law relating to heterosexual activities does), the law as it affects homosexual men largely condemns relationships which are entirely voluntary and consenting. Perhaps the most damaging effects are on the young men who enter into sexual relationships with others of their own age or with partners over the age of 21. In 1979 proceedings for homosexual offences were brought against seven boys aged under 14, 70 aged between 14 and 16 and 246 aged between 17 and 21. Although most received fines or suspended sentences, 13 were sent to prison.[6] The criminal statistics do not distinguish those cases which involved assault or rape, but the experience of organizations like NCCL, the gay counselling service Friend and the Albany Trust make it clear that the overwhelming majority of such prosecutions involve relationships in which no coercion at all is involved. In addition to those prosecutions, a substantial proportion of the 3089 prosecutions of men aged over 21 for gay offences in the same year involved partners below the age of 21 – who, even if they were not themselves prosecuted, may have suffered the humiliation and fear of seeing their lovers dragged through the courts.

As it stands, the law is peculiarly open to abuse through corrupt and unethical police methods. One consequence of the artificial definition of a 'private place' has been the extensive use of police spies in public lavatories. The case of 'John', who came to the NCCL for legal advice in 1975, was not uncommon. John, who is married with one daughter, was on his way home from a party one night when he went into a public lavatory, sat down in the cubicle and was reading a book on chess when a plain-clothes policeman burst his way in. A second officer kicked open the door of the next-door cubicle. John was charged with gross indecency with the man in the next cubicle and was apparently advised by the police to plead guilty in order to avoid publicity. He contested the charge, and the jury acquitted on a direction from the judge.[7] There is something extremely silly, as well as sinister, about requiring overworked police officers to hang about public lavatories, or even to spy on cubicles through holes in the walls or roof, in the hope of intercepting some sexual encounter between adult men. Even more objectionable is the use of police *agents provocateurs* to trap other men into criminal acts. In 1977, in a case at Winchester Crown Court, a man who stopped at a public lavatory on his way home from work was encouraged by another man to masturbate and was promptly arrested. The enticer turned out to be a police officer, who admitted under cross-examination that his actions were 'open to misinterpretation'. The defendant was acquitted. Later in the same year, in the West Midlands, a vicar was acquitted in a case in which he claimed that no fewer than four officers were operating in one public convenience.

In Scotland, where all male homosexual activity remained illegal after 1967, the Advocate operated a prosecutions policy under which no charge was authorized unless it would have been available under the English law. In 1980 an unexpected amendment to the Scottish Criminal Justice Bill moved by Robin Cook, MP, led to the extension of the 1967 Act to that part of the country. But in Northern Ireland pressure to reform the law was successfully warded off by Ian Paisley's 'Save Our Sons from Sodomy' campaign. In 1980 the European Human Rights Commission decided, in a case brought by Northern Ireland Gay Rights Association activist Jeff Dudgeon, that the law against homosexuality in Northern Ireland was contrary to the provisions of the Convention on privacy and discrimination on grounds of national origin.[8] Even then, the Government refused to introduce law reform and, in what has become a reflex action where European Commission decisions against the UK Government are concerned, referred the matter to the Court in the hope of obtaining a few years' more delay, if not a different judgment.

Lesbian women outside the armed forces have never been the target of the criminal law. There is no age of consent as such for sexual relationships between women, although indecent assault could be charged where one partner is under the age of 16. In 1921 an attempt to amend a Criminal Law Amendment Bill to extend the offence of gross indecency between men to activities involving women was defeated in the House of Lords and has not been revived.

But the absence of criminal sanctions against consenting sexual activity between women does not mean that the law ignores such activity. In 1928 Radclyffe Hall's moving but (in Vera Brittain's words) 'essentially lady-like' novel, *The Well of Loneliness*, was convicted of obscenity and the seized copies burned. The fears aroused in women whose sexuality is independent of men are most apparent in cases in which a separated or divorced mother who has become a lesbian claims custody of her children. It is not uncommon for the courts, when granting access to a lesbian mother, to impose a condition, at the father's insistence, that the mother's lover or women friends be barred from the house when the children are present. In one such case, however, the Court of Appeal refused to uphold the terms of the custody order, indicating that there was no point in granting custody to a parent and then imposing conditions on the people with whom that parent can allow the children to come into contact. Perhaps the most distressing aspect of such cases for the women concerned is the often salacious interest displayed by the court in the most minute details of their sleeping arrangements – an interest rarely displayed in cases in which one or both parents have remarried.

Lesbians who declare their homosexuality, like homosexual men who have 'come out', are likely to be the victims of prejudice and discrimination in their employment. In 1976 Veronica Pickles, who was employed as a midwife by a local council, had the offer of a place on a health visitors' course withdrawn after her gay rights activities were publicized in a local newspaper. She appealed against the decision, successfully. Others are less fortunate. A woman teacher was dismissed by her employing authority after two months simply because her doctor had disclosed to the authority that, in his view, a mild depression from which she had suffered was due to her lesbian relationship. When she challenged the decision, she was informed by the occupational health officer: 'A lesbian cannot be trusted to teach in a girls' school where some of the girls are very well developed.' No such fears, apparently, attached to men teachers at the same school. Although this teacher's work was highly recommended by her colleagues, she felt unable to fight or publicize her case for fear of prejudicing her chances of re-employment elsewhere.

The myth of the sexual predator pervades employers' attitudes towards homosexual men and women. There is no evidence at all to support the widely held prejudice that homosexuals are more prone than heterosexuals to feel sexual attraction for children or young people – or that even when they do feel such attraction, they are more likely to act on it. Sexual offences by adult men against girls and young women are all too common, but society draws no general conclusion that all men are untrustworthy. The belief that an openly homosexual man or woman is a threat to the young is a rationalization of a widespread fear of those who are different and of the challenge posed by homosexuality to the norm of hetero-sexual, reproductive relationships. Many seem to fear that even if a homosexual teacher, social worker or youth leader does not actually seduce the young people they work with, he or she will 'corrupt' them by example. Indeed, the main justification offered for retaining the higher age of consent for male homosexual activity is that homosexuality is a stage through which many, if not most, young men (and women) pass but in which they may become fixed if allowed to come into contact with openly homosexual, even happy, adults. Simply to state the position is to reveal the crudeness of the assumptions about human development. Surely heterosexuality is not so unattractive an option that it need fear the competition of an open, unoppressed homosexuality?

The arguments for retaining a higher age of consent (whether 21, as at present, or 18, as proposed by the Criminal Law Revision Committee in its recent report)[9] ignore the positive harm which is done by the laws against young male homosexuals. It is extremely difficult for young men and women who believe themselves to be homosexual or bisexual to obtain sympathetic and frank advice; for those who do, in fact, become mainly or exclusively homosexual, their development is made infinitely more painful by society's rejection of adult homosexuals who could have offered 'role models' which those young people are unlikely to find in their own families. In 1975 John Warburton was asked by his employers, the Inner London Education Authority, to sign an undertaking that he would never discuss homosexuality with his pupils except as part of a 'structured and authorized sex-education programme' after he had talked about his homosexuality to pupils who had taunted him for taking part in a gay rights demonstration. And yet the Inner London Education Authority is one of the few authorities with an official policy of not discriminating against gay teachers.

The law offers virtually no protection to homosexual employees. There is no anti-discrimination law equivalent to the Race Relations Act and the Sex Discrimination Act. And the law against unfair dismissal, which could and should have offered protection to homosexuals dismissed without good cause, has been severely undermined in a series of appeal decisions. John Saunders was employed for over two years by the Scottish National Camps Association as a maintenance worker at a camp for teenage school-children in Perthshire. There were no complaints about his work, no suggestion that he had made advances to any of the children, and he had no criminal convictions. But his employers discovered from a 'trustworthy' source that he was gay – as indeed he readily confirmed when asked. The Association's secretary, when he heard that John Saunders was homosexual, looked up the word 'bisexual' in his dictionary and dismissed him!

An industrial tribunal upheld John Saunders's dismissal in a finding confirmed by the Scottish Employment Appeals Tribunal.[10] It was enough that Mr Saunders was homosexual, that he worked in close proximity to children, that there was a 'body of opinion' which considered homosexuals to be a risk to children and that the employers had to take into account the 'probable' views of parents (whose views were never, in fact, ascertained). The *Saunders* decision not only left all homosexual employees, and particularly those who might come into contact with children, at risk of instant dismissal for nothing more than being homosexual but has also allowed employers to plead prejudice as a sufficient reason for dismissal in other cases as well. In the case of *Harper* v. *National Coal Board*,[11] involving the dismissal of an epileptic, Saunders was approvingly cited as a precedent.

In England and Wales the Employment Appeal Tribunal has followed the Scottish Tribunal's reasoning in their recent decision in the case of Gordon Wiseman.[12] Gordon Wiseman worked as a lecturer in drama therapy at the Salford College of Technology; his work was highly considered and his courses were nationally known. In December 1979 he was convicted of gross indecency with another adult man (although, as is so often the case with such convictions, the 'offence' took place behind locked doors). A newspaper cutting of the conviction was shown to the College authorities, who suspended Mr Wiseman and eventually sacked him. By a majority an industrial tribunal found his dismissal fair. In March 1981 the Employment Appeal Tribunal upheld the tribunal's decision, holding that although Gordon Wiseman's conviction was entirely unrelated to his work, and although there was no suggestion that he might 'corrupt' his students, other people's possible prejudices against his continued employment were sufficient reason for his dismissal. Bernard Levin's comment on the *Saunders* case is equally applicable to the *Wiseman* judgment:

> The case of Mr Saunders is an instance of injustice by people who ought to have known better and reinforced by people whose job was to put it right . . . some of the judges north of Berwick (and now, let it be added, south as well) appear to believe that Lord Goddard was a milksop, Lord Ellenborough an undercover communist and Judge Jeffreys a sentimental old fool. But what happened to Mr Saunders is one part of the scandal; the greater part lies in the fact that if he does not get legal redress, it will have been judicially established that a citizen who is wholly blameless may be punished because

some people believe that *other* people, not including the citizen in question, might, in certain circumstances, behave wrongly.[13]

The prejudice of the employer, or the employer's belief in the prejudice of other people, are now firmly established as grounds for dismissing a homosexual worker. But there is also a 'body of opinion' which holds that women, particularly married women, are unfit for employment, and another 'body of opinion' which considers black people essentially inferior to white. Their prejudices were explicitly ruled out by the Race Relations and Sex Discrimination Acts as adequate or acceptable grounds for dismissal or any other form of victimization. Similar protection for homosexuals is now urgently required.

In order to guarantee homosexual men and women their right to equality of treatment, the law on homosexual offences should be placed on the same basis as the law relating to heterosexual offences. In other words, the age of consent for homosexual men should be the same as that for heterosexual women, with a further proviso in both cases that no prosecution should be brought where two partners close in age are involved in consenting sexual activity, even though one or both partners is under age. The law in Northern Ireland should, of course, be aligned with that in the rest of the country, and the criminal offences specifically relating to the armed services and the merchant navy should be abolished. The notion of what is 'in private' should be redefined to ensure that consenting activity between more than two people, or activity in a place that is technically public but where no other member of the public is present, is not caught by the criminal law. The offence of 'gross indecency' between males should be abolished. One of the major defects of the 1967 Act was that it left untouched the offence of procuring or attempting to procure a *lawful* homosexual act, thus allowing publishers of contact advertisements to be convicted. (An equivalent offence relating to lawful heterosexual activity would make 'chatting up' as well as lonely hearts advertisements criminal!) Not only should those provisions of the 1967 Act be abolished; so too should the offence of conspiracy to corrupt public morals, the vague, judge-created law under which the publishers of *IT* were convicted. Its abolition has been recommended by the Law Commission and the Williams Committee on Obscenity, but, unfortunately, the Labour Government's Criminal Law Act of 1978, which reformed some other aspects of the conspiracy laws, ducked this issue.

The laws against homosexuality, and the law's failure to protect homosexuals from discrimination and harassment, cannot be justified by any social interest which could override claims of the homosexual minority to equal treatment and respect. Far from protecting society, the law demeans both its victims and those who enforce it. Gay men's right to privacy is invaded; consenting acts which harm no one are criminalized; public expressions of affection are taboo; gay organizations and meeting places have become the objects of police surveillance; and many homosexuals live in fear, their sexual preference stigmatized and derided. The enforcement of laws against homosexuality is accompanied by the most objectionable forms of surveillance and investigation, partly explained by the nature of the information required for a prosecution, but partly due to nothing more than prurience on the part of some police officers. Thus the law tramples on values which it should seek to protect and brings the law itself into disrepute.

IV

The United Kingdom and International Standards

10

Protecting Human Rights

In January 1981 the United Kingdom Government renewed the optional provision of the European Convention on Human Rights and Fundamental Freedoms which allows individuals to bring a complaint against the United Kingdom to the Human Rights Commission in Strasbourg. The renewal, which was for a further five years, was not achieved without opposition. The objections of a number of Conservative MPs to the 'interference' of foreign institutions with decisions of the British Parliament or British courts, together with the private resistance of Home Office officials to the prospect of having to continue to defend their record to unsympathetic European judges, were themselves a tribute to the growing effectiveness of Western Europe's human-rights enforcement procedures.

As the Foreign Office apparently recognized, the Government could not withdraw the right of individual petition to the Human Rights Commission without severely damaging its international standing. But it has been suggested for some time that more should be done than simply renewing the right of individual petition. Should the Government support measures to extend the scope of the Convention and to strengthen its enforcement procedures? Should the Convention – as Lord Scarman, among others, has urged – be used as the basis for a new Bill of Rights?

The European Human Rights Convention, signed in 1950 and ratified by the United Kingdom in 1951, was a product of the post-war desire for unity in Western Europe and for supra-national institutions which could help to prevent any recurrence of the previous decade's horrors. Modelled on the United Nations Declaration of Human Rights, it included, in general terms, a statement of the principles of civil and political rights which were by then conventional wisdom in moderate liberal circles. But its drafting was also influenced by Cold War thinking. Article 17 ('Nothing in this Convention may be interpreted as implying for any State, group or person any right to engage in any activity or perform any act aimed at the destruction of any of the rights and freedoms set forth herein or their limitation to a greater extent than is provided for in the Convention') was used in 1957 to uphold the banning of the West German Communist Party and could similarly be used to defend the same Government's notorious *Berufsverbot* or ban on 'extremists' in public service.

The Convention has been ratified by nineteen of the Council of Europe's twenty-one member states and signed by the remaining two, Spain and Lichtenstein. Fourteen recognize the right of individual petition, and fifteen, including the United Kingdom, recognize the jurisdiction of the European Human Rights Court, whose decisions are accepted as binding. The first fourteen articles of the Convention specify the rights and freedoms to be protected, including the right to life, freedom from torture or inhuman or degrading treatment or punishment, the right to a fair trial and the right to freedom of thought, religion, expression, peaceful assembly and association. Although the Convention does not prohibit race or sex discrimination as such, it provides in Article 14 that the rights and freedoms protected by the Convention must not be granted in a manner which discriminates on grounds of race, sex, colour, language, religion and so on. Indeed, the Commission has gone further in its interpretation of the Convention by holding[1] that racial discrimination may of itself amount to 'degrading treatment', which the Convention directly prohibits. Protocol 1, which the United Kingdom has ratified with certain reservations, protects the peaceful enjoyment of private possessions and the right to education and commits the member states to holding free elections by secret ballot. Protocol 4, banning imprisonment for civil debts, guaranteeing the right of a citizen to enter the country of his or her citizenship and protecting freedom of movement, has not been ratified by this country: since 1968 immigration controls have been designed to deprive certain United Kingdom citizens, primarily of Asian origin, of their right to enter this country, while the 1976 Prevention of Terrorism Act gives the Home Secretary the power, by executive order, to deny freedom of movement through the use of exclusion orders.

The only right absolutely protected by the Convention is the right not to be subjected to torture or inhuman or degrading treatment or punishment. The remaining articles contain their own exemptions, sufficiently widely drafted to give considerable scope for judicial caution. The right to life, for instance, may be denied without breach of the Convention if death results from the use of force which is absolutely necessary 'to effect a lawful arrest or prevent the escape of a person lawfully detained' (any arrest or any escape?) or to quell a riot or insurrection. Freedom of expression may be restricted

> as proscribed by law and [as] necessary in a democratic society, in the interests of national security, territorial integrity or public safety, for the prevention of disorder or crime, for the protection of health or morals, for the protection of the reputation or rights of others, for prevention of the disclosure of information received in confidence, or for maintaining the authority and impartiality of the judiciary.

Similar exceptions are provided in respect of peaceful assembly, freedom of conscience and religion and the right to respect for private life.

Furthermore, the Convention gives Governments the freedom to derogate from its provisions in times of emergency (with the exceptions of those articles concerning torture, protection from slavery, protection from retrospective criminal penalties and the right to life). But derogation is permitted only to the extent 'strictly required by the exigencies of the situation'. Thus, although Governments are given some leeway in deciding what measures are needed to deal with terrorism or other threats to a nation itself, emergency legislation may be scrutinized by the institutions of the Convention even where a derogation has been filed. Not only may an individual or another state challenge an action performed under the authority of emergency powers, but a Government which has derogated must keep the Council of Europe fully informed of its actions. Ireland's inter-state case against the United Kingdom, following the torture of detainees held under internment powers for which a derogation had been entered, illustrated the fact that some limitations are placed upon a Government even in emergency. Both the Commission and the Court found that the interrogation methods complained of violated the Convention, although internment itself was considered acceptable.[2]

It is impossible to construct a completely accurate 'league table' of the record of different countries under the Convention. Any such comparison would need to take into account not only population differences but also the question of whether alleged violations of the Convention can be made the subject of a complaint in each country's own courts. In the United Kingdom, of course, the Convention is not part of domestic law, and although its provisions may be used in argument to support a case, no action can be brought simply on the grounds that the Convention has been infringed. This failure to incorporate the Convention may itself be an infringement of the Convention, which requires 'an effective remedy before a national authority' for anyone who believes that his or her Convention rights have been breached. The point has not been decided by the Court. But the absence of any domestic remedy for many alleged infringements of the Convention must be one reason for the large number of complaints brought against the United Kingdom. Of the twenty-eight inter-state and individual complaints which have gone to the Human Rights Court since 1959, eight have been against Belgium, five against the United Kingdom and four against West Germany. Of 335 complaints registered by the Commission in 1978, 115 were against West Germany and ninety-seven against the United Kingdom; of 373 complaints registered in 1977, 148 were against the United Kingdom and ninety-five against West Germany.[3] Although a complaint will be registered only if it contains adequate facts to allow an examination, only a small proportion of registered complaints are eventually found to be admissible as disclosing a *prima facie* complaint. Of the 201 individual complaints declared admissible up to December 1978, sixty-seven were against the United Kingdom.

Even from a basic analysis of the figures, therefore, it appears that the United Kingdom has been on the receiving end of human rights complaints more ofen than any of the thirteen other countries (except West Germany and Belgium) which recognize the right of individual petition. And in case it is thought that the complaint were unimportant, it should be stressed that those cases which have reached a 'friendly settlement' or a decision against the United Kingdom are of very considerable significance. They include the Irish Government's complaints of torture of internees, the East African Asians' cases following the shameful 'shuttle-cocking' of United Kingdom citizens around the world, and several cases relating to the rights of prisoners and mental patients in institutions.

When the United Kingdom Government ratified the Convention thirty years ago, it presumably never imagined that subsequent Governments would be found in breach of the Convention's often bland provisions. The Convention's requirements – given the breadth of the exceptions – are indeed not strict, particularly when compared with the Bill of Rights of the United States of America: but the United Kingdom has repeatedly shown itself unable to meet even those standards which the Government in 1951 was willing to accept.

The Irish case was not the first time that British emergency legislation had been challenged in Strasbourg. In 1956 and 1957 Greece complained about emergency legislation and alleged torture for which the British authorities were responsible in Cyprus, although political agreements reached in 1959 between the countries concerned meant that the complaints were not pursued. In two applications made in 1971 and 1972 the Irish Government alleged numerous violations of the Convention by the United Kingdom Government in Northern Ireland, specifying the Special Powers Acts of 1922 and 1933, which were still in force, the internment powers, the treatment of internees and Army shootings of civilians. (The second application concerning retrospective criminal legislation was withdrawn after the United kingdom Government undertook not to pursue retrospective prosecutions.) In 1976, following a succession of hearings, the Commission reported that although detention without trial (the subject of a derogation notice) was compatible with the Convention, the use of the 'five techniques' (see page 157) amounted to torture. The Commission found that at Holywood Barracks, during the autumn of 1971, there had been not simply isolated incidents but 'a practice . . . [of] inhuman treatment in breach of Article 3'.[4] The Human Rights Court, to which the case was referred by the Irish Government, concluded in January 1978 that the interrogation techniques did not amount to torture but were nonetheless inhuman treatment in breach of the Convention, and it criticized the British Government's authorization of those and similar practices.[5] Long before the Court reached its ruling, the Government had announced that the 'five techniques' would no longer be used. But the limitations not only of Convention procedures but also of British legal and political remedies were underlined by the authorities' unwillingness or inability to bring proceedings against those who had ordered and conducted the assaults on the internees – or to reveal at what level of political and military command the techniques were authorized.

In 1978 the Northern Ireland issue was again referred to the Commission by a number of prisoners protesting against the British Government's withdrawal of 'special category' status from those convicted of terrorist offences (see page 163). The prisoners argued that the punishment imposed by the authorities in response to their refusal to wear prison clothes or to do prison work constituted inhuman and degrading treatment and, furthermore, that their rights to privacy, correspondence and freedom of association were interfered with. In 1980 a majority of the Commission decided that most of the complaints were manifestly ill-founded and ruled them inadmissible.[6] Only the issues of prisoners' correspondence and internal remedies were reserved for further consideration. But the Commission has remained involved, so far unsuccessfully, in attempts to resolve the dispute in the prisons.

One of the first individual complaints against the United Kingdom to be declared admissible, in 1971, was that of Mr Golder, a prisoner in Parkhurst who was accused by a prison officer of having assaulted him during the Parkhurst disturbances of October 1969. Mr Golder was refused permission by the prison authorities to write to a solicitor with a view to suing the prison officer for defamation and thus clearing his prison disciplinary record. He complained not only that his right to conduct private correspondence had been infringed but that, by being denied access to a solicitor, he had been refused a fair hearing of his complaint. In 1973, after the Commission had adopted a report finding in Mr Golder's favour, the Government referred the case to the Court, who in 1975 upheld both complaints.[7] In 1976 the Committee of Ministers (to whom the Court's judgment had been referred under Convention procedure) discharged the case, noting that the Government had amended the Prison Rules. In fact, the new Rules still required a prisoner to obtain the Home Secretary's consent before consulting a solicitor about possible civil proceedings, although the requirement to petition the Home Secretary was removed. Furthermore, consent would be refused if the proceedings concerned the prisoner's treatment in prison and if he had not exhausted the normal internal channels of complaining to the governor.

Between 1975 and 1978 a further forty prisoners complained to the Commission about censorship of their correspondence with MPs, relatives, friends and acquaintances on matters which included prison conditions, civil and criminal proceedings, business transactions and family problems. In 1977 the Commission selected seven of these cases, declaring them admissible. The Government argued that the prisoners failed to complain through internal prison channels about censorship of their correspondence – although, since the Prison Rules ban correspondence about prison conditions with any except a limited number of contacts, such complaints would be doomed to failure. The Commission's report in favour of the prisoners has been referred to the Court, from whom a decision is expected in 1981.[8]

The Court's decision in 1978 that judicial birching in the Isle of Man contravened the prohibition on inhuman and degrading punishment[9] led to sustained protests in that territory against foreign interference. Although the Westminter Government, which acts on behalf of the Manx Government in foreign affairs, finally renewed the right of individual petition for the Isle of Man in 1979, the renewal notice specifically excluded complaints under Article 3. Although no further judicial birchings have taken place, the Manx Parliament has refused to repeal the relevant legislation. Similar issues were raised by the complaints brought in 1976 by two Scots mothers against the use of corporal punishment with the tawse in Scottish schools. It is to be hoped that the distaste shown by the other European judges – most of whose countries forbid corporal punishment – in the Isle of Man case will extend to the regime in British schools.

The 1981 Contempt of Court Act was the result of another decision by the Court, in the case of the *Sunday Times*, holding that contempt laws which banned prior comment on pending civil litigation infringed the right to free exchange of information. But a further weakness in the Convention's procedures was revealed in the extraordinary dispute between the Lord Chancellor, Lord Hailsham – who insisted that the Bill, his 'little ewe-lamb', reformed the law in accordance with the Court's decision – and *The Times*'s legal advisers, who insisted that Lord Hailsham had simply misread the decision.[10] Instead of removing the law of contempt entirely from civil proceedings heard by a judge alone, the Act still leaves newspapers liable for comment designed to put pressure on parties to litigation.

In case after case the UK Government of the day has refused to give effect to a decision by the Human Rights Commission, insisting instead on a reference to the Court, from which, no doubt, it hoped for a more restrictive decision as well as further delay. In 1980 the Commission decided in favour of Jeff Dudgeon, a homosexual living in Northern Ireland, who had complained that the law in Northern Ireland (which makes any male homosexual act criminal, whatever the age of the participants and regardless of whether the act takes place in private) infringed his right to privacy and, furthermore, constituted discrimination against the people of one part of the United Kingdom.[11] Although the Commission's findings were clearly right and unlikely to be overturned by the Court, the Government refused to accept the Commission's decision, to face up to Ian Paisley's 'Save Our Sons from Sodomy' campaign and to bring the legal position in Northern Ireland into line with that in England, Wales and Scotland. The case was referred to the Court in 1981, but a hearing of the complaint was adjourned after a disagreement over the introduction of expert evidence.

Other cases pending before the Court include three complaints declared admissible by the Commission in 1980 from United Kingdom citizens who had been detained under the Prevention of Terrorism Act and released without charge after being interrogated, photographed and finger-printed. A further case challenging the same Act is being brought by a United Kingdom citizen from Northern Ireland, who was excluded by order of the Home Secretary and is therefore forbidden to live in any part of the country except Northern Ireland.

But cases brought against other countries may also affect the United Kingdom. The Court's decision in the *Klass* case,[12] concerning telephone tapping by the West German authorities, has made it clear that British law, which permits the police and security services to intercept telephone and mail communications on the Home Secretary's warant alone, is in breach of the Convention. A complaint on this issue is pending from Joseph Malone, who, when charged with receiving stolen goods, found that the evidence against him included a transcript of telephone calls he had made. Mr Malone appealed unsuccessfully to the High Court for a declaration that the interception was unlawful. In holding that telephone tapping was not prohibited under English law, the judge said that the absence of controls clearly violated the Convention and that the situation 'cried out for legislation'.[13] No doubt the Commission will agree.

As the *Malone* case indicates, the provisions of the Convention may be argued in the British courts even though no application may be founded directly on them. But the courts have rarely allowed themselves to be influenced by such arguments. Despite a Court of Appeal decision concerning the rights of patrial wives under the 1971 Immigration Act,[14] in which it was held that the powers of immigration officers should be exercised in accordance with the Convention, the guarantee of a fair hearing and protection against racial discrimination have had little effect on the administration of immigration control and have not prevented the House of Lords itself from denying *habeas corpus* to those held without trial on suspicion of being illegal entrants (see page 198).

The Convention's impact is undermined by the weaknesses of its wording and its enforcement procedures. As we have noted, the Convention provides a wide range of generalized exemptions to most of the rights which it protects, as well as permitting Governments to derogate from certain provisions in times of emergency. Although retaining a power to derogate, in many other respects the 1966 United Nations Covenant on Civil and Political Rights provides an improved formulation. Unlike the Convention, the Covenant does not permit the detention of 'persons of unsound mind, alcoholics or drug addicts or vagrants'; it prohibits any 'arbitrary' deprivation of life and specifically bans medical or scientific experimentation without the subject's consent. Its exceptions to freedom of expression and peaceful assembly are slightly narrower than those permited by the Convention, while its provisions on nationality specifically include the right of every child to acquire a nationality.

The United Kingdom's ratification of the Covenant in 1976 was accompanied by a note of reservation, which mainly related to the dependent territories but also reserved the right to legislate on citizenship in a manner which might breach the Covenant – a threat now realized in the 1981 Nationality Act.[15] Although the competence of the United Nations Human Rights Committee to receive a complaint by another state was accepted, the Optional Covenant, which provides a procedure for handling individual complaints, has not yet been ratified. Although the Government has argued that the Optional Covenant would duplicate the Convention procedure, there is no reason why individuals should not have a choice of remedies where the Convention and Covenant overlap, particularly since the Government's continued refusal to accept the Covenant's individual complaints procedure deprives people in this country of a remedy for the violation of rights protected by the Covenant but not the Convention.

The Council of Europe has itself recognized that some of the Convention's drafting is unsatisfactory and has begun to consider the possibility of bringing the Convention closer to the provisions of the Covenant. A second difficulty which has been recognized is that in some areas the Commission has had little or no opportunity to develop its interpretation of the Convention, simply because no appropriate complaints have been brought. Article 8's protection of the right to respect for private life might have been developed into a right of privacy, extending to the issue of personal records held by state and other agencies. But with the exception of the telephone-tapping case referred to earlier, Article 8 has hardly been tested. Fortunately, the Council of Europe itself took the initiative in drafting a new Convention specifically concerned with data processing and individual privacy (see page 44). The new Convention does not, however, provide any enforcement mechanism – although the Commission and the Court might decide, in an appropriate case under Article 8, to treat the new Convention as an elaboration of the right to respect for private life, thus giving individuals a direct remedy.

But even where the present Convention offers the possibility of challenging executive practice or powers, the aggrieved individual must overcome formidable barriers. The British legal aid system cannot be used for a complaint under the Convention, while the Commission's own legal aid system does not operate until the Government is asked for observations on admissibility or the complaint is put to the Commission for a decision on admissibility. But in order to arrive at first base, the complainant must exhaust all available domestic remedies, file his complaint within six months and persuade the staff of the Commission not to reject his complaint as manifestly ill-founded. At this vital stage the complainant must rely on private resources or find a private lawyer or organization prepared to handle the case without charge. Although many of the complaints to the Commission would be ruled out in any case, the very low proportion of initial complaints which are registered and the low proportion of registered complaints which are later declared admissible may partly result from the failure to provide proper legal assistance to the complainant at the start of the case. The Commission's own legal aid system not only comes into play after most complaints have been ruled out of order but also provides an entirely inadequate level of assistance. By averaging the level of legal aid provided in all member countries – some of which provide none at all – the Commission ends up with a scheme which covers little more than the out-of-pocket expenses of the complainant and his or her legal advisers. There are few organizations like NCCL, MIND or the Joint Council for the Welfare of Immigrants that are able to undertake European Convention cases without charge, and they can only handle a small number.

Perhaps the most serious defect is the time taken by the Commission and the Court. The disturbances which gave rise to Mr

Golder's complaint took place in 1969. The Commission's hearing was held in December 1971. Drafting of the report began in July 1972, the report being adopted a year later. In September 1973 the Government referred the case to the Court, which made its finding in February 1975. The *Sunday Times* complaint, lodged in January 1974, did not produce a report from the Commission until May 1977. The Court's decision was not made until six years after the injunction on publication of the disputed articles had been imposed. The delay is partly caused by Governments' failure to respond rapidly to requests for observations on a case but is seriously exacerbated by the fact that Commissioners are appointed part-time, cannot sit permanently and are serviced by an under-staffed secretariat.

Nor does it help that once the Commission has disposed of a complaint, the individual has no further standing in the case. It is up to the Commission itself or the Government involved to refer the case to the Court. It is the Commission, not the complainant, who argues the case to the Court, the complainant's lawyers only appearing at the Court if the Commission so requests. Although the *Sunday Times* lawyers were permitted to join the Commission's team at the Court hearing of the case, the NCCL's legal officer who represented the complainant in the Isle of Man birching case was refused permission to appear in front of the Court.

It is not only the complainant who has an interest in the case that is inadequately recognized under present procedures. The outcome of the complaint may have a major impact on the law or administrative practice of the country concerned. (The *Golder* case, for instance, led directly, albeit slowly, to a change in the Prison Rules.) Neither friendly settlement negotiations between the complainant, the Commission and the Government nor a hearing at the Court (from which the complainant may be excluded) is the best forum for ensuring that the wider issues raised by the case are adequately considered. The introduction of *amicus curiae* ('friend of the court') briefs from organizations with a public interest in the matter (for instance, from the National Union of Journalists and other groups concerned with press freedom in the *Sunday Times* and similar cases) would substantially reduce the risk of a Government's misleading the Commission or Court. Public debate of the issues raised by Convention cases, and an appreciation of human rights standards and methods for their enforcement, would be very considerably enhanced if the Commission would abandon its present rule that all pleadings in a case must be confidential.

Incorporation of the Convention into English law

The considerable defects in the Strasbourg procedures might be of lesser importance if the Convention were to be made part of the law of this country, so that the individual complaining of interference with rights protected by the Convention could bring an action in the British courts. The arguments in support of and against the incorporation of the Convention as a new Bill of Rights have been extensively dealt with elsewhere [16] and will be considered briefly here. Essentially, it is suggested that a new Bill of Rights would restrain Parliament from riding roughshod over basic rights of individuals or minorities; that it would provide the courts with more effective guidance as to the standards that they should adopt, particularly when dealing with the extensive powers of modern government, than the common law tradition can supply; and that it would give the aggrieved individual a more direct and a speedier remedy than that the Convention itself provides. For instance, a prisoner complaining of interference with correspondence would be able to apply directly to the High Court for a declaration of his rights and the appropriate order; [17] a defendant in criminal proceedings (for instance, under the Official Secrets Act) would be able to challenge the validity of the prosecution as an infringement of his Convention rights to impart and receive information – a question which could be referred to a higher court for a ruling before the prosecution could continue.

The effects of a new Bill of Rights would depend, first, on the substance of the rights and freedoms protected and, second, on its precise legal status. Although proposals have been made for a Bill of Rights drafted from scratch, [18] it is inconceivable that the political parties could agree on the need for, let alone the contents of, such a document. The only practical proposal for a new Bill of Rights remains the incorporation of the European Convention. The possible methods of its incorporation are discussed below. However, any proposal for incorporation implies an increase in the power of the courts as against that of Parliament and the executive.

It is quite true that Parliament's record of legislating against civil liberty principles is deplorable. The 1968 Commonwealth Immigrants Act, the 1971 Immigration Act, the 1972 Northern Ireland (Temporary Provisions) Act and the Detention of Terrorists (Northern Ireland) Order of the same year, the 1974 and 1976 Prevention of Terrorism Acts and the 1981 British Nationality Act

are particularly disgraceful examples of an elected majority's assent
to substantial increases in executive powers at the expense of the
rights of individuals and minorities. A few days after the passage of
the 1974 Prevention of Terrorism Act, Sir Leslie (now Lord)
Scarman said in a key contribution the the debate about a new Bill
of Rights: 'when times are abnormally alive with fear and
prejudice, the common law is at a disadvantage: it cannot resist the
will, however frightened and prejudiced it may be, of
Parliament.'[19] But fear and prejudice have also characterized a long
line of decisions by the courts in which the demands of state power
have been allowed to overrule the individual's rights.

More than any other judge, Lord Denning, the present Master of
the Rolls, is regarded as the champion of the ordinary individual
against the state. In two notable judgments he has indeed stood out
in support of hard-won rights: in his defence of the right of peaceful
assembly (see page 112)[20] and in his opposition to jury vetting (see
page 55).[21] In both cases, however, Lord Denning was in the
minority. More often, Lord Denning's championship of 'freedom'
has seemed positively perverse. The rights of television licence
holders,[22] tax-evasion suspects,[23] a Conservative education
authority[24] and a private airline company[25] have all been defended
against Government Ministers. But the rights of black immigrants[26] or an American journalist[27] to a fair hearing, the right of
social security claimants to a review of the decisions of administrative tribunals,[28] the rights of tenants to some measure of security,[29]
the rights of trade unionists to take part in peaceful industrial
action[30] – all have suffered at the hands of Lord Denning and his
colleagues. Nor is this a matter of individual personalities. Lord
Denning himself has often enough been overruled by the House of
Lords. But the House of Lords itself has been responsible for
judgments which show scant regard for human rights. The denial
of *habeas corpus* to black migrants settled here has already been
mentioned.[31] The *Sunday Times*'s complaint to the European
Human Rights Commission was necessitated by the House of
Lords extension of the law of contempt in that case. It has been
suggested by Lord Scarman that 'Had the House of Lords had the
advantage of a modern Bill of Rights, it would not have been led
into the formulation of a principle . . . which the European Court
believed to be . . . unnecessary in a democratic society.'[32] But 'a
modern Bill of Rights' need not have made any difference at all. The
House of Lords could have reached a very different decision in the
Sunday Times case, even without incorporation of the Convention

and could have referred to the Convention in justification of its decision (as Lord Scarman himself would have done, no doubt). But even if the Convention had been incorporated before the House of Lords came to judge the *Sunday Times* case, the court could still have reached the decision it did – and used the exceptions provided for in that Convention ('maintaining the authority and impartiality of the judiciary') to reach the decision so deplored by the Commission.

I am not, of course, suggesting that the decisions of the Court of Appeal and the House of Lords on civil liberties issues are all of a piece. But the roll-call of restrictive decisions leaves little room for optimism about the likely impact of incorporating the Convention. There is, too, a further problem. The judiciary is notoriously drawn from a very narrow section of the community, the bias of its background and legal training making it generally hostile to the collective exercise of rights and to state intervention designed to alter the balance of economic power.[33] Socialists are right to fear that the increased power conferred on the courts by a new Bill of Rights would be used to strike down, for instance, a wealth tax or a nationalization statute as contrary to the 'peaceful enjoyment of possessions' guaranteed to individuals *and* to corporations by Protocol 1 of the Convention. Interference with private property is indeed permitted by the Convention 'in accordance with law' and 'in the public interest', but the courts are scarcely the appropriate judges of what economic policies should be pursued in the public interest. Concern for civil and political rights is compatible with entirely conflicting views of private property and the role of the state. One may believe, as Sir Keith Joseph does,[34] that private property is the foundation of civil liberty, or take the view that state intervention to secure for all the necessities of life (employment, housing, income) is an essential part of a proper definition of human rights. But guarantees of civil and political rights – freedom of speech, association, assembly and communication – should keep open the means of achieving political change: they should not be hijacked in the service of one particular economic philosophy.

Both the risks and the benefits of a new Bill of Rights would depend not only on what it said but also on the constitutional importance given it. There are, essentially, three models on offer. The first, generally favoured by Lord Scarman, is the complete entrenchment of a new Bill of Rights, with a Supreme Court having the same power to strike down legislation as the Supreme Court of the USA enjoys. The second, adopted by the Standing Advisory

Commission on Human Rights in Northern Ireland,[35] gives the Bill of Rights a favoured status over other legislation, short of full entrenchment. The third, adopted by the House of Lords Select Committee on a Bill of Rights[36] and incorporated into the Bill introduced in that House by Lord Wade,[37] gives the Bill of Rights favoured status only over earlier legislation.

A fully entrenched Bill of Rights would require a new constitutional settlement, in which the present sovereignty of Parliament, already significantly eroded by the Treaty of Rome, would give way to the courts. Legislation held by the House of Lords (or a new Supreme Court) to be incompatible with the Bill of Rights would be nullified, and any amendment to the provisions of the Bill of Rights would require a special majority in Parliament or even a majority in a referendum. That Parliament has sometimes abused its power or that more effective curbs on executive action are needed is not in doubt. But the substitution of the unelected judiciary (with its own record of abuse of power) for an elected House of Commons cannot provide an acceptable answer.

The second model is the most satisfactory. Under the Standing Advisory Commission's proposals, the provisions of the Human Rights Convention would take precedence over both existing and subsequent legislation, unless Parliament specifically included in that legislation a clause stating that its provisions would take effect notwithstanding the Convention. If no 'notwithstanding' clause were included, anyone who believed that his Convention rights had been breached as a consequence of legislation would be able to apply directly to the courts in this country for the appropriate remedy. If, for instance, a complainant succeeded in a case challenging the validity of the Immigration Rules as they affect foreign husbands, on the grounds that the Rules breached the Convention provisions on family life and race and sex discrimination, the Government would have the choice of presenting to Parliament fresh Rules amended to bring them into line with the court's decision or re-enacting the Rules complete with a 'notwithstanding' clause – thus signalling beyond doubt its intention to breach the Convention. In the latter case the complainant would still be able to challenge the Rules in a complaint to the Human Rights Commission and, ultimately, the Human Rights Court, as he would be able to do in any case in which legislation was enacted which, from the outset, included a 'notwithstanding' clause.

Provided, of course, that legal aid were made available, incorporation of the Convention along these lines would considerably increase the use made of the Convention. The lengthy, expensive and rather remote proceedings at Strasbourg would become a last resort for a Convention case rather than the only resort. It is possible that as cases based on the Convention and the jurisprudence of the Commission and the Court were more commonly argued, the courts would become more sensitive to a broader, civil liberties approach. But this would not necessarily be the case. As I have tried to stress, the exceptions to the Convention are so opaque that any court wishing to uphold executive power would have no difficulty in so doing. A complainant who was met by a series of adverse interpretations of the Convention would simply find that his access to the Commission at Strasbourg had been seriously delayed – and, perhaps, that the Commission was more reluctant to find in his favour if that meant overturning the House of Lords than it might have been had the case come before it in the first place.

The Select Committee of the House of Lords – the only Parliamentary body to have reported on the possibility of a new Bill of Rights – was not prepared to go even as far as the limited degree of entrenchment implied by the second model. Holding that it was constitutionally impossible for one Parliament to bind its succesor and impossible to change the constitution, the Committee recommended instead that although a statute incorporating the Convention could overrule *previous* legislation, the Convention's provisions could only be used as a basis for interpreting *subsequent* legislation. Any subsequent legislation which could not be interpreted in a manner consistent with the Convention would, nonetheless, take effect and would be held, by implication, to have repealed any incompatible provisions of the Convention. It was a Bill drafted along these lines for which a Liberal peer, Lord Wade, obtained a second reading in the House of Lords in December 1979 and again the following year. Despite a suggestion from Lord Hailsham, the Lord Chancellor, that all-party talks might be held to reach agreement on the Bill, it is now clear that Lord Wade's Bill has no prospect of success. In view of its provisions, that is just as well. It would do almost nothing to hinder Governments from introducing and securing the passage of legislation violating the rights and freedoms which it claimed to protect, but it would seriously hinder the complainant's ability to take a case to the Human Rights Commission in Strasbourg.

The example of the Immigration Rules as they affect the foreign husband of a British woman again illustrates the point. Had Lord

Wade's Bill of Rights been in effect before the Immigration Rules, a woman who had been denied the right to be joined by her foreign husband would have had to apply to a British court for a declaration of her rights. The court would have been required to consider an interpretation of the Rules compatible with the provisions of the Convention. Since no such interpretation would have been possible, short of nullifying the provisions of the Rules which were complained of, the court would have been required to uphold the Rules anyway. The complainant, still separated from her husband, would have been forced to appeal to the House of Lords in order to exhaust her 'domestic remedies' before being able to bring her case, with some prospect of success, to the Commission.

A Bill of Rights and emergency legislation

Discussion of a new Bill of Rights is, within Britain, confined to a fairly narrow circle of academic and practising lawyers, some judges, a few politicians and civil liberties activists. In Northern Ireland, however, it has for many years been a matter of pressing public interest. Originally proposed as a remedy for discrimination against the minority in local administration and employment, a Bill of Rights later came to represent a hope for a political settlement of the troubles and means of eliminating the excesses of emergency legislation, if not all emergency legislation (see page 164). As Professor Kevin Boyle has rightly pointed out,[38] the agreement of the main political parties on the disagreement on virtually every other issue: a Bill of Rights may, in his words, 'protect a settlement, but not produce one'.

Nonetheless, Professor Boyle and others in Northern Ireland, including the Standing Advisory Commission on Human Rights, argue persuasively for the adoption of a Bill of Rights based on the Convention and, preferably, introduced throughout the United Kingdom. It is suggested, in particular, that incorporation of the Convention would involve a far greater degree of accountability on the part of the Westminster Government not only to Parliament but also to the courts, and that it would open the way for judicial scrutiny of emergency legislation and judicial decisions on whether or not such powers could be justified by the demands of the situation.

But there must be severe doubts as to whether a Bill of Rights would, in fact, achieve judicial scrutiny of emergency powers, let alone judicial limitation of those powers. Under either Lord Wade's Bill or the model proposed by the Standing Advisory Commission, the victims of administrative action unsanctioned by legislation – such as the torture of internees – would be able to bring a claim under the Convention's provisions in the British courts. Army operations involving the shooting of innocent civilians would, similarly, be open to challenge. But under Lord Wade's Bill, any emergency legislation re-enacted subsequently would escape judicial scrutiny except to the extremely limited extent that 'interpretation' of an ambiguous provision was required. Under the second model legislation which did not include a 'notwithstanding' clause would also be open to challenge, thus permitting someone detained or excluded under the Prevention of Terrorism Act to bring a case before the British courts.

Because the Government does not accept that the Prevention of Terrorism Act infringes the Convention, no notice of derogation has been entered and, presumably, no 'notwithstanding' clause would be included in any re-enactment of the Act's provisions. It is possible that a court would hold that the exclusion by executive order of a United Kingdom citizen from Britain to Northern Ireland was a deprivation of liberty contrary to Article 5 of the Convention and an interference with family life contrary to Article 8. But it is highly unlikely, in view of their previous record, that the courts would reverse the decision of a senior Minister, backed up (as is so often the case with emergency legislation) by a large parliamentary majority. The court would be more likely to hold that exclusion was not a deprivation of liberty, since it did not involve continuing detention, and that any infringement of family life was justified 'in the interests of national security'.

Where a notice of derogation has been entered, as it was, for instance, in 1971 and 1973 in respect of internment in Northern Ireland, it would be possible to create a special procedure allowing the domestic courts as well as the Commission to review the validity of the Government's decision that such measures were justified by the emergency. Again, however, it is unlikely that a British court would be any more willing than the Commission itself to override the assessment of the authorities on the spot as to the need for exceptional measures.

Conclusion

It is possible that incorporation of the European Convention in a form which preserved parliamentary sovereignty could provide a useful weapon for some victims of excessive executive power. A complaint to the British courts could offer a more rapid remedy than the Strasbourg machinery, although there is a very real risk that British judges, by taking a very narrow view of the Convention's provisions, would simply delay access to a more satisfactory decision at Strasbourg. Where an Act of Parliament specifically overrode the Convention, the individual's right to appeal directly to Strasbourg would remain intact. But where a Government decided that legislation was not in breach of the Convention and therefore included no 'notwithstanding' clause – as, for example, in the case of the Prevention of Terrorism Act 1976 or the Immigration Rules 1980 – or where the complaint related to executive discretion rather than statutory provision, the courts would have a very considerable power to review and overturn provisions held to be incompatible with the standards of the Convention.

But there is no prospect of either a Conservative or a Labour Government incorporating the Convention into United Kingdom law. Pressure from Northern Ireland is inadequate even to secure a Bill of Rights for that part of the country, and a weak Bill of Rights (such as that proposed by Lord Wade) would, by raising expectations which it could not fulfil, further weaken confidence in judicial independence. The Liberal party is committed to the introduction of a Bill of Rights, and the new Social Democratic Party might be expected to support them. However, if the proposal follows the terms of Lord Wade's Bill, which, as I have argued above, is seriously defective, it must be strongly resisted.

The rejection of proposals for a new Bill of Rights does not mean that no steps should be taken to improve the enforcement of international human rights standards in the United Kingdom. Three reforms are urgently needed. First, the Government should use its influence in the Council of Europe to make the procedures under the Human Rights Convention more open, speedier and more effective. Second, ratification of the Civil and Political Rights Covenant should be followed now by ratification of the Optional Protocol providing a remedy for individual complainants similar to that provided under the Human Rights Convention. Third, the Government should establish a Human Rights Commission in the United Kingdom, along the lines of that created in 1978 in New Zealand,[39] with the power to scrutinize legislation and ministerial decisions for their compatibility with the Convention and Covenant provisions and, where necessary, to provide legal assistance with complainants who wish to pursue their cases.

Notes

Chapter 1: Justice and the Criminal Law

1 *Report of the Royal Commission on Criminal Procedure*, Cmnd 8092 (London: HMSO, 1981); hereafter RCCP Report.
2 On this issue, see also Geoffrey Robertson, *Whose Conspiracy?* (London: NCCL, 1974).
3 *DPP* v. *Kamara* (1974) AC 104.
4 Robert Hazell, *Conspiracy and Civil Liberties* (London: Bell, 1974).
5 *per* Lord Diplock (1970) 3 All ER at 105.
6 *The Report of the Committee on Obscenity*, Cmnd 7772 (London: HMSO, 1979).
7 *Race Relations and the 'Sus' Law*, Second Report from the Home Affairs Committee, HC 559 (London: HMSO, 1980).
8 Sir Robert Marks, *In the Office of Constable* (London: Collins, 1978).
9 *Criminal Statistics 1978*, Cmnd 7670 (London: HMSO, 1979).
10 *Report of an Inquiry by the Hon. Sir Henry Fisher*, HC 90 (London: HMSO, 1977).
11 RCCP Report, para 3.72.
12 Part 1 of the Written Evidence of the Metropolitan Police Commissioner (London: New Scotland Yard, 1978).
13 Michael King, *Bail or Custody* (Cobden Trust, 1971).
14 Michael McConville and John Baldwin, 'Critics Have Missed the Point', *Rights*, vol. 5, no. 4, 1981.
15 *Breaking The Law* (Justice, 1974).
16 Part 1 of the Written Evidence of the Metropolitan Police Commissioner.
17 RCCP Report, para. 3.96.
18 RCCP Report, para. 3.96.
19 See page 165.
20 RCCP Report, para. 3.96.

21 *Report on Criminal Procedure in Scotland*, Second Report, Cmnd 6218 (London: HMSO, 1975).
22 *Criminal Investigation*, Report No. 2, Law Reform Commission (Sydney, 1975).
23 *Model Code of Pre-Arraignment Procedure* (American Law Institute, 1975).
24 British Institute of Human Rights, Report of a conference on *habeas corpus* (1980).
25 House of Commons, *Hansard*, 20 April 1980, col. 470.
26 *Guardian*, 10 December 1980; *Sherman and Apps* (1981) CLR 335.
27 Barrie Irving, *Police Interrogation: A Case Study of Current Practice*, RCCP Research Study No. 2 (London: HMSO, 1980).
28 RCCP Report, para 4.36.
29 *Guardian*, 9 March 1981.
30 Irving, *Police Interrogation*.
31 R. v. *Allen and others* (1977) Crim LR 163.
32 Walter Merricks, speaking at the University of Lancaster, 27 March 1981.
33 Dallin H. Oaks, 'Studying the Exclusionary Rule in Search and Seizure', *University of Chicago Law Review*, Vol. 39, no. 665, p. 755.
34 RCCP Report, para. 3.49.
35 *Report*, para. 2.26.
36 R. v. *McCormick* (1977) Northern Ireland Reports 105.
37 King, *Bail or Custody*.
38 *LAG Bulletin*, August 1981.
39 *Report of the Commissioner of Police of the Metropolis*, Cmnd 7238 (London: HMSO, 1978), Appendix 29.
40 R. v. *Nottingham Justices ex parte Davies* (1980) 3 WLR 15.
41 Imprisonment (Temporary Provisions) Act 1981.
42 *LAG Bulletin*, February 1980 and August 1980.
43 Howard Levenson, 'Uneven Justice – Refusal of Criminal Legal Aid in 1979', *LAG Bulletin*, May 1981.
44 ibid.
45 Ole Hanson, 'Justice Delayed – Justice Denied', *LAG Bulletin*, April 1980.
46 See Harriet Harman's study of compensation for wrongful imprisonment (London: NCCL, forthcoming).
47 Andrew Trollope, 'Justice for Prisoners', *LAG Bulletin*, September 1980.
48 *The Times*, 6 August 1981.
49 R. v. *Board of Visitors of Hull Prison/ex parte St Germain and others* (1979) 1 All ER 701.
50 Trollope, 'Justice for Prisoners'.
51 *Michael Sidney Williams* v. *the Home Office*, *The Times*, 10 May 1980.
52 A. v. *the United Kingdom*, No. 6740/74.

Chapter 2: Causing Problems for the State

1 Sir Robert Mark, *Policing A Perplexed Society* (London: Allen and Unwin, 1977), p. 12.
2 Sir Robert Mark, *In the Office of Constable* (London: Collins, 1978), p. 244. Cf. the remarks of James Anderton, Chief Constable of Greater Manchester, on the BBC 1 programme *Question Time* (16 October 1979): 'I think that from a police point of view . . . that basic crime such as theft, burglary, even violent crime will not be the predominant police feature. What will be the matter of greatest concern to me will be the covert, and ultimately overt, attempts to overthrow democracy, to subvert the authority of the state and, in fact, to involve themselves in acts of sedition designed to destroy our parliamentary system and the democratic government in this country.'
3 House of Commons, *Hansard*, 6 April 1978.
4 *Report of Her Majesty's Chief Inspector of Constabulary* (London: HMSO, 1978).
5 Martin Kettle, 'The Politics of Policing and the Policing of Politics', in Peter Hain and Brian Rose-Smith (eds.), *Policing the Police*, vol. 2 (London: Calder, 1980), p. 53.
6 Mark, *In the Office of Constable*, p. 293.
7 *Special Branch Security Records*, Initial Report to the Hon. Donald Allan Dunstan, QC, LLB, MP, by the Hon. Mr Acting Justice White (Adelaide, 1977).
8 Transcript of *Panorama*, BBC 1, 2 March 1981.
9 Michael Flood and Robin Grove-White, *Nuclear Prospects* (London: Friends of the Earth, 1978), p. 12.
10 See especially Duncan Campbell, 'Society Under Surveillance', in Hain and Rose-Smith (eds.), *Policing the Police*.
11 ibid., p. 80.
12 *Datalink*, 24 October 1977 and 13 December 1977.
13 Correspondence with NCCL.
14 Campbell, 'Society under Surveillance', p. 76.
15 *Report of the Committee on Data Protection*, Cmnd 7341 (London: HMSO, 1978), para, 8.08.
16 *Listener*, 8 March 1979.
17 *The Times*, 14 February 1977.
18 House of Commons, *Hansard*, 13 July 1979.
19 *Report of the Data Protection Committee*, para. 315.
20 See Alan Westin, *Privacy and Freedom* (New York: Atheneum, 1967), chapter 7.
21 Campbell, 'Society under Surveillance', p. 121.
22 *Police Review*, 21 April 1978.
23 Hansard, 5 February 1981, col 167.
24 Campbell, 'Society under Surveillance', p. 129.
25 Legal Action Group, *Bulletin*, July 1979.

26 *Le Canard Enchaîné*, 18 June 1980.
27 *The Interception of Communications in Great Britain*, Cmnd 7873 (London: HMSO, 1980).
28 Duncan Campbell, *Phonetappers and the Security State, New Statesman* Report No. 2, 1981, p. 45.
29 *The Interception of Communications in Great Britain.*
30 *Report of the Younger Committee*, Cmnd 5012 (London: HMSO, 1972).
31 *New Scientist*, 10 July 1975.
32 *Computers and Privacy*, Cmnd 6353 (London: HMSO, 1975).
33 *Computers: Safeguards for Privacy*, Cmnd 6354 (London: HMSO, 1975).
34 *Report of the Data Protection Committee.*
35 Organization for Economic Co-operation and Development, 'Guidelines Governing the Protection of Privacy and Transborder Flows of Personal Data' (c(80)58), August 1980.
36 The Convention will come into force three months after five member states have ratified its provisions.
37 See the official *Journal* of the European Parliament, 24 September 1979.
38 *Transnational Data Report*, vol. 1, nos. 1, 2, 5, 7, 1978.
39 *Malone* v. *the Commissioner of Police for the Metropolis*, judgment delivered by the Vice-Chancellor, 28 February 1979.
40 *Klass et al.* v. *the Federal Republic of Germany* (No. 5029/71), Judgment of the Court, 6 September 1978.
41 *The Interception of Communications in Great Britain*, Cmnd 8791 (London: HMSO, 1980).
42 *DPP* v. *Withers* (1975) AC 842.
43 See note 8.
44 Patricia Hewitt, *Privacy: The Information Gatherers* (London: NCCL, 1977), p. 63.
45 *Datalink*, 19 July 1979.
46 NCCL records.
47 Barry Cox, *Civil Liberties in Britain* (Harmondsworth: Penguin, 1975), p. 118.
48 John Griffith and Harriet Harman, *Justice Deserted* (London: NCCL, 1979).
49 *Guardian*, 20 September 1979.
50 *R.* v. *Sheffield Crown Court, ex parte Brownlow, The Times*, 4 March 1980.
51 *Justice Deserted: Postscript* (London: NCCL, 1980).

Chapter 3: Policing the Police

 1 Sir James Fitzjames Stephen, quoted in the *Report of the Royal Commission on Police Powers and Procedure*, Cmnd 3297 (London: HMSO, 1929).

2 E. P. Thompson, *The Making of the English Working Class*, rev. edn. (Harmondsworth: Penguin, 1968), pp. 88ff.

3 *R. v. Metropolitan Police Commissioner ex parte Blackburn* (1968) 1 All ER 763 at p. 769.

4 *R. v. Metropolitan Police Commissioner ex parte Blackburn* (1973) 1 All ER 324.

5 *Report of the Royal Commission on Criminal Procedure*, vol. 1, Cmnd 8092 (London: HMSO, 1981).

6 *R. v. Sang* (1979) 2 All ER 1222 at p. 1230.

7 *Report of the Royal Commission on the Police*, Cmnd 1728 (London: HMSO, 1962), para. 102.

8 Quoted in an unpublished paper, 'Police Accountability in England and Wales' (London: NCCL, 1980).

9 *Report of Her Majesty's Chief Inspector of Constabulary, 1979*, Cmnd 725 (London: HMSO, 1980), para. 7.10.

10 *In Evidence: the Sharp End*, ITV, 25 June 1980.

11 *Report of Her Majesty's Chief Inspector*, para. 7.21.

12 Geoffrey Marshall, 'The Government of the Police since 1964', in J. C. Alderson and P. J. Stead (eds.) *The Police We Deserve* (London: Wolfe, 1973).

13 ibid.

14 Merseyside Police Authority, *Role and Responsibilities of the Police Authority*, February 1980, para. 23; hereafter the Merseyside Report.

15 NCCL files 1980.

16 J. C. Harris, County Secretary, South Yorkshire County Council *Survey of Matters of Practice*; based on a 1976 survey of all police authorities carried out by the Working Party of the Association of County Councils and the Association of Metropolitan Authorities, 1977.

17 Marshall, 'The Government of the Police since 1964'.

18 Notes on police seminar organized by the Association of County Councils and the Association of Metropolitan Authorities, 16 and 17 March 1977; reproduced in the Merseyside Report.

19 *Report on Relationships Between the Police and Public in South Yorkshire*, South Yorkshire County Council, March 1979.

20 Ten-Minute Rule Bill, *Hansard*, 11 March 1980.

21 'The Control of London's Police', State Research *Bulletin*, vol. 3, no. 17, April–May 1980.

22 A proposal for non-statutory district police committees was made in Marshall, 'The Government of the Police since 1964'; Marshall was of the view, however, that 'there could, of course, be no legal obligation' on regional police officers to attend their meetings.

23 See also James Anderton, 'Accountable to whom?', *Police*, February 1981.

24 'Hands Off the London Police', *The Times*, 4 May 1981.

25 For instance, in his contributions to a seminar on the *Report of the Royal Commission on Criminal Procedure* organized by the *Poly Law Review* on 28 April 1981.

26 See, e.g., Discussion Document of the London Campaign for A Democratic Police Force (London Co-op. Political Committee, undated).

27 South Yorkshire did so in their most recent appointment.

28 *Police Complaints Board Triennial Review Report 1980*, Cmnd 7966 (London: HMSO, July 1980), para. 34.

29 *Southall: April 1979*, report of the Unofficial Committee of Inquiry (London: NCCL, 1980).

30 *Observations on the Triennial Review Report of the Police Complaints Board*, Justice, October 1980.

31 *Triennial Review Report*, paras. 60 and 61.

32 ibid., para. 97.

33 'Police Complaints', *The London Programme*, London Weekend TV, 6 February 1981.

34 Letter from the Secretary of the Police Federation to NCCL, 3 April 1981.

35 *Triennial Review Report*, para. 100.

36 *Report of the Police Complaints Board 1980* (London: HMSO, 1981).

37 *Sunday Times*, 16 March 1980.

38 *The Establishment of an Independent Element in the Investigation of Complaints against the Police*, Home Office Working Party Report, Cmnd 8193 (London: HMSO, 1981).

39 Geoffrey Robertson, 'The Fifty Per Cent Solution', *Guardian*, 14 January 1980.

Chapter 4: Censorship and Secrecy

1 *Chandler* v. DPP (1964) AC 763, (1962) 3 All ER 142, (1962) 3 WLR 702.

2 *R.* v. *Secretary of State for Home Affairs ex parte Hosenball* (1977) 1 WLR 776, CA.

3 Quoted in James Michael, *The Politics of Secrecy* (London: NCCL, 1979), p. 5.

4 *Report of the Franks Committee on Section 2 of the Official Secrets Act 1911*, Cmnd 5104 (London: HMSO, 1972).

5 *Reform of Section 2 of the Official Secrets Act*, Cmnd 7285 (London: HMSO, 1978).

6 Statement by the Home Secretary in the House of Commons, April 1978.

7 Michael, *The Politics of Secrecy*, p. 15.

8 ibid., p. 19.

9 *New Scientist*, 20 September 1979.

10 For a full discussion of the secrecy surrounding prison administration, see Laurie Taylor, *Prison Secrets* (London: NCCL, 1979).
11 Report on the work of the Prison Department, Cmnd 8228 (London: HMSO 1981)
12 Michael, *The Politics of Secrecy*, p. 12.
13 Quoted in ibid., p. 22.
14 *Attorney-General* v. *Jonathan Cape Ltd, Attorney-General* v. *Times Newspapers Ltd* (1976) QB 752, (1975) All ER 484, (1975) 3 WLR 606.
15 *British Steel Corporation* v. *Granada Television Ltd* (1980) 3WLR 774
16 'The Law and the Press: Breach of Confidence – How Far Should You Protect Your Sources?', paper delivered by Dr Peter North to the Law Society and the Guild of British Newspaper Editors, 27 February 1981.
17 *Attorney-General* v. *Times Newspapers Ltd* (1974) AC 273, (1973) All ER 54, (1973) 3 WLR 298, House of Lords.
18 *Sunday Times* case, Eur. Court HR Series A, vol. 30, judgment of the European Court of Human Rights, 26 April 1979.
19 *Report of the Committee on Contempt of Court*, Cmnd 5794 (London: HMSO, 1974).
20 Anthony Whitaker, 'Does The Act comply with the Convention?' *Times*, 27 August 1981.
21 *Attorney-General* v. *New Statesman* (1980) 1 All ER 644 QBD.
22 The Criminal Justice Act 1976, following the *Report of the James Committee on the Distribution of Business Between Magistrates and Crown Courts*, removed the option of jury trial from certain offences.
23 *Home Office* v. *Hormos* (1981) 2 WLR 310.
24 *Williams* v. *Home Office* (1980), *The Times*, 10 May 1980.
25 Thom Young and Martin Kettle, *Incitement to Disaffection* (London: Cobden Trust, 1976), p. 79.
26 *R.* v. *Arrowsmith* (1975) 1 All ER 463, (1975) 2 WLR 484.
27 *Arrowsmith* v. *the United Kingdom* (No. 7050/75), report of the European Commission of Human Rights, 12 October 1978.
28 A full acount of the case will be found in Young and Kettle, *Incitement to Disaffection*, pp. 85–90.
29 *The Report of the Committee on Obscenity*, Cmnd 7772 (London: HMSO, 1979); hereafter the Williams Report.
30 A full account of the development and operation of laws against obscenity will be found in Geoff Robertson's excellent book, *Obscenity* (London: Weidenfeld and Nicolson, 1979).
31 Appeal of Richard Handyside, Inner London Crown Court, 29 October 1971, transcript.
32 *Shaw* v. *DPP* (1962) AC 220.
33 Robertson, *Obscenity*, p. 216.
34 ibid., p. 219.
35 Williams Report, Appendix 7, Table 4.
36 *R.* v. *Lemon and Gay News Ltd* (1978) 3 All ER 175 CA.
37 Williams Report, para. 4.4.

38 ibid., Appendix 7, Tables 6 & 7.
39 ibid., para. 4.23.
40 Robertson, *Obscenity*, p. 286.
41 ibid., p. 102.
42 ibid., p. 106.
43 Post Office Act 1953, Section 11.
44 Williams Report, para. 6.55.
45 ibid., para. 12.45.
46 Robertson, *Obscenity*, p. 318.
47 Williams Report, Appendix 4.
48 *R. v. Metropolitan Police Commissioner ex parte Blackburn* (No. 3) (1973) QB 241, (1973) 1 All ER 324.
49 The Williams Report, para. 12.45.

Chapter 5: Peaceful Protest and Public Assembly

1 Thomas I. Emerson, 'The Right to Protest', in Norman Dorsen (ed.), *The Rights of Americans* (New York: Pantheon Books, 1970).
2 Thomas I. Emerson, *The System of Freedom of Expression* (New York: Vintage Books, 1970).
3 Sir Robert Mark, address to the Police College, Bramshill, 17 March 1975.
4 Supplementary evidence of Sir David McNee, Commissioner of the Metropolitan Police, to the Home Affairs Committee of the House of Commons, *Minutes of Evidence*, 18 February 1980, paras. 42–4; hereafter cited as *Minutes of Evidence*.
5 Written evidence of the Association of Chief Police Officers of England, Wales and Northern Ireland to the Home Affairs Committee, *Minutes of Evidence*, para. 7.
6 *Minutes of Evidence*, para. 32.
7 *Report of the Home Affairs Committee*, 756–1 (London: HMSO, 1980) para. 19.
8 *Report of the Commissioner of Police for the Metropolis*, 1978 Cmnd 8254 (London: HMSO, 1979).
9 *Hubbard and Others* v. *Pitt and Others* (1976) 1 QB 142.
10 *Minutes of Evidence*, Appendices A and B.
11 *Report of the Commissioner of Police for the Metropolis*, 1979 Cmnd 7932 (London: HMSO, 1980).
12 *Review of the Public Order Act 1936 and Related Legislation*, Cmnd 7891 (London: HMSO, 1980); hereafter cited as the Green Paper.
13 *Report of the Commissioner of Police for the Metropolis*, 1977 Cmnd 7238 (London: HMSO, 1980), p. 23.
14 A comprehensive analysis of public-order law may be found in Ian Brownlie, *The Law Relating to Public Order* (London: Butterworth, 1968).

15 Harry Street, *Freedom, the Individual and the Law* 3rd edn. (Harmondsworth: Penguin, 1972) p. 12.
16 *Report of Inquiry by the Rt. Hon. Lord Scarman OBE,* Cmnd 5919 (London: HMSO, 1975); hereafter Scarman Report.
17 Green Paper, para. 24.
18 Brownlie, *The Law Relating to Public Order,* p. 142.
19 Scarman Report.
20 *Minutes of Evidence,* para. 28.
21 *Minutes of Evidence,* para. 47.
22 *The Proper Limits to the Right of Assembly,* report of Justice Annual Members' Conference, 18 March 1978, pp. 14–15.
23 Decision of the European Human Rights Commission as to the admissibility of application No. 8440/78, p. 21.
24 *Kent* v. *Metropolitan Police Commissioner, The Times,* 15 May 1981.
25 NCCL records, 1981.
26 *Burden* v. *Rigler* (1911) 1 KB 337.
27 *Papworth* v. *Coventry* (1967) 2 All ER 41.
28 *Hubbard* v. *Pitt* (1976) 1 QB 142.
29 *Duncan* v. *Jones* (1936) 1 KB 218.
30 'A Barrister', *Justice in England* (London: Gollancz, 1938), pp. 250–60.
31 Brownlie, *The Law Relating to Public Order,* pp. 20–22.
32 *Arrowsmith* v. *Jenkins* (1963) 2 QB 561.
33 *Observer,* 23 March 1980.
34 Correspondence between NCCL and the Home Office Statistical Division.
35 For the most detailed account available of the events in Southall, see *Southall: April 23 1979: The Report of the Unofficial Committee of Inquiry* (London: NCCL, 1980).
36 It is sometimes suggested, inaccurately, that a power exists to ban election meetings: see, for instance, Joanna Rollo, 'The Special Patrol Group', in Peter Hain and Brian Rose-Smith (eds.), *Policing the Police, vol. 2* (London: Calder, 1980).
37 *Report of the Unofficial Committee of Enquiry,* chapter 9.
38 Green Paper.
39 *Piddington* v. *Bates* (1961) 1 WLR 162, (1960) All ER 660.
40 *Kavanagh* v. *Hiscock* (1974) 1 CR 282.
41 BBC v. *Hearn* (1978) 1 All ER 111.
42 *The Camilla M* (1979) Lloyds Rep. 26. The reasoning in this case was overruled by the House of Lords in NWL Ltd v. Woods (1979) All ER 614, HL.
43 *Express Newspapers* v. *MacShane* (1980) IRLR 247.
44 *United Biscuits* v. *Fall* (1979) IRLR 110.
45 'Strike and Be Sued', *New Statesman,* 24 April 1981.
46 Joe Rogaly, *Grunwick* (Harmondsworth: Penguin, 1977).
47 Paul Johnson, 'The Parasite State', *New Statesman,* 3 September 1976.
48 Sir Robert Mark, address to the Police College, Bramshill, 17 March 1975.

49 Statement by the Home Secretary to the House of Commons, 27 June 1979.
50 *Observer*, 12 April 1981.
51 Green Paper, para. 15.
52 The title of 'Operation Swamp' echoed the Prime Minister's pre-election statement that British culture was in danger of being 'swamped' by ethnic minorities.
53 See, for instance, *Police Against Black People* (London: Institute of Race Relations, 1979).
54 Green Paper.
55 *Report* of the Home Affairs Committee.
56 Scarman Report.
57 *Minutes of Evidence*, p. 57.
58 Statement to NCCL.
59 Green paper, para. 73.
60 ibid., para. 61.
61 *Report* of the Home Affairs Committee, para. 27.
62 *Kent* v. *Metropolitan Police Commissioner*.
63 *Report* of the Home Affairs Committee, para. 42.
64 *Report* of the Home Affairs Committee, draft prepared by Mr Alex Lyon, para. 22.
65 Green Paper, para. 78.
66 ·Legal Action group, *Recommendations to the Review of the Public Order Act 1936*, July 1980.
67 ibid.

Chapter 6: Civil Liberties and Northern Ireland

1 Polyvios G. Polyviou, *Cyprus: Conflict and Negotiation 1960–1980* (London: Duckworth, 1980), p. 23.
2 Tom Hadden and Paddy Hillyard, *Justice in Northern Ireland: A study in Social Confidence* (Cobden Trust, 1973), pp. 8–9. See also *Northern Ireland: The Plain Truth*, Campaign for Social Justice in Northern Ireland (1969).
3 *Disturbances in Northern Ireland*, Cmnd 532 (London: HMSO, 1969), para. 140.
4 *Northern Ireland: The Plain Truth*.
5 *Report of a Commission of Inquiry into the Special Powers Acts* (London: NCCL, 1936; republished 1972). The Commission's members were Edward Digby, KC, JP; Margery Fry, former secretary to the Howard League for Penal Reform; William McKeag, former Liberal MP and a solicitor; Edward Mallalieu, MA, a barrister and former Liberal MP. Its secretary was Neil Lawson, now Mr Justice Lawson.
6 *Why Justice Cannot Be Done*, Campaign for Social Justice in Northern Ireland (1964).

7 *Legal Aid to Oppose Discrimination – Not Likely!*, Campaign for Social Justice in Northern Ireland (1966).
8 Hadden and Hillyard, *Justice in Northern Ireland*, pp. 12–13.
9 ibid.
10 *Report* of the inquiry into allegations against the security forces of physical brutality in Northern Ireland arising out of events on 9 August 1971, Cmnd 4823 (London: HMSO, 1971).
11 Kevin Boyle, Tom Hadden and Paddy Hillyard, *Ten Years on in Northern Ireland: The Legal Control of Political Violence* (Cobden Trust, 1980), p. 66.
12 Hadden and Hillyard, *Justice in Northern Ireland*; see also *Prosecutions in Northern Ireland: A Study of Facts* (London: HMSO, 1974), pp. 31–3.
13 'Northern Ireland (Emergency Provisions) Act: Memorandum for MPs assessing the first year's operation of the Act' (London: NCCL, 1975).
14 It is sometimes argued that juries in Northern Ireland should be selected on sectarian lines and that defence challenges and/or prosecution 'jury vetting' would confirm this bias. The abolition of the property requirement and a scrupulously random system of selection would, however, go a long way towards dealing with this risk, while the Criminal Law Act 1976 has already reduced defence challenges to four. Although it is also feared that jurors would be an immediate target for terrorists, public support for the restoration of juries suggests otherwise; unlike members of the security services or those working in the prisons, jurors would be an extremely unpopular target.
15 Boyle, Hadden and Hillyard, *Ten Years on in Northern Ireland*, pp. 35–6.
16 *Guardian*, 17 March 1979.
17 *Northern Ireland: Report of An Amnesty International Mission*, (London: Amnesty International, 1978).
18 *Report of the Committee of Inquiry into Police Interrogation Procedures in Northern Ireland*, Cmnd 7497 (London: HMSO, 1979), para. 404.
19 Research into the cases of those detained under the Emergency Provisions Act and tried in the special courts is being carried out at Queen's University, Belfast, under the auspices of the Cobden Trust and the International League for Human Rights.
20 Boyle, Hadden and Hillyard, *Ten Years on in Northern Ireland*; see chapter 7, on which I have drawn extensively.
21 *Sunday Times*, 26 April 1981.
22 Parliamentary Answer to Lord Gifford, House of Lords, *Hansard*, 31 July 1981.
23 Boyle, Hadden and Hillyard, *Ten Years on in Northern Ireland*, list (p. 28) ten people shot dead by undercover Army patrols between December 1977 and November 1978. Of the ten, three were admitted by the Army to have been shot in error.

is below.

24 Boyle, Hadden and Hillyard, *Ten Years on in Northern Ireland*, pp. 93–5.
25 *McFeeley* v. *United Kingdom* (Application 8317/78); partial decision of the European Commission on Human Rights, May 1980.
26 *Bill of Rights (Northern Ireland) Act 1975*, Northern Ireland Civil Rights Association, April 1975.
27 *A Proposed Bill of Rights*, Ulster Citizens' Civil Liberties Centre, June 1975.
28 *The Protection of Human Rights by Law in Northern Ireland*, Cmnd 7009 (London: HMSO, 1977).
29 Parlimentary Answer by the Minister of State, *Hansard*, 5 November 1980.
30 Catherine Scorer and Patricia Hewitt, *The Prevention of Terrorism Act: The Case for Repeal* (London: NCCL, 1981), p. 59.
31 *Statistics on the Prevention of Terrorism Acts*, Home Office Statistical Bulletin, July 1981.
32 *Review of the Operation of the Prevention of Terrorism Acts 1974 and 1976*. Cmnd 7324 (London: HMSO, 1978).
33 Richard Rose, 'Ulster: What Can We Do?', *Sunday Times*, 11 January 1976.

Chapter 7: The Other Half

1 Mary Wollstonecraft's *A Vindication of the Rights of Women* was published in 1792, two years after her *Vindication of the Rights of Men*.
2 Bailey *et al.*, *Civil Liberties: Cases and Materials* (London: Butterworth, 1980), has a chapter on race discrimination but none on sex discrimination. Paul O'Higgins, *Cases and Materials on Civil Liberties* (London: Sweet and Maxwell, 1980) has a brief section on the treatment of aliens; the author apologizes in the introduction for the 'arbitrary exclusion' of sex discrimination.
3 Albie Sachs and Joan Hoff Wilson, *Sexism and the Law: A Study of Male Beliefs and Judicial Bias* (Oxford: Martin Robertson, 1978).
4 ibid., p. 6.
5 *Guardian*, 11 July 1981.
6 See Jo Richardson's speech on introducing her Bill to amend the National Health Service Act 1977, House of Commons, *Hansard*, 1 July 1981.
7 *First Report of the Home Affairs Committee on the Proposed New Immigration Rules and the European Convention on Human Rights*, HC 434 (London: HMSO, 1980).
8 Written Answer to Parliamentary Question 146, House of Commons, *Hansard*, 1 June 1981.
9 *The Taxation of Married Couples*, Cmnd 8093 (London: HMSO, 1980).

10 Department of Employment, 1980.
11 *R.* v. *Central Arbitration Committee ex parte Hu-Mac Ltd* (1979) IRLR 461.
12 *Meekes* v. *NUAWW* (1976) IRLR 198.
13 *Jenkins* v. *Kingsgate (Clothing Productions) Ltd* (1980) IRLR 6.
14 *Jenkins* v. *Kingsgate (Clothing Productions) Ltd, The Times,* 6 April 1981.
15 *Worringham and Humphreys* (1981) 1 WLR 950, European Court of Justice.
16 *Price* v. *the Civil Service Commissioners* (1977) IRLR 291.
17 A. Hunt, *A Survey of Women's Employment,* vol. 1 (London: HMSO, 1968.
18 M. Bone, *Pre-School Children and the Need for Day-Care* (London: HMSO, 1977).
19 Richard Titmuss, *Essays on the Welfare State,* (London: Allen and Unwin, 1963).

Chapter 8: Free and Equal?

1 Quoted in Anne Dummett, *A New Immigration Policy* (Runnymede Trust, 1978), pp. 58ff.
2 ibid., p. 59.
3 ibid., p. 61.
4 For instance, Harvey Proctor MP was the author of a Monday Club pamphlet on repatriation (published April 1981), for which Ronald Bell MP wrote the foreword.
5 *Hospital Doctor/On Call,* 9 April 1981.
6 Michael Dummett, *Immigration: Where the Debate Goes Wrong* (Action Group on Immigration and Nationality, undated), pp. 13–14.
7 Aliens Act 1905, Aliens Restriction Act 1914, Aliens Restriction (Amendment) Act 1919.
8 *Immigration from the Commonwealth,* Cmnd 2739 (London: HMSO, 1965), para. 2.
9 ibid., para. 9.
10 Op. cit.
11 The opinion of the European Human Rights Commission in the *East African Asians' Case* is reproduced in the *Report* of the Home Affairs Sub-Committee on Race Relations and Immigration, HC 434, 1981.
12 The present Rules are contained in HC 394 (London: HMSO, 1980).
13 See Larry Grant and Ian Martin, *Immigration Law and Practice* (Cobden Trust, 1981).
14 See 'Bring Anwar's Children Home', Friends of Anwar Ditta and Manchester Law Centre (undated).
15 *R.* v. *Secretary of State for the Home Department ex parte Phansopkhar* (1975) All ER 1087.
16 *Control of Immigration Statistics,* Home Office, March 1981, table 6.

17 *Annual Report* 1979/80 (Joint Council for the Welfare of Immigrants), p. 3.
18 Evidence by the Joint Council for the Welfare of Immigrants to the House of Commons Select Committee on Immigration and Race Relations; HC 303 II (London: HMSO, 1978).
19 Ted White, 'The Use of X-Rays for Age Determination in Immigration Control', Office of Lord Avebury, June 1981.
20 *Kolb* 1705/72 (67) (unreported); quoted in Grant and Martin, *Immigration Law and Practice*.
21 Separate figures for the admission of elderly relatives are not published by the Home Office. People admitted in this category are among the 'others' admitted for settlement in 1980.
22 *Official Report,* vol. 997, no. 35, 28 January 1981, cols. 980–1.
23 *Zamir* v. *Secretary of State for the Home Department,* (1980) 2 All ER 768.
24 See Dr M. A. Fazel, 'The Immigrants and their Basic Rights' (Trent Polytechnic, September 1979).
25 One immigration appeals adjudicator, Malcolm Hurwitt, resigned in protest at the system of hearing in London appeals from people living in the Indian sub-continent.
26 Quoted in *Annual Report 1978–79,* Joint Council for the Welfare of Immigrants, p. 10.
27 *Control of Immigration Statistics,* table 10.
28 *Annual Report 1979–80,* Joint Council for the Welfare of Immigrants, pp. 3, 10.
29 *R v. Secretary of State for Home Department, ex parte Mahmood* (1980) 3 WLR 312.
30 *British Nationality Law: Discussion of Possible Changes,* Cmnd 6695 (London: HMSO, 1977).
31 For a more detailed summary of an alternative citizenship law, see *British Nationality Law,* Action Group on Immigration and Nationality, October 1980.
32 Until the introduction of the British Nationality Act 1981, a foreign woman marrying a United Kingdom citizen was entitled herself to register as a citizen – a right retained even after divorce. Although the Government has argued that extension of the same right to a foreign husband would lead to marriages of convenience, it is unable even to provide information about the number of cases in which an extension of stay has been refused to a foreign husband on the grounds of an alleged marriage of convenience.
33 *Racial Violence in Britain* (London: Joint Committee Against Racism, 1980).
34 Section 5A of the 1936 Public Order Act as amended by the Race Relations Act 1976.
35 *The Red Lion Square Disorder of 15 June 1974,* Cmnd 5919 (London: HMSO, 1975).

36 Barry Cox, *Civil Liberties in Britain* (Harmondsworth: Penguin, 1975), p. 239.
37 ibid., p. 242.
38 *The Facts of Racial Disadvantage* (London: PEP, 1976).
39 *The Application of Race Relations Policy in the Civil Service* (London: Tavistock Institute, 1978).
40 David Smith, *Unemployment and Racial Minorities* (London: PSI, 1981).
41 *Looking for Work: Black and White School-Leavers* (London: Commission for Racial Equality, 1978).
42 Sally Tomlinson, 'The Educational Performance of Ethnic Minority Children', *New Community*, vol. 8, no. 3 (1980).
43 Little, Mabey and Whitaker, 'The Education of Immigrant Pupils in Inner London Primary Schools', *Race*, vol. 9, no. 4 (1968).
44 Yule, Berger, Rutter and Yule, 'Children of West Indian Immigrants, Intellectual Performance and Reading Attainment', *Journal of Child Psychology and Psychiatry*, vol. 16 (1975).
45 *Cause for Concern – West Indian Pupils in Redbridge* (London: Redbridge Community Relations Council, 1978).
46 C. Bagley, 'Social Environment and Intelligence in West Indian Children in London', *Social and Economic Studies*, no. 20, (1971).
47 G. Driver and R. Ballard, 'Comparing Performance in Multi-Racial Schools – South Asian Pupils at 16 Plus', *New Community*, vol. 7, no. 2 (1979).
48 Tomlinson, 'The Educational Performance of Ethnic Minority Children'.
49 *Race and Council Housing in London* (London: Runnymede Trust, 1975).
50 M. Ghodsian and J. Essen, 'The Children of Immigrants; Social and Home Circumstances,' *New Community*, vol. 8, no. 3 (1980), table 4.
51 Tavistock Institute, *op cit.*
52 *Regents of the University of California* v. *Bakke*, 483 US 265 (1978).
53 *Weber* v. *Kaiser Aluminium and Chemical Corporation* (1978) 99S Ct 720.
54 *Report on the National Advisory Commission on Civil Disorders* (Washington DC: US Government Printing Office, 1968).
55 ibid., p. 91.

Chapter 9: The Homosexual Minority

1 Devlin, 'The Enforcement of Morals' (1959); reprinted in Devlin, *The Enforcement of Morals* (New York: Oxford University Press, 1965).
2 H. L. A. Hart, *Law, Liberty and Morality* (London: Oxford University Press, 1963).
3 Ronald Dworkin, *Taking Rights Seriously* (London: Duckworth, edition 1978); see chapter 10.

4 *The Report of the Committee on Homosexual Offences and Prostitution,* Cmnd 247 (London: HMSO, 1957).
5 Quoted in Hyde, *The Other Love* (London, 1972), p. 303.
6 *Criminal Statistics 1979,* Cmnd 8098 (London, HMSO, 1980).
7 NCCL records and the unpublished report of an NCCL conference, May 1977; the same sources are used for other examples quoted in this chapter.
8 *Dudgeon v. the United Kingdom,* Application 7525/76.
9 *Working Paper on Sexual Offences,* Criminal Law Revision Committee, (London: HMSO, 1980).
10 *Saunders v. Scottish National Camps Association Ltd* (EAT 7/80); judgment delivered 14 April 1980).
11 *Harper v. National Coal Board,* (1980) IRLR 260.
12 *Wiseman v. Salford City Council* (EAT 417/80); judgment delivered 12 March 1981.
13 Quoted in Beer *et al., Gay Workers: Trade Unions and the Law* (London: NCCL, 1981), p. 27.

Chapter 10: Protecting Human Rights

1 Report of the European Human Rights Commission on the *East African Asians' Case*; reprinted in the *Report* of the Home Affairs Sub-Committee on Race Relations and Immigration, HC 434, 1980.
2 *Ireland v. the United Kingdom* (No. 5310/71); judgment of the European Court of Human Rights, 18 January 1978.
3 *Stock-Taking on the European Convention on Human Rights,* European Commission on Human Rights (Strasbourg, 1979).
4 *Stock-Taking,* p. 12.
5 *Ireland v. the United Kingdom.*
6 *McFeeley v. the United Kingdom* (No. 8317/78); partial decision of the European Commission of Human Rights, 15 May 1980.
7 *Golder v. the United Kingdom* (No. 4551/70); judgment of the European Court of Human Rights, 21 February 1975.
8 See page 26.
9 *Tyrer v. the United Kingdom* (No. 5856/72); judgment of the European Court of Human Rights, 25 April 1978.
10 *Sunday Times,* 1 February 1981.
11 *Dudgeon v. the United Kingdom* (No. 7525/76).
12 *Klass et al. v. West Germany* (No. 5029/71; judgment of the European Court of Human Rights, 6 September 1978.
13 *Malone v. the Commissioner of Police for the Metropolis* (1979) 2 All ER 620.
14 *R. v. Secretary of State for the Home Department ex parte Phapsopkhar* (1975) 3 All ER 1087.

15 The 1981 Act perpetuates the race discrimination of earlier immigration legislation; see pages 188–200.

16 See *The Protection of Human Rights by Law in Northern Ireland*, Standing Advisory Commission on Human Rights, Cmnd 7009 (London: HMSO, 1977); *Report of the Select Committee on a Bill of Rights*, HL 76 (London HMSO, 1978); Peter Wallington and Jeremy McBride, *Civil Liberties and a Bill of Rights* (Cobden Trust, 1976).

17 Even if the interference with the prisoner's correspondence breached the present Prison Rules, the courts would not interfere; see *Williams* v. *Home Office* (1980), *The Times*, 10 May 1980.

18 See, for instance, Joseph Jaconelli, *Enacting a Bill of Rights*, (Oxford: Clarendon Press, 1980).

19 Sir Leslie Scarman, *English Law – The New Dimension* (London: Stevens, 1974).

20 *Hubbard* v. *Pitt* (1976) 1 QB 142.

21 *R.* v. *Sheffield Crown Court ex parte Brownlow*, *The Times*, 4 March 1980.

22 *Congreve* v. *Home Office* (1976) 1 All ER 697.

23 *R.* v. *Inland Revenue Commissioners ex parte Rossminster* (1980) 2 WLR 1.

24 *Secretary of State for Education and Science* v. *Tameside Metropolitan Borough Council* (1976) All ER 665.

25 *Laker Airways* v. *Department of Trade* (1977) 2 All ER 182.

26 *R.* v. *Secretary of State for the Home Department ex parte Choudhary* (1978) 3 All ER 790; *R.* v. *Secretary of State for the Home Department ex parte Thakrar* (1974) 2 All ER 261.

27 *R.* v. *Secretary of State for Home Affairs ex parte Hosenball* (1977) 3 All ER 452.

28 *R.* v. *Preston Supplementary Benefits Appeal Tribunal ex parte Moore* (1975) 2 All ER 807.

29 See Peter Robson and Paul Watchman, 'Sabotaging the Rent Acts', in *Justice, Lord Denning and the Constitution* (London: Gower, 1981).

30 See notes to pages 128–35.

31 See note 26 above; see also page 199.

32 Lord Scarman, 'Human Rights: The Current Situation', in Colin Campbell (ed.), *Do We Need a Bill of Rights* (London: Temple Smith, 1980), p. 7.

33 J. A. G. Griffith *The Politics of the Judiciary* (London: Fontana, 1977).

34 See, for example, Sir Keith Joseph, *Freedom Under The Law* (London: Conservative Political Centre, 1975).

35 *The Protection of Human Rights by Law in Northern Ireland*.

36 *Report of the Select Committee on a Bill of Rights*.

37 Bill of Rights Bill, *Hansard* (HL), 25 November 1980, Col 415.

38 Kevin Boyle, 'Emergency Conditions', in Campbell (ed.), *Do We Need a Bill of Rights*.

39 Jerome B. Elkind, 'Application of the International Covenant on Civil and Political Rights in New Zealand', *American Journal of International Law*, vol. 75 (1981).

Bibliography

General

The standard text on civil liberties in the United Kingdom is Harry Street, *Freedom, the Individual and the Law*, 3rd edn., (Harmondsworth: Penguin, 1972). Barry Cox, *Civil Liberties in Britain* (Harmondsworth: Penguin, 1975) draws on the files and work of NCCL since 1934. Larry Grant *et al.*, *Civil Liberty: The NCCL Guide* 3rd edn., with revisions (Harmondsworth: Penguin, 1979) is a practical account of the operation of the law. Two casebooks have recently been published: Paul O'Higgins, *Cases and Materials on Civil Liberties* (London: Sweet and Maxwell, 1980), and S. H. Bailey, D. Harris and B. L. Jones, *Civil Liberties: Cases and Materials* (London: Butterworth, 1980). Both contain extensive bibliographies.

Dicey, *The Law of the Constitution*, is the classic work on the principles of the rule of law. A more modern account will be found in *Rule of Law in a Free Society* (Geneva: International Commission of Jurists, 1959). International human rights standards will be found in Ian Brownlie (ed.), *Basic Documents on Human Rights* (Oxford: Clarendon Press, 1971). The theoretical issues are discussed in H. A. Hart, *Concept of Law* (London: Oxford University Press, 1961); John Rawls, *A Theory of Justice* (Cambridge, Mass.: Harvard University Press, 1971); and Ronald Dworkin, *Taking Rights Seriously* (London: Duckworth, 1978).

1: Justice and the Criminal Law

The *Report of the Royal Commission on Criminal Procedure*, Cmnd 8092 (London: HMSO, 1981), its accompanying volume on Law and Procedure, Cmnd 8092–1 (London: HMSO, 1981), and the research studies commissioned by the Commission are an essential starting-point for a study of the criminal justice system. The Law and Procedure volume includes the Judges' Rules and Administrative Directions and reproduces the Home

Office circulars dealing with the right of a suspect to notify someone of his arrest (Criminal Law Act 1977, Section 62), medical examinations of suspects and the police complaints and discipline procedures. The research studies cover police interrogation; confessions in Crown Court trials; contested trials in magistrates' courts; police investigation techniques; tape recording of police interrogations; the use of arrest and summons; a survey of prosecuting solicitors' departments; and private prosecutions.

A large number of organizations gave evidence to the Commission, including the Home Office, the Association of Chief Police Officers, the Police Federation, the Metropolitan Police Commissioner, Justice, NCCL, the Legal Action Group, the Institute of Race Relations and Release. Copies of their evidence can be obtained from these organizations.

The *Report* of Sir Henry Fisher's inquiry into the Confait case, HC 90 (London: HMSO, 1977) is not only a fascinating study of the wrongful convictions of three young men, but also an invaluable account of the operation of the Judges' Rules.

Three useful studies of conspiracy law are available: Robert Hazel, *Conspiracy and Civil Liberties* (London: Bell, 1974); Geoffrey Robertson, *Whose Conspiracy?* (London: NCCL, 1974), and Robert Spicer, *Conspiracy: Law, Class and Society* (London: Lawrence and Wishart, 1981).

On the use of identification evidence and the dangers of wrongful conviction, the *Report of the Departmental Committee on Evidence of Identification in Criminal Cases* (the Devlin report), HC 338 (London: HMSO, 1976) is essential reading. Peter Hain, *Mistaken Identity* (London: Quartet, 1976) is an account of his own misidentification case as well as an analysis of the general problem.

The Cobden Trust has published two useful studies by Michael King: *Bail or Custody* (1971) and *The Effects of a Duty Solicitor Scheme* (1976). On the problem of refusal of costs to an acquitted defendant, see Howard Levenson, *The Price of Justice* (Cobden Trust, 1981). A number of studies of different aspects of the criminal justice system have been published by Justice (the British Section of the International Commission of Jurists). See also R. J. Sharples, *The Law of Habeas Corpus* (Oxford: Clarendon Press, 1976). On prisoners' rights, see Mike Fitzgerald and Joe Sims, *British Prisons* (Oxford: Blackwell, 1979); *Boards of Visitors of Penal Institutions* (London: Barry Rose, 1976) (the report of a Justice, Howard League and NACRO Committee on the prison disciplinary system); Stan Cohen and Laurie Taylor, *Prison Secrets* (London: NCCL/RAP, 1978); the *Report of the Committee of Inquiry into the United Kingdom Prison Services* (the May Report), Cmnd 7673 (London: HMSO, 1979); the Annual Reports of the Prison Department; and Roy King and Rodney Morgan, *Crisis in the Prisons: The Way Out* (Universities of Bath and Southampton, April 1979).

2: Causing Problems for the State

The Annual Reports of Chief Constables provide an excellent introduction to the police view of their role. (Often difficult to obtain, they may be inspected in the libraries of State Research and the Cobden Trust.) Sir Robert Mark's two books are illuminating: *Policing a Perplexed Society* (London: Allen and Unwin, 1977) and *In The Office of Constable* (London: Collins, 1978).

The major critique of police operations against 'subversives' remains Tony Bunyan's *Political Police in Britain* (London: Julian Friedmann, 1976). His material has been updated by the bulletins of State Research, reprinted annually as *Review of Security and the State* (London: Julian Friedmann, 1978, 1979, 1980). Both volumes of Peter Hain and Brian Rose-Smith (eds.), *Policing The Police* (London: Calder, 1979, 1980) are relevant, particularly the excellent essays by Duncan Campbell and Martin Kettle in volume 2. E. P. Thompson, *Writing by Candlelight* (London: Merlin Press, 1980) contains a number of relevant articles and essays. A comprehensive account of the technology of surveillance will be found in Carol Ackroyd, Karen Margolis, Jonathan Rosenhead and Tim Shallice, *The Technology of Political Control* (Harmondsworth: Penguin, 1977).

In the area of data protection and privacy, the two major official reports are the Younger Committee *Report,* Cmnd 5012 (London: HMSO, 1972) and the Lindop Committee *Report,* Cmnd 7341 (London: HMSO, 1978). The latter contains an updated version of the government's record of its own computer transactions involving personal information, originally published in the White Paper *Computers: Safeguards for Privacy,* Cmnd 6354 (London: HMSO, 1975). An account of the problems caused by the absence of privacy legislation is contained in Patricia Hewitt, *Privacy: The Information Gatherers* (London: NCCL, 1977), while NCCL's proposals for legislation are set out in a memorandum, *Legislating for Information Privacy* (London: NCCL, 1980). The most comprehensive source of information on developments overseas is the bimonthly*Transnational Data Report,* published by North Holland Publishing Co. (Amsterdam).

The Report of the Committee of Privy Councillors Appointed to Inquire into the Interception of Communications (the Birkett Report), Cmnd 283 (London: HMSO, 1957) was for many years the only official pronouncement on telephone tapping and mail interception. The Conservative Government published a White Paper with up-to-date figures on official warrants for interceptions, *The Interception of Communications in Great Britain* Cmnd 7873 (London: HMSO, 1980), and appointed Lord Diplock of the Security Commission to review the warrant procedure. His report was published under the same title, Cmnd 8191 (London: HMSO, 1981). The Post Office Engineering Union has published an excellent report, *Tapping The Telephone* (POEU, 1980), which makes detailed proposals for legislation. Duncan Campbell's *Phonetappers and the Security State* (New Statesman Report No. 2, 1981) is the most complete account of the tapping facilities available to the UK Government.

Little has been written about jury vetting except for John Griffiths's and Harriet Harman's *Justice Deserted* (London: NCCL, 1979; postscript, 1980) and an essay by E. P. Thompson in the collection referred to above. The story of the trial under the Official Secrets Act of Crispin Aubrey, John Berry and Duncan Campbell is told in Crispin Aubrey, *Who's Watching You?* (London: Penguin, 1981).

Other references under 'Censorship and Secrecy' will also be relevant.

3: Policing the Police

The 'official' history of the police will be found in T. A. Critchley, *A History of Police in England and Wales* (London: Constable, 1978). A more critical view is taken by Tom Bowden, *Beyond the Limits of the Law* (Harmondsworth: Penguin, 1978). Criticisms of proposals for more police accountability to elected bodies comes from the exponent of community policing, John Alderson, *Policing Freedom* (London: MacDonald and Evans, 1979); many of his arguments are dealt with by Ben Whitaker, *The Police in Society* (London: Eyre Methuen, 1979). Stuart Hall provides a brilliant analysis of the political role of the police in his Human Rights Day Lecture, *Drifting Into A Law And Order Society* (Cobden Trust, 1979).

During this century two Royal Commissions have considered the role and constitutional position of the police: the *Report* of the Royal Commission on Police Powers and Procedure, Cmnd 3297 (London: HMSO, 1929), and the *Report* of the Royal Commission on the Police, Cmnd 1728 (London: HMSO, 1962). The Annual Reports of the Chief Inspector of Constabulary and of the Police Complaints Board are useful sources.

The *Triennial Review Report* of the Police Complaints Board, Cmnd 7966 (London: HMSO, 1980), makes proposals for changes in the procedure for dealing with complaints against the police, most of which were dismissed by a Home Office working party, *The Establishment of an Independent Element in the Investigation of Complaints against the Police,* Cmnd 8193 (London: HMSO, 1981). Memoranda by NCCL and Justice on this issue are cited in chapter 3.

Both the South Yorkshire and the Merseyside Police Authorities have had somewhat stormy dealings with their Chief Constables and both have produced reports: *Report on Relationships Between the Police and Public in South Yorkshire* (South Yorkshire County Council, 1979) and *Role and Responsibilities of the Police Authority* (Merseyside Police Authority, 1980). The former is mainly concerned with substantive policing issues, the latter with the constitutional relationship between police and authority. The latter contains the notes of a police seminar organized by the Association of County Councils and the Association of Metropolitan Authorities in 1977.

4: Censorship and Secrecy

The Official Secrets Acts and the role of the security services are analysed in David Williams, *Not in the Public Interest* (London: Hutchinson, 1965). Those Acts are also the subject of Jonathan Aitken's *Officially Secret* (London: Weidenfeld and Nicolson, 1971). The obscenity laws, as well as official secrecy, are analysed in Paul O'Higgins, *Censorship in Britain* (Sunbury-on-Thames: Nelson, 1972). Crispin Aubrey, *Who's Watching You?* (London: Penguin, 1981) is a full account of the most recent Official Secrets Act trial. An excellent analysis of government secrecy will be found in David Leigh's *Frontiers of Secrecy: Closed Government in Britain* (London: Junction Books, 1980). A discussion of open government laws in other countries will be found in James Michael, *The Politics of Secrecy* (Harmondsworth: Penguin, forthcoming).

The Outer Circle Policy Unit (OCPU), a private research group which was wound up in 1981, has published extensively on secrecy and freedom of information. *An Official Information Act* (undated) contains a brief history of the movement for reform, a summary of the US legislation and proposals for a Freedom of Information Act. The *Official Information Bill* (OCPU, 1978) was the basis of the Private Member's Bill introduced that year by Clement Freud, MP, and, with amendments, by Frank Hooley, MP, in 1981. *A Consumer's Guide to Open Government: Techniques for Penetrating Whitehall* (OCPU, 1980) includes the text of the Croham Directive and an analysis of its effects, as well as material on the Public Records Office. Steward Dresner, *Open Government: Lessons from America* (OCPU, 1980) provides a useful account of the effects and limitations of American legislation.

James Michael, *The Politics of Secrecy* (London: NCCL, 1979) provides examples of information available in the USA but censored here, as well as proposals for reform of the Official Secrets Act and for a Freedom of Information Act. Trevor Barnes, *Open Up!*, Fabian Tract 467 (London: Fabian Society, 1980) proposes a staged introduction of freedom of information measures. Developments in the USA are described in Morton Halperin and Daniel Hoffman, *Top Secret: National Security and the Right to Know* (New Republic Books, 1977).

The *Report of the Departmental Committee on Section 2 of the Official Secrets Act 1911* was published as Cmnd 5104 (London: HMSO, 1972). The Government's response was eventually published in *Reform of Section 2 of the Official Secrets Act 1911*, Cmnd 7285 (London: HMSO, 1978), which was followed by *Disclosure of Official Information: A Report on Overseas Practice* (London: HMSO, 1979). Some indication of Labour Party thinking on the issue was given by Tony Benn, *The Right to Know* (Institute of Workers' Control, 1978).

Proposals for reforming the law of contempt of court were made in the *Report of the (Phillimore) Committee on Contempt of Court*, Cmnd 5794 (London: HMSO, 1974). The issue was also discussed in the Law Commission *Report on Offences Relating to Interference with the Course of Justice*, HC 213 (London: HMSO, 1979). The Government's response to Phillimore was set out in *Contempt of Court: A Discussion Paper* Cmnd 7145 (London: HMSO, 1978). A critique of Phillimore and the Government's Contempt of Court Bill 1981, together with proposals for reform, will be found in Andrew Nicol and Heather Rogers, *Changing Contempt of Court* (London: NCCL, Campaign for Press Freedom, 1981).

C. H. Rolph, *Books in the Dock* (London: André Deutsch, 1969) is a major study of the obscenity laws. Neville March Hunnings, *Film Censors and the Law* (London: Allen and Unwin, 1967) is a comparative study of film censorship which remains of interest, although now out of date. The *Report of the Commission on Obscenity and Pornography* (London: Bantam Books, 1970) is probably the most thorough inquiry into obscenity laws; its technical reports were edited and abridged by Alan Burns, *To Deprave and Corrupt* (London: Davis-Poynter, 1972). Tony Palmer's *Trials of Oz* (London: Blond and Briggs, 1971) is based on the transcript of the notorious obscenity trial of the 'Schoolkids' issue of *Oz* magazine.

The most comprehensive account of the obscenity laws and their operation is by Geoffrey Robertson, *Obscenity* (London: Weidenfeld and Nicolson, 1978). And proposals for reform are contained in the *Report of the Committee on Obscenity and Film Censorship*, Cmnd 7772 (London: HMSO, 1979).

5: Peaceful Protest and Public Assembly

The leading textbook remains Ian Brownlie, *The Law Relating to Public Order* (London: Butterworth, 1968). D. G. T. Williams, *Keeping the Peace: the Police and Public Order* (London: Hutchinson, 1967) is also valuable. Additional material will be found in the relevant chapters of the two casebooks on civil liberties; in *Civil Liberty: The NCCL Guide* (Harmondsworth: Penguin, 1979); in Harry Street, *Freedom, the Individual and the Law* 3rd edn. (Harmondsworth: Penguin, 1972); and Barry Cox, *Civil Liberties in Britain* (Harmondsworth: Penguin, 1975). R. Benewick and T. Smith (ed.), *Direct Action and Democratic Politics* (London: Allen and Unwin, 1972) is particularly useful for the modern development of freedom of assembly. Detailed discussion of particular aspects of restraints on demonstrations will be found in Peter Wallington, 'Injunctions and the "Right to Demonstrate"', *Cambridge Law Journal*, no. 35 (1976), and William Birtles, 'The Common Law Power of the Police to Control Public Meetings', *Modern Law Review*, no. 34 (1973).

Accounts of the law relating to industrial picketing and other forms of industrial action will be found in Otto Kahn-Freund, *Labour and the Law*, 2nd edn. (London: Stevens, 1977), and P. Elias, B. Napier and P. Wallington, *Labour Law: Cases and Materials* (London: Butterworth, 1980). A practical guide to the law on industrial action is contained in Jeremy McMullen, *Rights at Work* (London: Pluto Press, 1978) and its supplement, *Employment Law under the Tories* (London: Pluto Press, 1981). The Government's proposals in this field are contained in the Department of Employment *Working Paper on Secondary Industrial Action* (February, 1980) and the Green Paper on *Trade Union Immunities* (London: HMSO, 1981).

The Government's proposals for amending the law on public order generally are set out in the Green Paper *Review of the Public Order Act 1936 and Related Legislation*, Cmnd 7891 (London: HMSO, 1980). A parallel review of the law was conducted by the Home Affairs Committee of the House of Commons, whose report was published as HC 756–1 (London: HMSO, 1980). The *Minutes of Evidence* taken by the Committee (London: HMSO, 1980) are a useful guide to the views of the Metropolitan Police Commissioner, the police associations and a wide range of voluntary organizations. The reports of the Metropolitan Police Commissioner and of other Chief Constables also contain relevant material. Police thinking on public order is reviewed by Martin Kettle, 'The Politics of Policing and the Policing of Politics', in Peter Hain and Brian Rose-Smith (eds.), *Policing the Police*, (London: Calder, 1980).

A detailed account of the events in Red Lion Square in 1974 is contained in Tony Gilbert, *Only One Died* (Kay Beauchamp, nd). The report of the official inquiry, established under the 1964 Police Act, is published as *The Red Lion Square Disorders of June 15, 1974; Report of an Inquiry by the Rt Hon Lord Justice Scarman OBE*, Cmnd 5919 (London: HMSO, 1975). No official inquiry was established into the events in Southall in 1979. An unofficial committee of inquiry was set up by the NCCL; its reports are *Southall: April 23 1979: The Report of the Unofficial Committee of Enquiry* (London: NCCL, 1980), and *The Death of Blair Peach; The Supplementary Report of the Unofficial Committee of Enquiry* (London: NCCL, 1981).

A comprehensive review of constitutional protection for freedom of protest in the United States of America is contained in Thomas I. Emerson, *The System of Freedom of Expression* (New York: Random House, 1970). An analysis of the Skokie case, in which the American Civil Liberties Union upheld the freedom of the American Nazi Party to march through a suburb of Chicago containing 7000 refugees and survivors of Nazi concentration camps, was written by the ACLU's then director, Aryeh Neier: *Defending My Enemy; American Nazis, the Skokie Case and the Risks of Freedom* (New York: Dutton, 1979).

6: *Civil Liberties and Northern Ireland*

Perhaps the best political history of Ireland is Robert Kee's *The Green Flag* (London: Weidenfeld and Nicolson, 1972; reprinted in three volumes by Quartet Books, 1976). A vivid account of the development of the present troubles, during 1970 and 1971, is provided by the *Guardian* reporter Simon Winchester, *In Holy Terror* (London: Faber and Faber, 1974). Robert Fisk, who reported on Northern Ireland for *The Times* during much of the decade, has produced an extremely valuable analysis, *The Point of No Return* (London: André Deutsch, 1975).

The last twelve years have been punctuated with official reports, the first being that of the Cameron Commission, appointed to investigate the disturbances in Northern Ireland between October 1968 and March 1969, Cmnd 532 (London: HMSO, 1969). The *Report* of the Scarman Tribunal on Violence and Civil Disturbances in Northern Ireland in 1969, Cmnd 566 (London: HMSO, 1972), took much longer to be published. The allegations of torture by some of the internees detained in August 1971 were investigated by the Compton Inquiry, whose *Report*, Cmnd 4823, (London: HMSO, 1971), concluded (with a biting dissent from Lord Gardiner) that the interrogation techniques used were permissible. The shootings of unarmed civilians by the Army on 30 January 1972 ('Bloody Sunday') were investigated by the Widgery Tribunal; its *Report*, HC 220 (London: HMSO, 1972) was strongly criticized by an unofficial inquiry conducted by Sam Dash, later a Watergate prosecutor, whose report was published as *Justice Denied* (London: International League for the Rights of Man and NCCL, 1972). The *Report* of the Parker Committee on Methods of Interrogation, Cmnd 4901 (London: HMSO, 1972), was followed by the *Report* of the Diplock Committee on Legal Procedures to deal with Terrorist Activities, Cmnd 5185 (London: HMSO, 1972), which led to the introduction of the Emergency Provisions Act 1973. That Act was in turn considered by the Gardiner Committee, Cmnd 5847 (London: HMSO, 1975). Further allegations of brutality after the ending of internment were investigated by the Committee of Inquiry into Police Interrogation Procedures, Cmnd 7497 (London: HMSO, 1979).

The operation of the earlier Special Powers Acts was investigated by an unofficial committee of inquiry established by NCCL in 1936 (London: NCCL, 1936; republished 1972). The administration of justice in the 1960s and up to 1972 was thoroughly assessed by Tom Hadden and Paddy Hillyard in *Justice in Northern Ireland: A Study in Social Confidence* (Cobden Trust, 1973). The Government's comments on that report were contained in *Prosecutions in Northern Ireland: A Study of Facts* (London: HMSO, 1974). That work was developed in Kevin Boyle, Tom Hadden and Paddy Hillyard, *Law and State: The Case of Northern Ireland* (Oxford: Martin Robertson, 1975), and the same authors were responsible for a detailed assessment of the Emergency Provisions Act, *Ten Years on in*

Northern Ireland: The Legal Control of Political Violence (Cobden Trust, 1980).

The operation of the Prevention of Terrorism Act was considered by Lord Shackleton, Cmnd 7324 (London: HMSO, 1978). A detailed criticism of the Act is contained in Catherine Scorer and Patricia Hewitt, *The Prevention of Terrorism Act: The Case for Repeal* (London: NCCL, 1981).

The Annual Reports of the Standing Advisory Commission on Human Rights in Northern Ireland provide useful information, as do the reports of the Commissioner for Complaints and the Northern Ireland Housing Executive. The Standing Advisory Commission is also responsible for the excellent study of proposals for a Bill of Rights, *The Protection of Human Rights by Law in Northern Ireland*, Cmnd 7009 (London: HMSO, 1977). The question of a Bill of Rights is also considered in Colin Campbell (ed.), *Do We Need a Bill of Rights?* (London: Temple Smith, 1980).

The following titles are all relevant to further consideration of the political future: Richard Rose, *Northern Ireland: A Time of Choice* (London: Macmillan, 1976); F. Burton, *The Politics of Legitimacy* (London: Routledge and Kegan Paul, 1972); G. Bell, *The Protestants of Ulster* (London: Pluto Press, 1976). The best study of the prison protest is by T. P. Coogan, *On the Blanket: The H-Block Story* (Dublin: Ward River Press, 1980).

7: The Other Half

A comprehensive guide to the law as it affects women's rights will be found in Anna Coote and Tess Gill, *Women's Rights: A Practical Guide* 2nd edn. (Harmondsworth: Penguin, 1977). An analysis of how the law has treated women in the USA and in this country is developed in Albie Sachs and Joan Hoff Wilson, *Sexism and the Law: A Study of Male Beliefs and Judicial Bias* (Oxford: Martin Robertson, 1978). The bibliography in the latter publication is especially strong on North American material. Women and the criminal law is the subject of Carol Smart's *Women, Crime and Criminology* (London: Routledge and Kegan Paul, 1976).

The Annual Reports of the Equal Opportunities Commission contain a wealth of material on the enforcement of the Sex Discrimination and Equal Pay Acts. The Commission also publishes a regular research bulletin, the first volume of which summarizes statistical material concerning the position of women in the UK.

Further information concerning the pay and job segregation of women will be found in the monthly *Gazettes* of the Department of Employment.

The most detailed analysis of the operation of the Sex Discrimination and Equal Pay Acts, together with an account of affirmative action in the USA and proposals for similar schemes here, will be found in Sadie Robarts *et al.*, *Positive Action for Women* (London: NCCL, 1981).

An account of developments in the last decade will be found in Anna Coote and Bea Campbell, *Sweet Freedom: The Struggle for Women's Liberation* (Oxford: Blackwell, 1982).

8: Free and Equal?

The fullest and most up-to-date guide to immigration law will be found in Larry Grant and Ian Martin, *Immigration Law and Practice* (Cobden Trust, 1981). An account of the development of immigration controls and their operation is contained in Robert Moore and Tina Wallace, *Slamming the Door: The Administration of Immigration Control* (Oxford: Martin Robertson, 1975); the treatment of the Ugandan Asian refugees is described in Derek Humphry and Michael Ward, *Passports and Politics* (Harmondsworth: Penguin, 1974).

Further material on immigration control is available in the Annual Reports and bulletins of the Joint Council for the Welfare of Immigrants and of the United Kingdom Immigrants Advisory Service. Briefing papers issued between 1978 and 1981 by the Action Group on Immigration and Nationality will be of assistance to those wanting further information on both immigration and nationality law.

A brief but cogent critique of immigration policy is contained in Michael Dummett, *Immigration: Where the Debate Goes Wrong*, (Action Group on Immigration and Nationality, undated). Anne Dummett's *A New Immigration Policy* (Runnymede Trust, 1978) examines the immigration policies of other countries and proposes alternative policies.

Official thinking on nationality law will be found in the Labour Government's Green Paper *British Nationality Law*, Cmnd 6795 (London: HMSO, 1977) and the Conservative Government's White Paper *British Nationality Law*, Cmnd 7987 (London: HMSO, 1980). The use of medical techniques for immigration control is considered in the report by Sir Henry Yellowlees, the Chief Medical Officer, *The Medical Examination of Immigrants* (Department of Health and Social Security, 1980); a detailed critique of that report is contained in a memorandum by Edward White, 'The Use of X-Rays for Age Determination in Immigration Control', Office of Lord Avebury, 1981.

One of the earliest studies of race relations in Britain, not since equalled in its scope, is E. B. Rose and associates, *Colour and Citizenship* (London: Institute of Race Relations and Oxford University Press, 1969). W. W. Daniel, *Racial Discrimination in England* (Harmondsworth: Penguin, 1968) is based on the results of the first major Political and Economic Planning (PEP) survey of racial prejudice. Derek Humphry's and Gus John's *Because They're Black* (Harmondsworth: Penguin, 1971) also contains a vivid account of racial discrimination.

Accounts of the law against racial discrimination will be found in Bob Hepple, *Race, Jobs and the Law in Britain* 2nd edn. (Harmondsworth:

Penguin, 1970); Anthony Lester and Geoffrey Bindman, *Race and Law* (Harmondsworth: Penguin, 1972); and Ian A. Macdonald, *Race Relations – The New Law* (London: Butterworth, 1977). The Commission for Racial Equality has also published useful summaries of statistical information, *Ethnic Minorities in Britain* (revised December 1978).

A transcript of the Supreme Court ruling in *Bakke* and a discussion of the judgment is contained in *Towards An Understanding of Bakke* (United States Commission on Civil Rights, 1979).

The journal of the Institute of Race Relations, *Race and Class*, and that of the Race Today Collective, *Race Today*, are both invaluable. Accounts of research in the field of race relations and discrimination are published regularly in the journal of the Commission for Racial Equality, *New Community*. Vol. 8, no. 3 of that journal contains an extremely useful summary of the research material on educational disadvantage.

An early study into relations between the police and the ethnic minority communities by John Lambert published as *Crime, Police and Race Relations* (London: Institute of Race Relations and Oxford University Press, 1970). Derek Humphry and Gus John, *Police Power and Black People* (London: Panther, 1972) draws extensively on NCCL files and other case material in building up an account of the black community's experience of police harassment. A more recent account of the same problem will be found in the evidence of the Institute of Race Relations to the Royal Commission on Criminal Procedure, *Police Against Black People* (Institute of Race Relations, 1979).

An analysis of relations between police and the black communities is contained in NCCL's evidence to Lord Scarman's Inquiry into the events in Brixton in April 1981, *Civil Liberties and Civil Disorder* (NCCL, 1981).

9: The Homosexual Minority

The *Report of the Committee on Homosexual Offences and the Law Relating to Prostitution* (the Wolfenden Report), Cmnd 247 (London: HMSO, 1957) is the key document for a study of the law reform which followed in the 1960s. An account of the campaign for reform is given by Anthony Grey, 'Homosexual Law Reform', in Brian Frost (ed.), *The Tactics of Pressure* (London: 1975). More recently, the Policy Advisory Committee on Sexual Offences and the Criminal Law Revision Committee were invited to consider this area of the law: see the Policy Advisory Committee's *Working Paper on the Age of Consent in Relation to Sexual Offences* (London: HMSO, 1979), the CLRC's *Working Paper on Sexual Offences* (London: HMSO, 1980) and the Advisory Committee's *Report on the Age of Consent in relation to Sexual Offences*, Cmnd 8216 (London: HMSO, 1981). The Home Office Research Study 54, *Sexual Offences, Consent and Sentencing* (London: HMSO, 1979), is also relevant.

Jeffrey Weeks, *Coming Out* (London: Quartet, 1977) is an invaluable account of the history of prosecution and persecution of gay men and women and the development of the gay liberation movement; it contains an extensive bibliography.

NCCL has produced a number of campaigning reports on this subject: *Homosexuals and the Teaching Profession* (NCCL Report No. 8); *Homosexuality and the Social Services* (1977) and Beer *et al.*, *Gay Workers, Trade Unions and the Law* (1981).

10: Protecting Human Rights

Ian Brownlie (ed.), *Basic Documents on Human Rights* (Oxford: Clarendon Press, 1977) brings together all the international documents on human rights standards.

Sir Leslie Scarman, *English Law – the New Dimension* (London: Stevens, 1974) is the text of Sir Leslie's Hamlyn Lecture, in which he proposed a Bill of Rights as part of a new constitutional settlement. Peter Wallington and Jeremy McBride, *Civil Liberties and a Bill of Rights* (Cobden Trust, 1976) propose incorporation of the European Convention of Human Rights and include a model Bill and an extensive bibliography. Michael Zander, *A Bill of Rights?*, 2nd edn. (London: Barry Rose, 1979) also supports incorporation of the Convention. Colin Campbell (ed.), *Do We Need a Bill of Rights?* (London: Temple Smith, 1980) contains the papers given at a conference sponsored by the Standing Advisory Commission on Human Rights in Northern Ireland during 1980; that body's own report, *The Protection of Human Rights by Law in Northern Ireland*, Cmnd 7009 (London: HMSO, 1977), is the most comprehensive discussion of the issues available.

Before the Standing Advisory Commission reported, the Home Office produced its own discussion document, *Legislation on Human Rights* (Home Office, 1976). A Bill introduced in the House of Lords by Lord Wade to incorporate the Convention was referred to a Select Committee of the House, whose *Report* of the Select Committee on a Bill of Rights HL 176 (London: HMSO, 1978) sets out proposals for incorporation of the Convention with a very restricted degree of entrenchment. Joseph Jaconelli, *Enacting a Bill of Rights* (Oxford: Clarendon Press, 1980) discusses the alternative proposals, favouring a 'tailor-made' Bill of Rights, of which he sets out a draft. John Griffith, *The Politics of the Judiciary* 2nd edn., (London: Fontana, 1981) makes a strong case against any increase in the power of the judges.

Francis Jacobs, *The European Convention on Human Rights* (Oxford: Clarendon Press, 1975) provides a very detailed account of the Convention's provisions and the jurisprudence of the Commission and the Court. Ralph Beddard, *Human Rights and Europe*, 2nd edn., (London:

Sweet and Maxwell, 1980) provides a briefer but useful discussion of the impact of the Convention. The *Decisions* of the Commission and the Court, together with the Commission's *Yearbook* and a regular *Stock-Taking* are available from the Commission itself.

Table of Statutes

Table of Cases

283

Index

'Sus', 6

Tavistock Institute, 212
Telephone tapping, 41–3, 47, 238
Thomson Committee, 14
Time Out, 51
Tobin, Michael, 52

Wade, Lord, 245–9
Walden, Brian, MP, 44
Watch committees, 59, 62
Warburton, John, 225
Well of Loneliness, 223
Wesler, Johann, 83
Whitehouse, Mary, 98
Whitelaw, William, MP, 41, 64, 141
Williams Committee, *see* Obscenity
Williams, Michael, 93, 94
Wiseman, Gordon, 226
Wolfenden Committee, 220, 221
Women, 171–86
    abortion, 172, 173

children, 184–6
citizenship, 173–5
domestic violence, 172
education, 180–2
employment, 177–86
Equal Pay Act, 177–80
immigration, 173–5
lesbians, 223, 224
matrimonial property, 172
social security, 175, 176
suffrage, 172
tax, 173, 175–7
Wootton, Baroness, 94

X, Michael, 205

Yellowlees, Sir Henry, 195
Yorkshire Ripper, 11, 63, 102
Younger, Sir Kenneth, 44, 45

Zamir, Mohammed, 198, 199
Zander, Professor Michael, 25
Zimbabwe,
    sanctions busting in, 88